LOST Humanity:

The Mythology and Themes of LOST

by Pearson Moore

By Pearson Moore

LOST Humanity:
The Mythology and Themes of LOST

LOST Identity:
The Characters of LOST

Cartier's Ring
A Novel of Canada

Direwolves and Dragons
Volume 1.01
Symbolism and Thesis

Direwolves and Dragons
Volume 1.02
Bran and Jon

LOST
Humanity

The Mythology and Themes of LOST

Pearson Moore

LOST Humanity:

The mythology and themes of LOST

ISBN: 978-1-46354-870-4

For Kim, my Constant.

Table of Contents

INTRODUCTION

**Chaos and Identity:
An Introduction to 'LOST Humanity'**

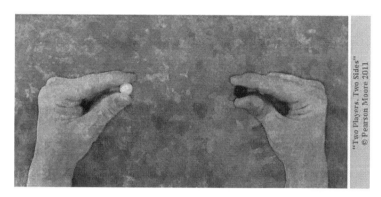

"What if everything that happened here happened for a reason?"

The inspector shook his head, stopped under a tree, and took a swig from his water bottle. He trained his gaze on the bald man whose words had disturbed the silence. His eyes narrowed into a frown and he sighed. "I heard you say that in this same spot, seven years ago. Maybe there was a reason, but none of it made any sense."

The four of them stood in silence while the inspector drank his fill. The young woman leaned her rifle against the tree, reached up with both hands and worked her hair into a bun. The man of olive skin and dark curly hair focussed on the bald man, then peered at the inspector.

"Sense can be hard to find," he said with his thick Iraqi accent, "when everything is chaotic."

The inspector fastened the cap on his water bottle and returned it to the holster on his belt. He nodded and smiled at the Iraqi. "Finally, a man who knows it was all nonsense."

The bald man looked into the sun and squinted. "He means everything made sense—you just have to look at it the right way."

The inspector laughed. "I've heard that one before, too. 'Not intelligent enough. You have to try harder, do more research'—or my favourite: 'It's about the characters. It wasn't supposed to make sense.'" He laughed again. "I have a bachelor's degree in economics, a master's in business adminstration, and you think I'm not smart enough?"

The bald man shrugged. "I don't have a degree in anything. I figured it out just fine."

The inspector pursed his lips and stared daggers at the bald man.

The young woman, her brunette hair wrapped in a bun, took a step toward the inspector. "You're smart enough. We all are. And it was always about more than just the characters."

The bald man pulled a mango from his pocket. "Says the woman who never watched television."

"I watched 'North of 60.'"

The bald man frowned. "That what they got for entertainment in Iowa?"

"It's about a town in Northwest Territories."

"What's that got to do with our Island?" He pulled the knife from the sheath at his belt and began skinning the mango.

The Iraqi folded his arms. "Strong women, men who fought over stupid things—'North of 60' was chaotic, too."

"Didn't make sense either, huh?" the inspector asked.

"No," the dark-skinned man said, "it rather made perfect sense."

"You see," the inspector fumed, "that's why I never understood Lost. It didn't made sense, no one agreed on anything, people said things that—"

The Iraqi pointed to the woman. "Show him your tapestry." He motioning toward her daypack.

She pulled out the strap over her left shoulder and dropped the daypack to the ground. "It's not a tapestry."

The bald man rolled his eyes and cut a slice of mango. "Jacob wove tapestries, she weaves—"

"I **make** embroideries," she said, withdrawing light-coloured fabric from her pack. "They're not woven."

The dark-skinned man frowned at her. "Does it make any difference that—"

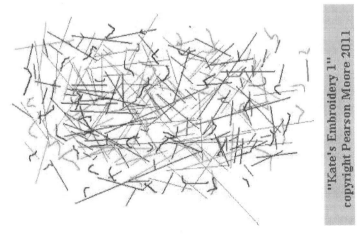

"Kate's Embroidery 1"
copyright Pearson Moore 2011

"No." She unfolded the white fabric. An aimless array of different coloured threads appeared, scattered across the surface of the cloth. "It's just that he's the one—with his 'faith in the Island' and 'sacrifice the Island demanded'—he's the one who caused more grief in our lives than anyone else."

The Iraqi man laughed. "Great White Hunter over there is dead. Seems like you came out of this with a much sweeter deal than any—"

"Jack's dead, too," she said, gritting her teeth. "You think being a widow is some kind of picnic?"

The bald man pointed to the cloth in her hands. "Just show him the tapestry."

"Embroidery."

The dark-skinned man exhaled noisily. "Whatever."

The inspector stared at the cloth, trying to discern some pattern in the dense collection of random threads. "What does it mean?"

"It's chaos," the former torturer said.

"Is that the only word you know?" the inspector asked. He frowned, stared at the fabric, then glanced at the young woman. "How long did you work on this?"

"Two years," she said.

He looked at her with questioning eyes.

The bald man threw the pit into the tall grass and wiped the knife on his pants leg. "She's a widow. She has time."

The former soldier stared at the bald man and shook his head. "And they said *I* was the heartless zombie."

The inspector grimaced. "Two years?"

She nodded. "I worked on it every day."

The inspector's eyes scanned the embroidered surface from one end to the other, along the edges, through the middle, top to bottom. He pursed his lips and looked into the young woman's eyes. "I don't know much about embroidery, but I don't see any pattern here. And I don't want to be disrespectful, but I think I could finish something like this in a couple hours. It certainly wouldn't take two years."

"I watched her," the bald man said. "Last few months, anyway. She worked hard on it."

The Iraqi took a step forward and pointed to a violet thread, then drew his finger to a pink thread. "You see, it's not the individual threads that make any difference—it's their relationship to each other—the way they're connected—that makes the composition beautiful."

"*Beautiful?*" the inspector squealed, his eyes bulging out of their sockets.

The woman nodded. "He's right. It took two years to understand the relationships between threads."

"You people." The inspector shook his head and laughed. "No wonder I never understood Lost."

The soft-spoken man from Iraq made a circular motion with his hand. "Turn it around. Let him see the other side."

Still grasping the fabric, the young woman passed one hand over the other, revealing the opposite side of the fabric. The inspector gasped. The young woman smiled.

"Wow." The inspector stared, stunned into silence by the design.

"That, my friend," the former torturer said, "is an aperiodic, scale-independent, iteratively repelling complex polynomial fractal quotient in the Julia set."

The bald man returned the knife to its sheath. "You coulda just said it's a chaotic design."

The Iraqi nodded. "Yes, but I did not want to hear him tell me again that I know only one word."

The young woman, still smiling, shifted her gaze to the bald old man. "I hate to say it, but I agree with you."

The old man snorted and laughed.

She turned to the inspector. "He's right. You don't need a degree in anything to understand Lost. All you need is an open mind. You just need to be open to looking at things from a fresh point of view."

"What she's sayin'," the bald man said, "is that you've been lookin' at Lost the wrong way. You have all the information you need—you just need to put it together differently."

"I don't need to watch every episode five times?"

"No," the young woman shook her head. "I haven't even watched every episode once."

"Really?"

"This guy," the old man said, pointing to the Iraqi, "never watched it. Still figured it out."

The inspector's mouth dropped open.

"Death due to C4 explosion on a submarine tends to bring new perspective to things," the dark-skinned man said.

IDENTITY

The young woman led the way down the well-worn path toward the caves. Her stride was fast but seemingly effortless, and the inspector had a difficult time keeping up with her. The old man and his Iraqi sidekick were far behind them.

"So," she asked, not breaking stride, "you're from the University of Michigan?"

"Yes," the inspector said, raising his voice so she could hear. "Ann Arbor campus, Department of Modern Literature."

She looked back, her brow knitted into a frown. "Not the Economics Department?"

He shook his head. "Literature. They're lookin' to add Lost to the curriculum, but only if I give it the thumbs up. They told me if I understood, anyone could understand."

She laughed. "They insulted you and you agreed to help out anyway?"

He smiled. "It wasn't the worst insult. Seems they talked a pharmaceutical chemist into writing the book they're gonna use for the course."

"Must be a smart guy." The young woman bent a branch forward so it wouldn't whip back in the inspector's face.

"They said he's dumb as a bag of rocks. Doesn't know anything about literary theory. He's got weird ideas about 'metadrama' and 'strange attractors' and 'identity.'"

The young woman pointed to a puddle in the path and the inspector jumped around it. The path took a turn east and they began the approach toward the caves.

"Well," she said, "Sounds like he's got it right, even if he's not so smart. Identity's what it's all about, isn't it?"

"Identity?" he said, his voice an octave too high.

The young woman stopped and turned around. "Yes. Identity. The show's called 'Lost,' remember? It's about people who don't know who they are. They find out on the Island."

"That's it?"

"What do you mean 'that's it'?"

"I just thought it was more... complicated than that."

"And you think identity isn't complicated?"

The inspector brought his hands to his hips and frowned and squinted at her. "Everyone knows who they are. You don't need to crash on an island with mysterious powers to figure it out."

"No," she said. "You need much more than that. That's why it took six years to tell the story."

The inspector shook his head and snorted.

"Look," the woman said, "You say you're an inspector, from Ann Arbor. Literature Department sent you. Well, I don't mean to be flip, but—so what? Being an 'inspector' is not your identity. What you believe, why you believe it, the way you express your beliefs in relationships and actions—that's your identity."

"Relationships?"

The young woman nodded.

The inspector shook his head. "There you go again with that 'it's all about the characters' crap. We're back to saying the mysterious Island was meaningless. They might as well have been trapped in an elevator for six years if it was 'all about the characters.'"

She looked down to the brown dirt, smiled, and exhaled. "That's not how it is."

"And how is it?"

"The Island was the most important character in the show," she said, peering up at him. "All of it mattered, just like Jack said. Everything we did on the Island was important. The story could not have been told without the Monster and Widmore's mercenaries and the green pill and everything else."

LIFE, DEATH, REBIRTH

"The green pill?"

"In the Temple. Dogen gave Jack a green pill for Sayid, remember?"

"Oh, right. The poision pill—to kill Sayid." He laughed. "The guy writing the book talked about the green pill—said it was the symbol of 'life, death, and rebirth.' Completely bonkers."

"No, he got it right." She grunted. "I'm going to have to read that book."

"Wait a minute." The inspector frowned, bit his lip, opened his mouth, then closed it again. He looked around in the trees and finally returned his gaze to the young woman, a deep frown embedded in his face. "How could a little capsule full of poison symbolise 'life, death, and rebirth'? It makes no sense. The pill could only kill—it couldn't give life or birth or anything—just death."

"So, then, if Sayid knew it was poison, and he swallowed it, he would die?"

"Well, yes, of course."

"You're sure?"

"Yes!" His voice was so loud he must have scared a bird in the tree above them. It screeched and flew off toward the ocean.

"I suppose if he had a stick of dynamite in his hand and lit the fuse he also would have died?

"Yes." His eyes grew big and his brow wrinkled. "No! I mean... wait! This is... he was a Candidate. The dynamite wouldn't have killed him because he couldn't commit suicide—it was one of Jacob's rules."

"So, if Jack gave Sayid the pill, and Sayid knew it was poison, and he swallowed it, he would die, right?"

The inspector gazed down into the long grass, frowned, then laughed and looked into her eyes. "How did you do that?"

"It's all about the way we look at things—and the way the characters perceived things, too." The woman turned around and began walking again. The inspector followed close on her heels. They were only a few metres away from the entrance to the first cave. "If Sayid knew the pill was poison, and swallowed, the pill could not have harmed him, because he was not allowed to commit suicide. But if he believed the pill harmless and swallowed, he would have died a long, agonising, painful death."

"It's an interesting idea," the inspector said.

"It's all about perception—like my embroidery. Just as Locke said, you have all the information you need—you gotta look at it in new ways, and you'll understand."

"You mean I can understand every single mystery—just by thinking about it in different ways?"

She nodded.

"But how does the pill symbolise 'life, death, and rebirth'?"

"Jack could tell you... but didn't you say you read that pharmaceutical guy's book? Isn't the answer in there?"

"Yeah, I suppose, but—" The inspector heard the swishing of a branch behind him and he jumped and pivoted around.

The old man and the Iraqi stood two metres behind him. The old man's face wore a sheepish grin.

"Sorry," the bald man said. "We were trying to be quiet."

The dark-skinned man turned to the young woman. "Where are you taking him?"

"I thought I'd show him the casket."

TWO PLAYERS. TWO SIDES.

The four of them stood at the foot of the dark mahogany casket, its brass handholds gleaming in the light of the bald man's torch.

The inspector stared at the casket. "I thought Jack smashed his father's coffin to pieces after—"

"After he chased the White Rabbit," the bald man said. "Jack's father led him to water... 'he leadeth me beside the still waters... Yea, though I walk through the shadow of the valley of death—"

"Oh, please," the Iraqi fumed. "Get it right. It's 'Yea, though I walk through the valley of the shadow of death,' not 'through the shadow of death valley or—"

"Those aren't the words I used. The old man crossed his arms over his chest. "I said—"

"Whatever," the former torturer said. "You didn't get any of it right. The waters here are not still, as you can see. They're fed by a waterfall, and it's a moving stream, not a still pool. But that's beside the point."

"And what *is* the point?" the bald man asked.

"The point," the Iraqi said, " is that it wasn't Jack's father who led him here—it was the Smoke Monster, and he was trying to lead Jack off a cliff, not to water."

The young woman shook her head. "That's not what Jack said happened."

"Oh?" The former soldier peered into the young woman's eyes.

The inspector reached down to the top of the casket and pulled it up. The door creaked on its hinges as the inspector gently brought it up and around, opening the coffin to their eyes. The cream-coloured linen inside was uncreased, as if never used. The casket was empty.

"No," the young woman said. "He told me this was the Island's greatest mystery—that it had to do with the light and dark stones. That's why the casket ended up here, near Adam and Eve."

"That's right," the inspector said.

Everyone looked at him. The Iraqi man, in particular, seemed perplexed. "And just how do you know this?" he said, staring at the inspector.

The inspector grinned and crossed his arms. "It's the only thing I remember from the book I read—the one they're gonna use at the University of Michigan."

"The one the drug company guy wrote?" the young woman asked.

He nodded. "It's the greatest mystery. The empty casket is due to 'two player, two sides.'"

The old man frowned. "Jacob and the Man in Black?"

"No." The inspector laughed. "Not even close."

"Who, then?" the Iraqi asked.

The inspector, a broad, silly grin across his face, turned to the young woman. "Do you wanna tell 'em?"

She laughed. "Sure."

They sat down around her, and she spoke. Her tongue did not fail her, even as the light outside the cave grew dim, as the crickets chirped. She spoke well into the night, into the morning, until dawn broke in the east and bathed the jungle in light. The inspector recorded her words, writing "Blue and yellow make green..."

Blue and yellow make green.

LOST is about the human need to belong, and the personal need to struggle. To achieve these conflicting ends, to find ourselves, we face disorientation, paradox, impossibility, and triumph, and all of these in the context of deep relationships, hurtful and healing, with those who make us into the people we become. The core of who we are—struggle and surrender, integrity and iniquity—is expressed in our relationship with others.

The contradictions are unrelenting. An intelligent, evil entity—immortal, impervious to bullets and missiles, invulnerable to rock and spear—could not be destroyed. Yet Jack and Kate killed the Smoke Monster. Juliet used her last bit of strength to smash Jughead's nuclear core, but there was no explosion, no return to pre-Island lives. We ought to account the Incident a failure, yet the Candidates were catapulted thirty years into the future to fight the battle that would destroy all time loops. Faraday's plan succeeded in ways unpredicted.

Forces and furies unrelated converged to explode into events unforeseen. Blue had no relation to yellow, but working together, they made green.

LOST presents a bewildering array of complex ideas, dense mythologies, interconnected events, and layers of thought and imagination woven into the most baffling and entertaining series ever produced for television. With so many characters and plot threads we feel overwhelmed, perhaps even convinced that the series made no sense, that it left too many questions unresolved. Our confusion is real, inevitable, and necessary. But it is not the final stage in our understanding. Hundreds of questions outstanding are resolved into a few major ideas. The major ideas meld into a single core, which is the thesis of LOST. The colours of the rainbow, the complexities of LOST, are all driven into light of a single wavelength, the kernel of an idea, that is the central tenet of the series.

The book you hold in your hands combines light and dark, blue and yellow, fate and freewill, good and evil, into a sure means of distilling coherence from ambiguity, confusion, and paradox. These were some of the guiding dramatic methods used in telling the story of LOST. The storytelling techniques were more advanced than any ever before applied to television, and with good reason. The creators of LOST were attempting to generate a work of enduring significance, an audacious statement about the condition of our humanity and the value of human civilisation.

This book is for anyone who has enjoyed LOST but wishes to gain fresh appreciation for the interrelated nature of its rich ideas. This book is for all of you who followed the series faithfully through most or all of the six years, but found yourselves disenchanted or confused or frustrated. You were not alone in your bewilderment and vexation—I was there, too. With several thousands of hours of research dedicated to the task, I found my way through the confusion and into a new state of understanding. In less than ten or twenty hours, having read this book, you will find a deeper and more rewarding sense of the Island, without having to read advanced texts in differential equations, literary theory, or quantum physics. You may find yourself at times annoyed or amused. You may concur with my analyses or disagree with my interpretations, but you will not complete this book without becoming exposed to new ways of thinking about and exploring LOST.

THE ADVENTURE OF LOST

This six-year adventure became the most monumental endeavour in the history of television. Millions of us around the world spent hours each week, not watching a programme so much as engaging our senses, immersing ourselves in an experience unlike anything ever presented on the small screen. We attended online lectures by professors of linguistics, Egyptology, and quantum string theory. The tome in Sawyer's hand or the thin volume on the Swan Station bookshelf became our weekly order from Amazon. We listened to Al Trautwig, Carmel, Mr. James, Iain Lee, and Doc Jensen. Lostpedia was our bible, Vozzek69 our prophet.

We scoured every scene for clues. Hurley is buying Ho-Hos. Hurley and Jack play horse, but they proceed only as far as HO before Jack decides to leave. Hurley is in the recreation room, and behind him, conspicuous to our fanatical eyes, a plastic sculpture of the letters HO. This is rich fare for a guy who spends sixty hours a week in pharmaceutical laboratories, and I immediately reach for the periodic table in my mind's eye. Holmium, a heavy metal, a lanthanide, atomic symbol Ho. Can't say I know much more about it than that--it is obscure, even to a professional chemist. So I turn to the chemist's best friend: Google. Holmium has the highest magnetic susceptibility of any element, several times more magnetic than iron. The Swan Station has peculiar and extreme magnetic properties. Is Holmium the key to understanding the significance of the Swan Station?

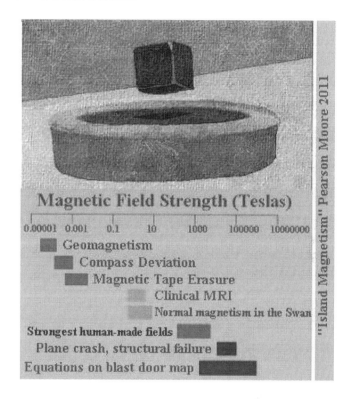

No.

I know this because of my acquaintance with Mr. Friendly. To his complete amazement, I'm sure, I explain to him every nuance of mutually-orthogonal four-dimensional electromagnetic space, and how the unusual concentration of unstable energy at the Swan explains not only the local magnetism, but also the strange light scattering properties of the Island, which are due to shifts away from the normal range of Mie and Fraunhofer diffraction. Five hours later, when I've explained every detail of electromagnetism in the Land of Mittelos, Mr. Friendly just shakes his head in amusement. "That's not what the Island's about, Pearson."

What is the Island, then?

I'm going to apply the Mr. Friendly Rule to the remainder of this book. If a concept useful to full understanding of the core reality of the Island requires graduate-level expertise in a physical science, then the concept is not essential to that understanding. Studying the non-intuitive etiologies deriving of Schrödinger's Cat and other quantum phenomena is entertaining, but at least for the purposes of my discussion, I'm going to bring the question to Tom Friendly and Flight Attendant Cindy Chandler. If they can't figure out what I'm talking about, it probably is not relevant to the deeper aspects of the story. The Island is not a Mr. Wizard science freak show.

What is the Island?

The question is daunting. The series generated over five hundred questions, thousands of details that must be woven together to figure out just what Jacob's Eye of Horus might signify, why it contains important Egyptian and Greek elements, and why nine individuals are depicted as bowing in obedience to the Eye. Jacob's tapestry, laboriously spun from wool and woven on a hand loom, is symbolic of the tremendous investment in time we must give to reconciling unusual phenomena, extreme and unpredicted events, and most of all, the strange circularity and interconnectedness of Island, people, and time.

Much more than science is required to understand the Island. We gain important clues to the deeper appreciation of Mittelos' significance from the narrative structure of the story itself.

Normal storytelling does not work on the Island, because LOST cannot unfold in linear fashion. The chronologies of cause and effect were difficult to track long before the time travel of Season Five, before Daniel Faraday demonstrated the bizarre curvature of spacetime around the Island in Season Four, before even we heard Mama Cass exhorting Desmond Hume to make his own kind of music in Season Two.

NONLINEAR STORY

Why is the story nonlinear?

A woman's body is found unmoving in a pool of blood in a basement apartment. A neighbour calls the police, detectives arrive, interview tenants, landlord, husband. They search telephone calls, internet usage, medical records. Police identify suspects, assign motives, make an arrest, and there's a trial. The bad guy goes to jail, and the world is safe again. Best thing is, it took only forty-three minutes (not counting seventeen minutes of commercial messages) to tell the whole story from start to finish.

"Meandering River" Thanachaporn 2011 CC SA 3.0

Law-And-Order storytelling could not possibly work on Jacob's Island. I suppose one might imagine LOST as a simple story of good versus evil, much in the manner of CSI, Law and Order SUV (Or is it CSI-SVU?) or any of the other programmes that seem to fill prime time in North America. But LOST brings much more to our dialogue: Free Will versus Destiny, Destiny versus Fate, the philosophical imposition of Rousseau, Locke, Dogen, Burke, Bentham, and the religious sensibilities and histories of Islam, Christianity, Judaism, Hinduism, and Buddhism. Even Greek mythology and ancient Egyptian religion are heavily represented. The story alludes to modern stories, classic literature, and archaic texts. It invokes ancient civilisations, timeless themes, and current culture.

As Lex Luthor said thirty-three years ago, "Some people can read War and Peace and come away thinking it was a simple adventure story. Others can read the ingredients on a chewing gum wrapper and unlock the secrets of the universe." LOST is not a simple adventure story. A bare-bones recitation of the dialogue alone consumes 3800 pages. If LOST were rendered in novel form with the required narrative support the story would fill over ten thousand pages. The story was complex, with dozens of major themes, hundreds of characters, thousands of interconnected pieces. Only the concerted application of several forms of analytical technique, aimed at illuminating key interrelated facets of the story, will allow us to unravel the deeper significance of this television masterpiece.

The Island operates on a hierarchy of values. Any valid thesis regarding LOST must account for the vital and mortal truths of Mittelos. Theses addressing only scientific phenomena, character relationships, or pure mythology will fall short of identifying the most potent and enduring of LOST's ideas.

LOST must be presented in a nonlinear, non-chronological, non-causal manner because of the complexity of the hierarchy. Most of the time Cerberus (the Smoke Monster) can mind his own business, curl up under the Temple and contemplate getting off the rock he has been stranded on. Sometimes he gets ornery; knowing when the Man in Black is in a bad mood--and where he is at the time--constitutes useful information to anyone interested in prolonging her stay on the Island. Sometimes the rules of the Island or his own constitution and caprice dictate that he will kill. Being aware of the conditions that oblige Smokey to execute the full force of Island law or to fulfill his personal objectives is a matter of life and death.

LOST MYTHOLOGY

The mythology of LOST is not a single strand. It is a grand tapestry, with warp composed of literature ancient and classic, with weft comprising the strongest cords of spiritual sentiment and tradition. We cannot follow a single strand of this woven masterpiece and hope to elucidate every nuance of significance. In fact, if we do not take into consideration the rich and sometimes conflicting facets of the work, we will never attain to an appreciation of the deepest meaning of the series.

The Swan Station was built by modern scientists but it referenced the Greek mythology of the sun god, Apollo, and it incorporated Egyptian mythology into the counter clock. The station studied electromagnetic phenomena, but its primary purpose, post-Incident, was to prevent the extreme effects of a massive and uncontrollable discharge of electromagnetic energy. But the overarching mythology of the station belonged to LOST, with the creation of the doomsday Valenzetti Equation. The word "Valenzetti" was never spoken during the six years of LOST, and it appeared only once as feeble scratchings in the midst of hundreds of notations on an immense blast door map. But such is the depth of mythological association that we cannot understand the Swan Station and the concepts it represents without first gaining a full appreciation of the doomsday equation.

We cannot consider events or characters from a single point of view. The Smoke Monster provides an excellent example in this regard, but we might equally consider the case of any of the major characters or occurrences.

Consider the complexity of the Man in Black. He is the black death, evil incarnate, a representation of the unholy depravity that holds the hearts of women and men. We have seen him before, we think: The Invisible Man of H.G. Wells, the night-abiding evils of the vampire, the werewolf, the goblins and monsters of fantasy and lore. If so, then we can categorise him, define him, place him into a pigeonhole and in this way determine the significance of every single interaction in which he ever participated. But we will miss crucial strands if we do this. The Dharma Initiative knew the Man in Black as Cerberus, from the Greek myth of the guardian of the gate between Hades and Earth. He inhabited the underworld—the Island Hades—under the Temple, the place where Montand lost his arm. The place where Rousseau lost her sanity. We saw the great pillar of smoke stand in judgment of Juliet, of Ben, of Mr. Eko.

Weaving these strong strands into the tapestry we find ourselves no longer sure of our original assignment. Is the Man in Black evil incarnate? Is he a "security system"? Is he an arbiter of law, a judge of the hearts of women and men? Guardian of the Temple? Is he all of these things, or something else entirely? Only a careful consideration of every one of these marvelously woven strands, and the way they are connected to the larger embroidery, will allow us to come to a determination of his significance.

The goal of LOST is not creativity for the sake of innovation. LOST is the most creative programme ever produced for television, but this is not its unique or most important objective. Neither is it intended as Lex Luthor's adventure-story interpretation of War and Peace. The intention is to create an idea of permanent value. The story created, conflicted, and ultimately resolved hundreds of plot threads and concepts in breathtaking fashion, establishing enduring purchase in the literary world.

The genius of LOST is its profound connection to our awareness as human beings, to the deepest sensibilities of our nature. A story becomes literature, I think, when it engages the reader, plunges her into the story, and forces her to examine and perhaps even reconsider her own values in light of choices made by the characters in the difficult situations created by the author. Literature best achieves these ends when it weaves into the story elements of thought immediately recognisable to the reader.

MYTHIC PERFECTION

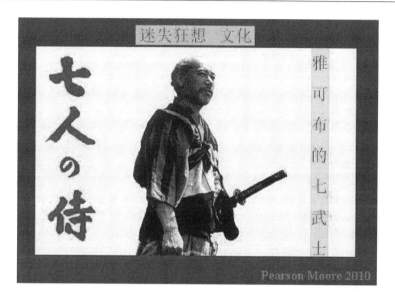

His name is Kambei Shimada, a ronin who lived five hundred years ago. He is an aged, balding, unemployed swordsman, symbol of a dying breed of men useless in an age of muskets. His story required only two hundred seven minutes of celluloid. We think we know him: hero, defender of peasants, leader of men. But his story does not end with one year's barley harvest, or even an entire nation's movement into the modern age. If we are to understand LOST, we must have a deep appreciation of Kambei Shimada and his significance to Akira Kurosawa's masterpiece, "The Seven Samurai."

Kambei Shimada did not act alone to save the farmers from marauding thieves and bandits. Akira Kurosawa did not restrict himself to self-referential creations. The master storyteller reached back to over a thousand years of Japanese history to invoke themes and ideas that have stood these many years, proof to wars, plagues, and all manner of human imperfection. Kurosawa examined poverty, nobility and altruism, gratitude—and the lack of it—and the injustice of a class-based society, among the grand themes of the film.

Kurosawa gave us memorable characters, most notably in Shimada, the balding leader past his prime who, on first attempt, failed to convince other ronin to follow him to the village. But more than memorable characters and situations, the director wove his story from the strong yarn of enduring culture. His film stands not only as an irreplaceable pillar of modern Japanese culture, but is considered by many the greatest film ever produced.

Few in North America have experienced the genius of The Seven Samurai, but the most frequently offered movie on American television is familiar to almost everyone on the continent: The Magnificent Seven.

Set in 1880s Mexico, seven unemployed gunslingers agree to risk their lives for twenty dollars to protect a village of farmers. The lead role of Chris Adams, an aging bald man past his prime, was played by Yul Brynner. John Sturges' characters were as memorable as Kurosawa's, most notably in Chris Adams, who, on first attempt, failed to convince gunslingers to follow him to the village.

The story of the Seven Samurai works perfectly well in any culture because the enduring and necessary elements of any culture transcend time and place. One of the notions that works equally well in sixteenth century Japan, nineteenth century Mexico, or the twenty-first century South Pacific, is the idea of perfection. In both the Kurosawa classic and the American remake, perfection is expressed in a number: Seven. In Japanese, Hebrew, and Western cultures, the number seven is perfect. The perfect number of selfless men to protect a village? Seven. The perfect number of selfless individuals to protect an Island?

The very stressed characters on Jacob's Island were striving toward some better condition. They strove toward perfection. As Jacob said, "It only ends once. Anything that happens before that—it's just progress."

Six survivors: Shephard, Austen, Reyes, Jarrah, Kwon, Littleton. Six Swan Station numbers: 4, 8, 15, 16, 23, 42. Six Candidates: Locke, Reyes, Ford, Jarrah, Shephard, Kwon. But six did not prevail against the Smoke Monster. Six could not defend the Island. All of Jacob's plans, all the Temple Master's work, the hopes of Jin and Sun, the faith of Jack and Locke, were found wanting in the end.

If you are reading these lines, it is almost certainly because you have seen most or all of the 121 episodes. Perhaps with millions of us around the world, you have absorbed repeated viewings not only of the episodes, but every one of the mobisodes, the Hanso Foundation commercials, and the hour-long "Mysteries of the Universe" series. You own copies of the Sri Lanka video, the Norway video, the Hanso Industries film. But even if you have not immersed yourself to this extent in LOST lore, you may be reading these words with a degree of scepticism in your thoughts. "What do you mean, Pearson, when you say 'the plans and hopes and faith of Jack and Locke were found wanting'? Jack killed the Man in Black. The plan worked."

I do not dispute the objective truth that the Man in Black was defeated. I do dispute the view that Jacob's original plan succeeded and that his vision was sufficient to determine the outcome of the 2000-year-old game of Senet. In the end, neither Jacob nor Jack prevailed. Something much grander occurred, and it is the aim of this book to come to terms with the eloquence of the profound statements that LOST made about us in those final minutes on the lava cliffs.

Many of us with degrees in language or literature share an interesting hubris: We believe we enjoy not only innate curiosity regarding the nature of the human condition, but also an obligation, essentially a moral imperative, to find the means to engage others in a contemplation of the meaning of existence.

Usually the artist is thwarted in her attempts to engage the audience. She must feed herself, after all, and employers are not interested in art for art's sake, they're interested in selling a product or service. Radically new ideas, risky by definition, are not generally seen as worthy of investment. So the artist becomes a waitress, or sells commodities at the Chicago Board of Trade, or works sixty hours a week in a pharmaceutical laboratory... and the sculpture goes unseen, the screenplay unread, the great symphony unheard.

Sometimes the artist gets lucky. A small work gains attention, a former employer earns a profit on the artist's work, a second employer, willing to take a risk, agrees to feed the starving artist while she whips up another small creation. That was the intention with LOST, as far as I can tell. But something unexpected occurred: 18.6 million viewers.

What does an artist do when she's given a nice salary and carte blanche? Building 23 at the ABC complex in Los Angeles was full of cartes blanches, and for nearly six years the writers filled them with scenarios, plot developments, character arcs, storylines, and most of all, cultural references.

Darlton (Damon Lindelof and Carlton Cuse) knew the best way to engage the audience was to weave LOST into the very fabric of our lives. They were able to do this only because the basic material was already there. The greatest demonstrable skill of the artist is not the creation of new ideas. Ideas are a dime a dozen. The greatest skill is the ability to engage an audience. If, in order to achieve this end, the artist must use fabric already present in the viewer's psyche, she must endeavour to choose the strongest, most enduring yarns from that fabric, then re-weave them into something new. The bottom line for us: Regardless of any story innovations, LOST must rely on cultural motifs we all recognise. The necessary connections between culture and the completed plotline provide a basis for a reasonable understanding of the story.

THE ISLAND

The Island is Shangri-La and LOST is James Hilton's Lost Horizon, updated to the internet age and stuffed with a hundred-fold more cultural references and statements regarding our humanity than Hilton ever thought to include in his masterwork. The Darlton Shangri-La surpasses Hilton's creation in ways critical to the telling of the story. Most importantly, Mittelos is a multi-cultural, multi-ethnic Shangri-La with origins in Tibet, Mesopotamia, Egypt, Hawaii, and Japan, deep spiritual roots in Judaism and Christianity, and mythic roots in Ancient Greece and Ancient Egypt. Those in the Western world will recognise elements of Eden: Adam and Eve, harmony with nature, timelessness (e.g., Ricardus' immortality), inaccessibility (a trait shared also with Lost Horizon), guardian angels (the Man in Black and Jacob). Mittelos references myths from around the world because this is a story for the entire world—for all of humanity.

But this is only a small portion of the reality of the Island. We must also understand the literary strands, the references to William Shakespeare and Stephen King, C.S. Lewis and Lewis Carroll, Joseph Conrad and Joseph Heller, and a hundred other authors and works, from the Epic of Gilgamesh to The Third Policeman. We need to understand Jacob's connections to The Wizard of Oz and Star Wars, the Man in Black's connections to Jurassic Park and Lord of the Flies.

We will see that the Island is far richer than any particular strand of mythology, literary allusion, or reference to religion, history, or philosophy. Even the characters of Mittelos are more complex than any ever before seen on television, and we will explore exactly how this is so. This book is only an introduction to the intricacies of thought that must be applied to this fictional structure to glean the deepest possible enjoyment of the series.

WHAT THE ISLAND IS NOT

The Island most emphatically is not Cheech and Chong's pot-smoking, hippie-infested free-love paradise. The Temple Master's assistant, Lennon, may have worn love beads around his neck, but he felt no emotion of any kind when he relayed the command to exterminate prisoners. Lennon was one of the final representatives of the hippie counter-culture. Darlton have made clear to us their unreserved disdain for any organisation on the island expressing hedonistic ideals. Hedonism in LOST is a ploy, a diversion used to mask the true agenda of those in command, and that agenda is the acquisition of power over others. Culture, on Darlton's Island, seeks the Common Good. Counter-culture seeks to concentrate power into a single dictator and her minions. Counter-culture is what it implies: a radical opposition to culture. It is the purest expression of evil because it rejects everything of humanity that endures and is worthy of being held as ideal and exemplar of thought and behaviour.

DISORIENTATION

One of the most useful realisations we can bring to the comprehension of LOST is the necessity of confusion. We need to be confused because LOST assaults and tears down many of the assumptions we apply in attempting to understand drama, causality, and human nature. LOST makes unique statements in all of these areas. If we are to accept, appreciate, and finally admire these novel proclamations, we first need to be willing to part with the deep biases that inhibit our ability to synthesise radically novel ideas from the dramatic material supplied by the series. Allowing ourselves to succumb to the disorientations of frenzy, chaos, and conceptual disorder, we are stripped of useless preconceptions and we have new eyes with which to begin the piecing together of insights and epiphanies that will become the foundation for true understanding.

Much of the complexity of LOST was attained through a bewildering array of disorientation techniques: lies, incomplete thoughts and actions, long-term misdirection and deception, short cons, long cons, and the disorienting effects of unexpected events and strange connections between people, mythologies, and unusual occurrences. I found confusion and severe disorientation became the normal state of mind after an episode of LOST. Disorientation spurred research on the internet and at the library. We sought clues not only to plot elements, but tried to find enough supporting information about a book, line of dialogue, or image on the Island to make sense of the current disposition of the story so we would be ready for the next week's bewilderments.

At the beginning of Season Three, Jack, then Ben's prisoner on Hydra Island, asked, "What do you want from me?" Ben's response: "I want for you to change your ... perspective." He was speaking to every one of us viewer-participants.

The effort to disorient viewers was not accidental, but very much intentional on the part of writers and directors. They did not seek shock and awe so much as they truly hoped to effect a change in the way we perceived the story. In fact, as I will relate later in this book, those of us who came to understand the series were not viewers at all, but participants in the story. This claim might sound rather fanciful, but as I will demonstrate, there is in performance art a long and quite respected tradition of forcing those attending a performance to cast themselves in the role of participants—fellow actors in the drama—in such a way that passive attendance at the event is not possible. If you are not actively involved in LOST, you will never understand it. Thus, disorientation—the aggressive attempt to knock us free of conventions of perception and understanding—was an essential component of the LOST experience.

The struggle between science and faith was a major theme of the series. During the first four seasons Locke and Jack clashed on an almost daily basis. While Jack grew in faith, Locke became progressively less sure of himself, to the point that he was ready to take his own life. Given the task of returning the Oceanic Six to the Island, he died believing he had failed. But John Locke proved to be the greatest of the LOST prophets, and the man responsible for the Oceanic Six's return to Mittelos. Jack died considering Locke his spiritual master.

Although LOST pitted Locke and Jack against each other, they were not the primary exemplars of faith and science. The series made crucial statements about the validity and utility of both the scientific- and belief-based worldviews. As with most of the work's themes, the final statements were not black and white, but heavily nuanced and derivative of the show's primary themes. Our goal of understanding the full import of LOST's thesis and core statements will become achievable only if we commit ourselves to a robust analysis of this important leitmotif.

TRUST

Trust, especially as it related to John Locke, was a recurring theme. LOST made challenging statements regarding the value of trust and its place in human civilisation. We will give a full chapter to this theme, as it provides the basis for the more important concepts of faith and the Constant.

Trust did not enjoy plentiful or wide distribution on the Island. Several factors had direct bearing on this poor representation of a crucial virtue. Certainly the perceived value of the Island and its abilities had striking effect on the ambitions of people like Charles Widmore, but he was far from unique in having an agenda that replaced trust and good will with expediency and single-mindedness as daily protocols toward his objective. With as many as five different groups simultaneously competing for resources to fulfill unrelated or opposing goals, courtesy and cooperation were not often the first thought when groups came into contact. Trust was risky and often dangerous. Lack of trust was no less dangerous, and proved deadly on at least three occasions. LOST proposed a means of escaping the dilemma posed by trust in a dangerous and contentious environment.

FAITH

Although the motif of faith is often coupled with religious symbols, the concept of faith in LOST is independent of sentiments and doctrines of any organised religion. The accoutrements of the LOST variant of faith are not all that different from those of any other system of knowledge and belief grounded in spiritual trust rather than scientific logic. I will attempt to resolve those elements relating to faith from the sometimes closely aligned constituents that tend more toward the province of religious symbol, mythological tradition, or literary allusion.

I will devote some effort to defining and categorising types of allegory and allusion, as these ideas are important to an understanding of LOST's type of faith. We will see that LOST is rich in literary, religious, and mythological allusion, and more often than not these elements intersect and build upon each other. Gaining an appreciation for the multi-tiered nature of faith-related elements will help us in analysing the grand themes and the final thesis of the series.

THE CONSTANT

The writers of LOST devoted nearly a quarter of Season Six to development of the idea of the Constant, and with good reason. The concept superficially seems no different than the modern-day notions of soul mate or partner. Although the ideas are not unrelated, they are nevertheless distinct. In fact, with this theme LOST makes a new statement with far-reaching effects within the story, but also provides rich food for thought regarding the nature of friendship, marriage, and the spiritual bonds between people.

The Constant became a major theme in Season Four with the story of Desmond's spiritual bond to Penny. By the final episode in Season Six, most of the main characters, both living and dead, congregated in Constant-pairs inside the church. The pairings seemed entirely natural developments based on stories in both the sideways and Island realities, but there was something odd about the Constant-pairs. With more happy couples than one is ever likely to find in the pages of the most saccharine romance novel, one would expect to find the word "love" and like terms in high abundance in the corpus of LOST. In fact, though, the word "love" occurs only 267 times throughout the whole six years, including the mobisodes. The word "believe," often closely associated with the idea of faith, occurs 275 times. I will take a close look at this disconnection between the Constant and the traditional idea of love since the distinction carries great relevance to the major themes of the work.

LEADERSHIP

LOST presented us with a diverse ensemble cast and a wide range of leaders of several varieties. Some of the leaders fit into traditional roles. Charles Widmore was the autocratic tyrant, Sayid Jarrah was the martyr to a just cause, John Locke was the natural expedition captain who led by example and experience, Michael Dawson was the father who sought the best for his son at great expense to himself. That these characters fulfilled traditional roles does not at all diminish the richness of their stories or their essential contribution to the main plot.

It is in the category of leadership that LOST made some of its most original contributions to television fiction. Sawyer was a self-absorbed renegade, but he had been a voracious reader his entire life. When he met Juliet, hidden talents made their way to the fore. Sawyer, the confidence man, became the most effective leader of the entire series. The leadership style of the Man in Black, in his perfection of the art of deception, and more importantly, in his unconscious acquisition of sentiments not entirely his own, will require the most research of any of the characters. We plumb the depths of LOST only by going through the deep well of this disembodied entity's character.

Finally, Kate and Jack present unique leadership traits that require their own in-depth analysis. The scope of this book does not allow the full treatment that Jack, Kate, and the dozens of other characters deserve. But we do not understand LOST without studying each one of them, and this will be done in my second book, "LOST Identity," to be published about three months after the book you hold in your hands appears in stores.

MAGNIFICENT TAPESTRY

Even the most profound expressions of philosophical inquiry start with simple and common ideas. We will begin our analysis with traditional, "linear" examinations of key concepts in LOST. The thesis of LOST, defined in Chapter Two, will serve as a guide for the following seven chapters devoted to "linear themes." These are analytical essays of the type that might be found in any of the popular companion books treating LOST. I have included them because I believe the themes covered in these chapters are necessary or useful to an understanding of the later, "nonlinear" chapters addressing multi-dimensional aspects of the series.

Chapters Ten through Thirteen examine the storytelling tools themselves: Disorientation, literary structures, metadrama, and nonlinear character relationships unique to LOST that I refer to as "Strange Attractors." Having studied these strange and fascinating aspects of the story, we will move on to examine advanced topics. These include concepts requiring the nonlinear methods described in earlier chapters. We will look at topics such as literary connections to the Seven Samurai, the significance of the green pill, and the meaning of the Valenzetti Equation. Most importantly, we will use these advanced studies to deepen our understanding of the core ideas of LOST, their attachment to the thesis, and the impact they have on our conception of human life.

We may believe that the blue colour of Dharma vans and jeeps is real, that it represents something attainable. In like manner, we may believe the yellow colour of the Light is something we already possess. But these are incomplete, linear, and practically meaningless depictions of reality, as we shall see. The only reality we can attain is the truth of the green pill. Science (Dharma blue) and faith (the yellow Light) make us complete. Blue and yellow make green. This book will approach our green reality from four distinct directions.

LOST is unlike anything you have experienced on television, in cinema, in fiction—in life. The series is about a band of survivors on a tropical island, but more than that, the show concerns all of us: our conflicting cultures, our shared humanity. LOST makes bold statements, unique to fiction, regarding the nature of human aspirations and human civilisation.

You must get LOST.

Getting LOST is not for the lukewarm, the faint of heart, the casual viewer. You do not "watch" LOST. You experience it. Absorb it. Put your mind and heart and soul into it. You must let go, succumb to confusion, allow yourself to be carried by the story.

Welcome to the adventure. Prepare to get LOST.

"The Island" copyright Pearson Moore
2011 Kindle-compatible version

LOST is not a story of good versus evil. When Kate and Jack killed the Smoke Monster no dramatic music played. The credits did not roll. The greater part of the story remained.

LOST is not a story of freedom versus destiny. Jack "chose" to become Protector of the Island, but only because he recognised the office as his destiny. The entire story was built on a continuous assumption of ultimate purpose; free will was given short shrift. But the story was not about fate per se.

LOST is not a story of science versus faith. Once Locke freed Jack from the shackles of logic, the deepest part of the story remained. We discovered with Jack his true purpose, the purpose of the Island, our purpose as human beings.

LOST is the story of our humanity and the cultural elements comprising its essential core. LOST tells us the unceasing perpetuation of civilisation is the source and final goal of all culture, all humanity, all divinity. If we cannot live together, if we die alone, we are lost. But if we recognise and honour the call to civility, allow the Light inside to guide us, we find our way to each other, and we are not lost.

A simple idea. A one-hour Hallmark special ought to suffice. Hell, even a Histori.ca minute oughta do it, right? No. Six years were required, and for good reason. This will not be a short chapter.

LIVE TOGETHER, DIE ALONE

Jack framed a crude, initial statement of the thesis in Episode 1.05, "White Rabbit." The emphasis is mine.

"It's been six days and we're all still waiting. Waiting for someone to come. But what if they don't? We have to stop waiting. We need to start figuring things out. A woman died this morning just going for a swim and [Boone] tried to save her, and now you're about to crucify him? We can't do this. *Everyman for himself is not going to work*. It's time to start organizing. We need to figure out how we're going to survive here. Now, I found water. Fresh water, up in the valley. I'll take a group in at first light. If you don't want to go then find another way to contribute. Last week most of us were strangers, but we're all here now. And God knows how long we're going to be here. *But if we can't live together, we're going to die alone*."

These are easy words to preach, they are most difficult principles to practice. For one thing, not everyone's needs and abilities are identical. When needs are great and resources are few, conflict is inevitable. These two elements, differing needs and dearth of resources, are further exacerbated by the natural human tendency toward selfishness. A breakdown in civility could be expected on the basis of any two of these three destructive elements. In a conventional story, these are the only three elements that would be addressed. A power struggle could be expected, and the story would end with the establishment of a chosen, appointed, or assumed leader, and an Island government. The leader, acting as arbiter of the Common Good, would make decisions on the allocation of food and resources, work schedules, communal projects, and any other activities required for the general welfare.

But LOST is not a conventional story. Appointing a leader for the survivors, finding a replacement for Ben, completing the process of turning a Candidate into the Protector of the Island were not the final objectives of the show. If they had been, that one-hour Hallmark special would have done the trick. The problem is much deeper, and required a few years of intense development and discussion.

JACK OF THE NUCLEAR AGE

One of the more interesting philosophical positions on the scenario of a stranded group of individuals was developed by William Golding in his 1954 masterpiece, "Lord of the Flies". At the very end of the novel, the boys' island engulfed in flames, Ralph on the verge of being murdered by Jack Merridew and his lawless gang, a British Royal Navy officer appeared on the beach.

With the arrival of the officer in his dazzling white, perfectly pressed uniform, the boys realised the extent of their depravity. Living without the order imposed by civilisation, the boys had reverted to barbarism, or something that might even be considered closer in character to a pre-human, animal existence. But instantly, with the return of civilisation, represented by the just-so uniforms of the Royal Navy, all was well again.

I believe LOST accepts the notion of selfishness, but I am certain it adamantly rejects Golding's starched uniform ideal. Golding's novel was pessimistic. If people are taken outside their normal social milieu, they will succumb to their basest instincts, which are entirely selfish, destructive, and disrespectful of human life itself. All that is needed to restore order are the outward trappings of civilisation: Uniforms tailored, laundered, and pressed just so, British Common Law, a jolly game of cricket, tea time at four o'clock sharp, and a rousing chorus of God Save the Queen. Meanwhile, inside the pressed uniform, the depraved desires are tensed, waiting for their moment to escape the artificial constraints of Victorian sensibility to unleash whatever urges and excitements appeal at the moment.

LOST rejects this idea. The starched uniform is not important and is not the defining aspect of civility. Civility is not external, but very much internal. The body, mind, and soul inside the uniform is what concerns LOST. It is the enormous depth that LOST attempted that rendered it entirely unsuited to the limited format of a brief novel or two-hour movie. LOST started with Golding but would go much, much farther in establishing and delineating its unique thesis.

PRISTINE SNOW BLANKETING PUTRID DUNG

Jack Merridew of the Nuclear Age was inherently depraved. Jack Shephard, the New Jack, was not inherently or even essentially evil. Darlton's Jack—representing each one of us—was inherently and essentially good.

If we are to understand the ramifications of the thesis of LOST, we must first understand what LOST believes about the nature of humanity. Simply saying "LOST believes we're all good at heart" will not suffice, because the show took pains to explain its position on humanity. The need to plumb the depths of the human soul inevitably requires that we employ the language of religion. I beg the reader to understand, as I begin delving into religious territory, that I do this within the context of the television programme. It is not my intention to provide commentary on any particular religious tradition or to advocate one strain of religion over any other.

According to apocryphal citation, adherents of some religious traditions have held that human nature is best compared to a seething, putrid dung heap. I advise again that I do not claim that any particular tradition currently embraces this comparison, or that any tradition ever did use this imagery in its teaching, or that the teaching is without religious merit. But the image is powerful and appropriate to this discussion because it relates a way of thinking about humanity helpful in better understanding LOST. According to this apocryphal tradition, the redeeming grace of the Creator can be thought of as a pristine layer of snow, forever covering the dung heap. The disagreeable odour of the dung is replaced by the clean scent of fresh snow, and all of the vile aspects of the dung are hidden, replaced by the beauty of the perfectly white (perfectly clean, without even the smallest stain of sin) powder from heaven.

The powerful imagery is predicated on theological understandings of human nature and the nature of divine grace. According to this way of thinking, not even the omnipotence of the Creator is sufficient to change the essentials of human nature. We are depraved, treacherously sinful creatures, with or without the divine intervention of grace, redemption, or salvation. The covering of our sins by the Creator's perfect grace (the snow in the apocryphal analogy) is sufficient to render us suitable for redemption or the afterlife or whatever rewards might accrue to a life lived in the Creator's grace.

I believe this understanding of human nature to be entirely at odds with the view expressed in LOST. I believe LOST proclaims that there is an unalterable basis for positing the inherent goodness of human nature. Further, I believe LOST conveys the idea that tendencies toward evil can be changed; even if the fundamental disposition of an individual is toward evil, with appropriate and effective intervention at the spiritual level, that disposition can be redirected toward constructive intentions and pursuits.

THE SOURCE

The Source is the point of contact with the Divine. We might think of it as something akin to the Burning Bush, but the comparison is feeble. The Burning Bush was a divine apparition in a form suitable to Moses' human understanding. The Source is raw, unfiltered divine power. It is the Burning Bush, but it burns not only with bright light, but with heat, with angry red judgment, with the full majesty and fury and terror of a million suns, with the complete force of divine will.

The Creator is Source of all power, and Her strength is not subject to the whims or puny syllogisms of the most intelligent human mind or the most powerful engine humans could ever create. There is but one way to come into the presence of the Source, and that is through sustained commitment. Theology expresses this commitment in the form of "Covenant." In Western monotheistic tradition, one of the most important of these civilisation-wide commitments was expressed as a set of Ten Commandments carved onto stone tablets. The material instrument of Covenant in LOST was the Cork Stone, carved in ancient script with the most important axioms of human civilisation. We meet the Source by coming into Covenant. The Cork Stone was humanity's statement of adherence to the highest values of civilisation. By placing the Cork Stone into the centre of the Source, the Protector established the only conceivable connection between humanity and that which is divine, and that connection was predicated on and created the fertile ground for the propagation of human civilisation. The pledge of civility was humanity's Covenant with the Divine.

THE LIGHT

It is by the power of the Source working through the etched-in-stone precepts of civilisation on the Cork Stone that we are allowed to enjoy the chief benefit of the filtered, raw divine energy that we experience as the comforting Light of the Source. Not the "energy field created by all living things" of Star Wars or pantheism, the Light that each one of us carries in our hearts ("a little bit of this very same light is inside of every man," according to the Guardian in "Across the Sea") is present inside us only because of our communal commitment to the responsibilities of civilisation.

Chicago Union Station January 1943
Jack Delano, Farm Security Administration, WMC PD

The Light is that aspect of reality that we share with the Creator. The first book of the Hebrew Bible, Genesis, speaks of humanity's likeness to the Creator: "God created human beings in the divine image; in the divine image God created them; male and female God created them." (Gen. 1:27) Human beings, in the Hebrew tradition, are the Image of the Creator. We share with the Creator some ineffable, undefined aspect or substance or quality that imbues us with inherent worth. Our value is not a function of utility, expression, or function in life. Our worth is independent of intellectual or creative accomplishment, and cannot be calibrated against or thought to wax or wane with crimes committed or great works performed. All of us, whether prince or pauper, saint or criminal, bear the divine image and are therefore, of all creation, closest in likeness and actual substance to the Creator; human beings are therefore sacred, inviolate. In the language of LOST, we are all bearers of the divine Light, and our dignity expresses itself in our commitment to the humble and yet earnest maintenance and propagation of that Light. That is to say, commitment to the responsibilities and benefits of civilisation is the source and final objective of our identity and our human dignity.

It is because of the Light that Jack (and all of us) carry the divine spark of goodness in our hearts. The Light renders us inherently good. The Light is always present, so that at any moment we might choose to orient our thoughts and intentions and choices and actions along a fundamental disposition toward the responsibilities and freedoms of civilisation.

If Jack was inherently good, if he worked diligently, even past the point of exhaustion, even to the point of transfusing his own blood to save a dying man, how could LOST possibly say that Jack was in any way insufficient to the position of leader of the survivors, or the office of Protector of the Island? Why did Jack have to endure a three-year ordeal, a series of psychological and spiritual trials that nearly killed him, before he was deemed ready for the great responsibilities of Protector?

Boone was dying. Nothing Jack Shephard did, no course of action available to him on the Island, would lead to any but the most dreaded outcome. Boone would die, had to die, regardless of any of Jack's many heroic actions. Jack worked ceaselessly, hour after hour, ignoring his own physical needs, giving every ounce of his strength and even his own blood in an attempt to pull Boone away from the clutches of death.

This was not the first time Jack had been forced into a position of confronting the full reality of death. The first instance occurred during their initial night on the Island. Federal Agent Ed Mars, a jagged slab of metal imbedded in his abdomen, could not possibly survive without immediate, state-of-the-art surgical procedures unavailable on the Island. Jack refused to surrender, tending to his dying patient night and day. It was only Sawyer's botched attempt at euthanasia that eventually accelerated Mars' demise, though painfully so, as Jack explained to Sawyer. If not for Sawyer's well-intentioned action, Jack would have spent even more of his precious time tending to a patient who instead should have been triaged into the care of a lesser-trained person.

Jack's refusal to admit defeat was driven by two important events in his past. The more immediate, and possibly the more important of the two, was the intensely emotional scene of Charlie's resuscitation after his hanging.

Many consider this scene, fraught with deep, unsettling, raw emotion, the most moving moment in the six years of LOST. Kate, driven to wretched pain and tears by Charlie's death, implored Jack to stop pummeling Charlie's chest. He was dead. Nothing Jack did was going to change that. Jack stopped for only a moment, pulled back his own tears, and then raised a strong, angry arm into the air and pulled down the full weight of his fury, beating Charlie's chest with inhuman force. He did it again. And again. And again. Against all the laws of medicine and physics and nature, Charlie's heart started. By indefatigable force of will, Jack brought Charlie back from death.

The issue in all three of these incidents was not the extent of Jack Shephard's medical prowess or depth of his human passion. He was by any standard a most gifted physician and expert surgeon. The issue for LOST was Jack's intent. He did not exert superhuman heroics with the intention of saving Ed Mars or Charlie Pace or Boone Carlyle. Jack went to extraordinary lengths with the intention of serving his own ends. He had to "fix" every patient because to do otherwise was a personal (not a professional) failure that would, he believed, count against him in his father's eyes. The well-being of his patients was a distant secondary concern to Jack Shephard. Serving his own selfish urge to prove his father wrong, to prove himself always personally and scientifically superior, was the overwhelming force motivating the good works of Dr. Jack Shephard.

In the world of LOST, "being a good person" is not always enough. The measure of a human being is seen in and composed of the same Light. But for those who seek leadership, much more is required. Leadership, of the variety that bears on human endeavour, requires intimate engagement with the primal stuff of our humanity, requires single-minded and sacrificial commitment to the foundations of human civilisation.

Jack, until his enlightenment, lacked commitment. He was not engaging with the essential elements of humanity because he was consumed with the urge to satisfy his unquenchable personal needs for proof of perfection.

Worse, Jack, with all of us, was conditioned to accept as normative, and not only acceptable but expected and desired, behaviours and ways of thinking that he later understood to be antithetical to the best traditions of human civilisation. Somehow Jack had to overcome his perverse, regimented, and useless way of looking at the world. The Island found a means by which Jack could achieve this end: Disorientation.

DISORIENTATION

Contortion Backbend
No Attribution, WMC PD

The full truth of the Swan Station eventually became too much for even John Locke's mind to accept. He thought himself re-awakening to reality when he marched into the geodesic dome and violently threw the ancient computer to the concrete floor, proving, or so he thought, the lack of meaning behind the numbers and the decades-long practice of entering the six-integer sequence every 108 minutes. Only when steel containers and metal knives flew through the air and the fillings in his teeth threatened to pull loose did Locke realise his error.

There are in this world special places of extraordinary significance, loci of unexplained power and unimaginable beauty: the gigantic Easter Island statues, the perfectly symmetrical Peruvian desert drawings, the "impossibly" perfect Mayan architectures of the Chichen Itza temples. These structures, whose fabrication would tax modern capabilities, were completed hundreds of years ago using materials and methods entirely unknown and apparently as advanced as any modern equivalents.

We rebel at thoughts such as these, conditioned as we are to believe that certain levels of scientific capability must precede any creations such as those we observe on Easter Island, in the Peruvian desert, and on the Yucatán. The rules of cause and effect tell us that some advanced science must have been created to allow the design and execution of drawings several kilometres in length and breadth. At the very least, the ancient desert dwellers must have had access to aerial or satellite photography to ensure straight lines. Our minds cannot fathom alternatives (the artist dreamed the correct orientation of lines over hill and dale, across stream and field; shamans led the construction effort, using knowledge of medicines to predict proper shape of the drawings; etc.).

When Locke told Jack the Island was special, that bizarre communication elevated Locke to a certain level of disequilibrium in Jack's estimation. When only a couple months later Locke told him the Island had to be "protected," Jack felt entirely justified in his conclusion that Locke had completely lost touch with reality.

But then the Island disappeared from the ocean, leaving not a trace behind.

Jack saw his dead father, alive, in the jungle, leading him beside fresh waters--and to the casket that contained no body, but only a mystery. Even Locke had conversations with Jack's dead father, told Jack the old man said hello.

At some point the burden of so many occurrences unexplainable by any rational means became too much for poor Jack. Disorientation was the painful but very necessary means of loosing Jack from the comfortable scientific straight jacket he had spent a lifetime engineering for himself. He came to understand, as the result of one painful or inexplicable event piled on top of another and then yet another, that science could explain only a small and increasingly irrelevant sampling of the important events in his life. The particulars of his connection to the world that carried greatest significance to him were those unfettered by any relationship to logic: his love for Kate, the Island's hold over his thoughts, the growing awareness that Locke had been right—about everything.

COGNITIVE PARTIALITY

Disorientation was intensified and broadened by the fact that only rarely could two people agree on anything: the significance of an event transpired, the action that should be taken in response to a problem or threat, the meaning of so many unearthly occurrences on this strange island. No one had a complete understanding of the Island. Ben claimed to know everything, but of course, he did not.

Did even Jacob himself understand how the Island had healed Locke's paralysis and Rose's cancer? No one had all the answers, but everyone had an axe to grind, an agenda to pursue, a mission to fulfill. The needs and desires of every one of the major players on the Island coloured their understanding of the meaning of Island phenomena and their significance to the group. Differing agendas, the strange nature of the Island, the fear and threat of death looming in unexpected places, engendered confusion, mistrust, and very quickly created hostility, open aggression, and occasionally outright genocide. An entire village was consumed by the Guardian's wrath. The Dharma Initiative, at Ben's behest, was wiped out.

Other than the Hansos (Magnus and great-grandson Alvar), who were almost certainly motivated by greed, and the United States Army, which was motivated by discovering another island they could turn into radioactive waste, no one came to the Island by choice. Upon arrival, the survivors or refugees or captives made a decision to find a route off the Island, find a means of exploiting the Island's powers, or find a way to eliminate competitors or those deemed a danger or a hindrance. These were the primary motivators, and for untold centuries, Jacob found not a single soul motivated by the desire to serve the Island's needs.

We found ourselves stranded on the Island after the crash of Flight 815 on September 22, 2004. But with the advantage of an almost global view (relevant stories told from four dozen points of view over six years), we pieced together a certain feeling about the Island only short episodes after Locke made his earliest pronouncements on the Island's import. Long before Locke told Jack the Island had to be protected, we felt the truth of this in our hearts. We had to go through the same disorientation as Jack and Locke. Our thought processes had to be adjusted. We had to come to the realisation that polar bears roamed the Island, illnesses were miraculously cured, the DI continued to make food drops decades after Hanso's group had virtually ceased to exist as an entity, at least on the Island. None of it made any sense, and no answers were anywhere in sight. We never gave up seeking those answers, but over time we also came to appreciate Locke's wisdom: The most important aspects of Island life would simply have to be accepted on faith.

Disorientation is integral to the process of preserving human civilisation. History is the ongoing story of our attempts to progress along a path toward more complete harmonisation with the fundamental expectations of civil society. Inevitably, some of our experiments are well-intentioned failures that only serve to pull us away from our goal. Some of the experiments turn out to be deceptions, fabrications intended to serve the selfish needs of a particular group, but serving instead to sever human connection to civility. More often than not, these groups are led by the Charles Widmores, Martin Keamys, and

Stuart Radzinskys of this world. Through the pain of disorientation, we come to understand the folly of selfish greed, we come to see its false allure, the inevitable destruction it causes to culture, humanity, and the civility from which every good aspect of human life draws sustenance and meaning.

A CULTURE OF TRUST

LOST is about the elements of our humanity that precede and supersede life itself. Our common humanity has a value greater than life. LOST argues that there must be a fertile ground into which we place the fragile seeds of our human existence. This ground is rich in trust, empathy, compassion, respect, and the desire to serve the needs of others. This is our perfection.

Locke, though he was long dead, was essential to the endgame of LOST. Jack, lowering Desmond down to the Source, said, "Turns out [Locke] was right about most everything. I just wish I could've told him that while he was still alive."

If he was so important to the end of the show, Locke must have evinced some quality distinguishing him above every other character. His impact on the endgame was not the result of his fondness for knives, the fact that he was confined to a wheelchair, his natural teaching ability, or any other of the accidentals associated with his existence. There was something about Locke that made him, and no one else, essential to Jack, and therefore essential to the Island.

Locke was connected to the Island. He knew when the rain would fall. He seemed to be able to track anything through the jungle, as if he knew the place, as if he didn't even need his eyes to make a way through the forest. The Island healed him, restored his ability to walk, gave him boar to hunt, and provided him insight into the Island. Not because the Island felt sorry for him, or saw a "sucker." No. The Island healed him because Locke, by his very nature, understood the Island. He had an intuitive grasp of the Island's essence long before Flight 815 crashed near the water. Among other strong bits of evidence, his depiction of the Smoke Monster, committed to a charcoal drawing at the age of five, constituted overwhelming proof of his connection. All of this relates directly to the single aspect of character that is present in John Locke in greater abundance than in any other human being to have walked trail or shore.

The strength of character to which I refer is trust. John Locke trusted, almost without hesitation. You may argue that Locke's trusting nature was not a virtue, it was gullibility, plain and simple. He was possibly the most gullible personality ever explored on network television. All of this is true. Nevertheless, LOST wishes us to believe that Locke's ability to trust was essential to the outcome of the story. There was something good and pure and efficacious in Locke's trusting nature.

LOST tells us that Trust is essential. It is the core cultural value on the Island. But there must be some basis for trust. Even if Locke's ability to trust was a virtue, nevertheless the trust could be abused so that the person trusted could bend the situation to her advantage and even visit harm upon the one trusting.

At least superficially, the Island seemed to be the most unlikely location to establish a culture of trust. Everyone, it seems, lied. There were people on the Island who lied about things large and small, things trivial and essential, things of life and even things of death. Some people, like Benjamin Linus, seemed to have progressed through life and come into positions of authority entirely on the basis of a complicated structure of lies.

Ben was not alone in his reliance on falsehood. Sawyer also made a career out of deceit. The Smoke Monster lied about a great many things for a long time. Every major character in this six-year drama lied at one time or another, some much more than others. Even Hurley, great saint of honesty and truth, agreed to the Great Lie that Jack fashioned before they were rescued after the first three months on the Island. When he had a choice between telling the truth and remaining subject to Ben's manipulations or telling a lie and ending up in prison for the remainder of his life, incarcerated for multiple murders, Hurley chose to lie.

If everyone lies--that is, if everyone attempts to deceive others and violate their trust--how could trust ever be possible, especially on the Island? This is a valid and useful question that goes to the heart of LOST's development of both trust and faith, and I will address this question in detail in Chapter Three.

LOVE

Kiss   Briseis Painter ca 480BC Louvre PD

The sixth season of LOST launched a continuing series of cultural virtues: Love, Trust, Faith, Honesty, Hope, and in Hurley's episode (6.12), Charity. But by far, the greatest of these, the virtue to which lavish attention was given, was Love.

As best I can tell, only two individuals received invitations for unaccompanied passage to the "pre-moving-on" party in the sanctuary of the Church of the Holy Lamp Post at the end of the series: John Locke and Boone

Carlyle. Everyone else, apparently, had to bring her significant other—her Constant—or she was not allowed entry. My conclusion was that a Constant was the prerequisite to passage onward to the next level (to "heaven"?). The fact that Locke was unaccompanied made sense; his Constant was the Island, and he was connected to it both bodily (his body was buried on Boone Hill, after all) and spiritually. Boone's case was more difficult. The only valid hypothesis I could muster was a shared Constant: both Boone and Sayid must have considered Shannon their Constant.

The essentiality of the Constant to individuals and to the Island society struck me as a radical statement of the series. In the religious tradition I try to follow, significant others are not a pre-requisite to any aspect of communion with the Deity. If one does cultivate a reciprocal love, romantic or otherwise, this is considered all to the good, but it is certainly no requirement. Single people, married people, those in committed relationship, even hermits with no relationship, are welcome at the table of heaven according to the tradition in which I participate. I am married, and I would like to believe that this fact qualifies me, in my religious tradition, to certain perks. I cannot imagine, for instance, that marriage ends with the death of the human body. But marriage does end at death, at least according to the religious teachings in my faith tradition. In heaven there is no beer, and in heaven there is neither husband nor wife. I can't say I appreciate or understand or agree with this long-held teaching, but nevertheless, it is integral to the theological positions of many religious traditions. There are no heavenly perks for married people. When you die, that gold band stays on the finger of your rotting corpse—you can't take it with you.

It is from this faith background that I consider LOST's position on love to be radical. But in examining the Season Six sideways statements concerning Faith, Honesty, Charity, Hope, and especially Trust, this radical and possibly unique statement regarding Love fits perfectly, and becomes the seamless expansion of an essential clause in LOST's thesis statement.

The essential aspects of civilisation that must be safeguarded, even at risk of life and limb, are these:

Trust
Love
Faith
Honesty
Hope
Charity

There are no "isms" worthy of preservation in the world of LOST. The liberalism of Jacob ("It only ends once. Everything else is just progress") gives way to the conservatism of Hurley ("That's not cool, dude," as Hurley often said; Hurley has rendered many decisions regarding what he considers inappropriate behaviour by others—behaviours that probably would have been accepted by the more liberal Jacob.), but neither is a virtue as far as I can tell on the Island of Mittelos. The Protector is apparently given virtual carte blanche regarding her leadership and government style. "That's how Jacob ran things," Ben told Hurley. "Maybe there's another way. A better way." Ben recognised the wide latitude the Island gave the Protector.

The unifying characteristic of these aspects of civilisation is their expectation or requirement for human collaboration and broad participation. A life grounded in faith is preferred over existence based on science. There are many reasons for this, but surely one of the major reasons for favouring faith must be centred on the horizontal nature of faith (all share equally in the Light; multiple approaches are invited—"You do what you do best, Hugo"), compared to the rigid, sceptical, show-me-the-proof, hierarchical nature of logic-based science.

DESTRUCTIVE CULTURES

One might well imagine Island civilisation whole-heartedly embracing broadly-accepted human cultural ideals, such as La Déclaration des droits de l'Homme et du Citoyen of the French Revolution, or the more modern version, The Universal Declaration of Human Rights, as promulgated by the United Nations in 1948.

LOST appears to condemn certain features of historic cultures. The Dharma Initiative is seen as not only flawed, but almost laughably so. Science in general is considered inadequate to complete understanding of civilisation and culture. Any human activity destructive of collaboration or the essential tenets (faith, love, trust, etc.) would certainly be condemned. Selfishness of any kind, antithetical as it is to healthy civilisations, would be considered the worst of the offences against humanity, an attitude shared with many matricentrist and aboriginal civilisations. In some aboriginal cultures, extreme selfishness was a capital offence. The most selfish players in the series (Charles Widmore, Stuart Radzinsky, and Martin Keamy) were not given invitations to the big fête at Our Lady of the Foucault Pendulum, and Keamy died, even in the sideways reality. Poof! He ceased to exist. In heaven there is no beer, and in heaven there is no Martin Keamy. I would guess, in the theology of LOST, anyone pursuing selfish agendas damaging to the human condition might expect the same final outcome as the one dealt to Keamy.

A CULTURAL THESIS FOR LOST

Two players. Two sides. One is light. One is dark.

The world's longest running game of backgammon was a life-or-death struggle for control of the Island, for control of the destiny of humankind.

Damon Lindelof, co-creator of LOST, summed up the programme's philosophy in an interview with IGN in January, 2007:

"This show is about people who are metaphorically lost in their lives, who get on an airplane, and crash on an island, and become physically lost on the planet Earth. And once they are able to metaphorically find themselves in their lives again, they will be able to physically find themselves in the world again. When you look at the entire show, that's what it will look like. That's what it's always been about."

The nuanced view of Lindelof's vision is breathtaking. As we will see in this book, the journey will require that we reconsider the range and breadth of human interaction and relationship. LOST enjoins new requirements, never before imposed by a work of fiction. LOST creates vibrant new relationships, of a type never before imagined. LOST calls us to a profound commitment to the ideals of humanity and an abiding optimism for our future.

The Thesis of LOST: *We find ourselves not through abstract ideas, but in our deep connections with each other. Women and men must live and work together, both in harmony and in conflict, to preserve the personal and social connections that are the basis of human civilisation.*

While this simple statement may seem bland or even uninspired, LOST insists on a most radical interpretation of the idea. As we shall see, the journey toward connection and civility, according to LOST, requires a set of relationships never before created in fiction. Each one of the major characters was required to establish not only a Constant, but an opposing and even deeper connection with a "Strange Attractor."

There is nothing conventional about LOST's understanding of human relationships, causal connection, and the basis for society and civilisation. It is this strange but compelling view of humanity, and not any appeal to the well-worn ideas of right and wrong, free will and fate, or good and evil, that makes LOST the most stimulating and fascinating fictional work presented on television.

The foundational theme of LOST is trust.

Those who dispute this statement will have to construct an argument worthy of toppling the enormous weight of evidence presented in Episode 6.14, "The Candidate." Until that episode it may have been possible to argue that trust was a straw man, a misrepresentation of Locke as exemplar when he was meant to be understood as a failure. After all, Locke died in weakness, a bitter, lonely, frustrated, and defeated man. That trust was John Locke's primary virtue could only mean that the attribute had to be considered nothing more than a polite way of indicating gullibility. Wasn't blind trust the defect of character that had led to the bulk of the survivors' tribulations?

Episode 6.14 taught otherwise. If Sawyer had been able to trust, he would not have pulled the leads from the Smoke Monster's bomb on board the submarine, the bomb would not have been detonated, and Sayid, Sun, and Jin would not have died. Events would have gone very badly for Smokey, and much more quickly, if the submarine survivors had been able to work together toward his demise.

Trust was the core concept underlying even faith. A leap of faith is preceded by trust in the elements of belief. Jack trusted the Rules of the Island enough to know that if he lit the fuse on a stick of dynamite no explosion would occur in his presence. The Rules transcended and bent to their own ends the lesser so-called "laws" of physics. The Island was greater than physics, greater than science, greater than any logic, because it was the point of contact with the Source, that aspect of reality sometimes referenced as "divine will." In almost every Island event of any significance, trust was the dominant issue.

The word "Trust" occurs 178 times throughout the corpus of Lost. Only a few words carrying conceptual weight outrank Trust in frequency of occurrence. The most heavily-used concept word in Lost is "Believe," at 275 occurrences. "Love" is close, at 267 entries throughout all episodes and mobisodes.

Frequency	Word
347	Dude
275	Believe
267	Love
219	Remember
213	Together
204	God
178	Trust
116	Promise
26	Faith

An argument could be made that the concept of Faith, as represented in the word "believe," is the dominant leitmotif of the series. I would argue that as we approached the final and pivotal scenes of the series, and especially as we approached the Light and the Source, the idea of trust came to occupy the central position in Lost's hierarchy of values, and not just on the Island.

Faith was situational. As seen in the diagram below, the occurrence of the primary faith-related word, "believe," was highly variable throughout the six season of LOST.

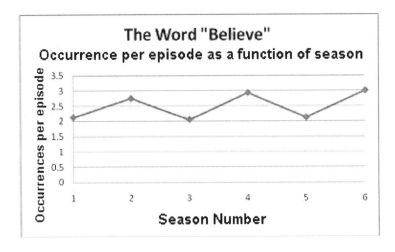

Faith was a primary topic of discussion in the early days after opening the hatch to the Swan Station. Relative to Season One, faith became a focus of concern in Season Two, and this is seen in the dramatic increase in the frequency of the occurrence of the word "believe." During the heat of battle in

Season Three, and the Dharma days of Season Five, faith was not a central concept.

On the other hand, trust was nearly absent in the early days on the Island, but gained prominence during Season Three and held its importance through the remainder of the series.

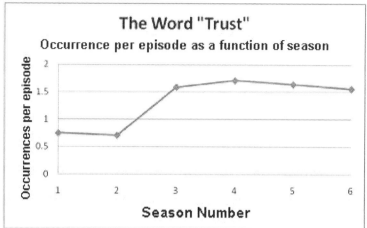

The critical difference between the themes of trust and faith, as demonstrated by these computations of concept-related word frequency, is situational dependence. Once the survivors began to trust each other, and implore confidence in each other, progress could be made toward building faith and cooperation and all the other virtues that would be required to wrest control of the Island from the dark power of the Smoke Monster. Trust remained a valued resource independent of the situation the crash survivors found themselves facing. Faith, on the other hand, experienced ebb and flow depending on the surroundings and times.

THE SIDEWAYS VALUE OF TRUST

Trust was also the dominant theme holding together the sideways world.

In the scene leading to Sayid's enlightenment, Hurley raised the issue, elevating it to the central theme in Sayid's life. He also continued to skew word frequency analysis with the use of his favourite word (dude)—twice in only four lines!

SAYID: What are we doing here?
HURLEY: I'm not allowed to tell you.
SAYID: What do you mean you're not allowed?
HURLEY: There are rules, dude.
SAYID: Whose rules?
HURLEY: Don't worry about it. Just trust me, okay? I trust you.
SAYID: And what, may I ask, have I done to deserve your trust?
HURLEY: I think you're a good guy, Sayid. You know, a lot of people have

told you that you're not. Maybe you've heard it so many times you started believing it. You can't let other people tell you what you are, dude. You have to decide that for yourself.

Trust was the dominant theme in the sideways reality for all of the characters. It dominated Season Six. But it had strong roots going all the way back to the very beginning of the series.

TRUST: CIVILISATION'S CONSTANT

Trust was the basis of every relationship in Lost.

In an empty football stadium late at night, a man and a woman extend their right hands toward each other in Western civilisation's greatest symbol of trust: the handshake. The lighting is dark, and it is difficult to discern enough features to hazard a guess regarding the characters' identities, but they are alone in the stadium. Perhaps you believe such a handshake could not carry much significance. Isn't this a normal expression of agreement, solidarity, or trust between individuals? Isn't this gesture performed billions of times every day?

No. Not in a dark, empty stadium late hours after sunset. If you are a woman, ask yourself how much trust you would place in a man who approaches you in this defenceless and vulnerable place, far from the safety and constraints of civility. And yet she trusted him immediately. Her name of course was Penny, and the man she met in this dark stadium, for the first time in her life, was the person who would become her best friend, her love; in the parlance of Lost, her Constant.

Penny and Desmond became the symbol of Lost's version of Love. Love starts with trust and it becomes that which no one can put asunder. True love is Constant because it is the union of two souls to become one. Love is not subordinate to trust, but it begins with trust. Without trust, there is no faith, no hope, no love. Without trust there is no Constant.

Any philosophy that posits the necessity and efficacy of trust will have to overcome the unpleasant facts of the real world. Even the best of societies harbours in its ranks those who would take advantage of the trust others place in them. If there is no honour among thieves, no virtue among the greedy, how can we fairly expect trust to result in anything other than the rapid corruption of civilisation?

BASIS FOR TRUST

Jack has come to a fork in the road. Ahead are two paths, one guarded by Hugo Reyes, the other guarded by Benjamin Linus. One path leads to Shambala, the other path leads to a dark valley where a ferocious monster kills every person who passes by. Jack doesn't know which path leads to Shangri-La, but he knows the guards know each other and they are familiar with both paths. After several years of gathering clues, he knows one of the two guards always tells the truth, and the other guard always lies, but he again doesn't know which is the truth teller and which is the source of false statements. Even though he doesn't know which guard to trust, Jack decides to ask Hugo the single question he is allowed to pose. What is the question Jack asks?

It's an elementary school logic puzzle, but it gets to the heart of the question of trust as it played out on the Island. Jack doesn't know whether he can trust Hugo or Ben, but he knows he can trust one of them. More importantly, he can trust the rules of the game.

He poses this question to Hugo: "Which way would Ben say is the road to Shambala?" Just as Jack can trust the dynamite not to explode, he knows that in Hugo's answer, regardless of whether he lies or tells honestly, Jack will find the truth.

In the same way, Jack relied on his firm grasp of the Rules of the Island to determine the best response to the presence of a bomb in his backpack after he boarded the submarine in Episode 6.14. He didn't have to trust the Smoke Monster. He had to trust the Island. Jack understood, not intuitively as John Locke did, but by brute force logic, that he had to trust the Island. It was this trust that allowed him to win the millennia-old backgammon game, making the last move that erased the Smoke Monster's supernatural advantage, rendered him mortal, and finally ended his wretched existence.

Some of the survivors had neither intuitive nor brute-force understanding of the Island. Sawyer, unfortunately, was among the unenlightened, and it was his action that caused the bomb to explode. But it was not his fault. The nature of the game and the way it was played over the millennia by two very imperfect creatures incapable of love were the elements most worthy of blame.

Trust the Island, Locke said. Jack listened, and he discovered the correct Road to Shambala. The Island civilisation instituted by Jack and continued by Hurley and "Number Two" Ben Linus was based on trust. "I trust you, dude," Hurley told Sayid in the sideways reality. It was the mantra of Season Six.

It was trust in the Rules of the Island that allowed Jack to refuse surgically "fixing" young Ben after Sayid shot him (Lost 5.11). "You know, when we were here before, I spent all of my time trying to fix things. But...did you ever think that maybe the island just wants to fix things itself? And maybe I was just...getting in the way?"

Perfectionists, like the pre-Dharma Jack, believe they have to "fix" everything themselves because they cannot trust anyone else to do it. Jack's refusal to operate on the young teenager was the strongest possible assertion of trust from an expert surgeon. That reliance on trust had become the primary counsel of LOST's protagonist meant the concept occupied the central position in the philosophical system underlying the series. Trust was the first rule of civilisation carved into the Cork Stone. Civilisation begins when two people, without history or precedent, without any basis whatever for agreement or solidarity, extend hands toward each other and place their trust in each others' good will. This is the position from which LOST would have us start.

THE AUDACITY OF TRUST

The pill contained enough poison to kill five men.

In Episode 6.03 Jack swallowed the pill and Dogen rushed into action, performing the martial arts equivalent of the Heimlich Manoeuvre, dislodging the green capsule from Jack's throat and forcing it out of his mouth. Thank goodness for clear thinking and fast action, you say. Indeed. But let us imagine a hypothetical situation in which Jack consumed the pill in private, without Dogen's knowledge. What would have happened to Jack?

Nothing. Jack would have gone about his business, suffering no ill effects whatever.

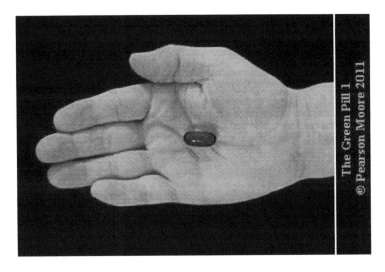

You read this thinking "Pearson has lost touch with reality—again. The pill would kill even a person in perfect health." I do not argue; the pill would indeed kill a person in good health. Death would be instant; the person taking the pill might as well have been holding in his hand a stick of dynamite, fuse lit, sparks flying, seconds left... A person in good health would have been blown to bits, but Jack... not a hair on his head was harmed. The green pill could have had no more physical effect on Jack than the dynamite had in the belly of the Black Rock. Candidates, remember, could not commit suicide.

But what would have been the effect of the green death on Sayid?

Even before Jack swallowed the green pill, he had solid reason to believe the gelatin liner contained poison. By swallowing the pill, he was essentially committing suicide. According to the rules of the Island, those designated potential Protector ("Candidates" in Jacob's parlance) could not die of natural causes or by their own hand. The Protector, Protector-Candidates, and the Consigliere (Richard and Ben after him) were granted eternal life on the Island. Therefore, as Jack was aware of the pill as potentially deadly, the Island would have prevented him from ingesting it, or he would have suffered no enduring ill effect from consuming it.

On the other hand, if Dogen had given Jack no reason to believe the pill was dangerous, or if he had tied Jack down, forced his mouth open, intubated him, and forced the capsule down his gullet, Jack would have died, because murdering a Candidate, as unsavoury as it might otherwise be, was nevertheless allowed by the rules of Mittelos.

The status and significance of the green pill becomes even more complicated when we bring Sayid into the discussion.

[Jack unfolds the paper and exposes the capsule.]
SAYID: What's that?
JACK: They want you to take it. It's medicine, according to them.
SAYID: What about according to you?
JACK: I don't know. And you know, before when you... when you thanked me for saving your life, I, I didn't have anything to do with it Sayid. I didn't fix you. They did.
[Jack takes the capsule in his right palm.]
SAYID: I don't care who fixed me. I only care about who I trust. So, if you want me to take that pill, Jack, I'll do it.

We believed at first Sayid to have been reborn. In the physical sense, apparently he was. The Man in Black or some other powerful entity, if we are to believe the most likely interpretation of events, was somehow empowered to bring back to life those in his sphere of influence. This was a power that even Jacob lacked, but we cannot deny that the Smoke Monster was, in at least one important sense, closer to the Source than Jacob was. Logically, if Sayid regained life through the action of an unclean source, he ought to become tainted, too. In the words of Rousseau, he should be considered to have the "sickness."

Yet we found ourselves aware of new life—new spiritual life—in Sayid. When Dogen and Jack had their private talk, the Temple Master told Jack he must give Sayid the green pill. Jack demanded to know the contents of the pill, and when Dogen said Jack had to give Sayid the medicine, for the sake of his life, Jack countered with "He already died." This seemed a rare and strange place for a healer to place himself. Jack seemed to be hoisting a list of ingredients to a higher plane than Sayid's life. Dogen expressed concern about Sayid's "infection," while Jack insisted on broadening his knowledge of herbal medicines, and all the while, a man who miraculously regained consciousness and complete healing of wounds was dismissed as one who "already died." The strange discussion seems askew, the priorities grossly misplaced.

But this was not the only instance of Sayid's life being accorded less value than abstract concepts. When Jack presented Sayid with the green pill, Sayid's response was Biblical: "I only care about who I trust. So if you want me to take that pill, Jack, I will."

This was breathtaking in its audacity. Neither Sayid nor Jack knew the contents of the pill. Sayid placed unrestrained faith in Jack, and now a crushing burden fell on the healer. This was no longer abstract. Sayid may have died if he took the pill. The only useful question at this point in the episode: What was Jack Shephard made of? What value does he place on life, on trust, on knowledge?

As I watched Jack throw the pill in his mouth and swallow, my jaw dropped open and I could not process the event through my shock. The sequence of events remained askew. The problem was not that Jack was placing higher value on Sayid's life than his own. The problem for me, as I struggled to make sense of this most intense scene, was that Jack was not placing greater value on Sayid's life. Something else, apparently something carrying an importance more profound even than life or death, was in play.

Jack couldn't give Sayid the pill. He was planning to do so. He had every intention of doing so. He resolved to tell Sayid the complete truth, and that was what he did. But then Sayid said those words: "I care only about who I trust. So if you want me to take that pill, Jack, I will."

RUTH AND NAOMI

Ruth and Naomi
Pieter Lastman 1614 PD

56

The Book of Ruth in the Hebrew Bible relates a story about a pagan woman named Ruth who showed kindness to a Hebrew woman named Naomi. When it was time for them to go their separate ways, Naomi encouraged Ruth to return to her pagan village.

"Look," said Naomi, "your sister-in-law is going back to her people and her gods. Go back with her."

But Ruth replied, "Don't urge me to leave you or to turn back from you. Where you go I will go, and where you stay I will stay. Your people will be my people and your God my God. Where you die I will die, and there I will be buried. May the Lord deal with me, be it ever so severely, if anything but death separates you and me."

Ruth just gave up everything: family, village, her former gods, everything she ever knew–turned her back on all of it, and gave herself over to Naomi and her God. Ruth discovered something of greater value than even her own life.

Jack couldn't give Sayid the pill. Not because he valued Sayid's life. He certainly did value the man's life, and his own. But life did not carry greatest value in this scene. Jack was able to risk his own life by swallowing that pill because he placed greater importance on something other than his own life. Jack placed highest value on the trust Sayid had placed in him.

Sayid and Jack placed greater value on their trust of each other than on their own lives.

This is audacious. Rare. This is story that burns deep into the soul, engages every faculty of spirit and sense and wonder.

With the intensity of this scene we began to get a glimpse into the innermost core of LOST. This is not a show about good versus evil. It is not about free will versus determinism. It is not about time travel or electromagnetic anomalies or spacetime displacement. It is about our very humanity. It is about who we are at the very centre of our conscious selves.

The audacity reaches even deeper than this, however, as we now know:

The physical effects of the pill depended entirely on the recipient's understanding of the provider's intent.

If the Candidate understood the provider of the pill to have malevolent intent, the pill, if self-administered, could have no ill effect. If however, intent was misunderstood as remedial or beneficial, the pill would have caused immediate death upon ingestion. That is to say, deadly intent would lead to life, and expectation of salutary remedy would lead to death. In the end, whether Sayid lived or died upon consuming the pill was entirely a consequence of what he believed about the intentions of those who fabricated and provided the green capsule.

Imagine now that Jack offers and Sayid accepts and swallows the pill. We cannot know a priori the outcome of this action. In order to predict with any certainty the effect on Sayid, we must have unfettered access to the complete range of his thoughts in the moments around the discussion of the pill, immediately before he takes the pill, and during the time his stomach is dissolving the non-toxic gelatin shell containing the green poison. If at any point in this chronology Sayid believes his life to be in danger, the pill will have no adverse consequences, or some Island-created situation will lead to his body's rejection of the poison in a way that will protect him from ill effect.

THE COLOUR OF TRUST

LOST redefined causality. Expectation of death instead brought life. Knowledge of life brought death.

LOST redefined symbol. Yellow is life and death and rebirth. Green is trust and honour and commitment. The green pill, like the Source itself, was at the same time life and death. The pill was symbol of rebirth: of new trust between Jack and Sayid, of deeper rapport between Jack and Dogen, of Jack's recommitment to all of his people, even one considered to be the intractable agent of his deadly foe.

Just as green is the most prominent colour of the Island, trust is the most prominent expectation among the children of Mittelos. Trust is the virtue that protects and sustains all the other truths of the Cork Stone. It is the virtue passed down from Locke to Jack to Hurley.

We can sum up LOST as Life and Death in Green, or simplify even further to the essential core: Life and death and rebirth are the precursors and the final result of trust. Trust is the basis of human civilisation, the commitment that allows the Source to give Light. It's what keeps the Island afloat. It's what makes the world go 'round.

"Christian's Lantern"
© Pearson Moore 2011

Demanding, unforgiving, yet life-affirming. Faith is the supreme virtue in the Island world, the excellence upon which all other perfections establish their value, strength, and perpetuity. Yet faith is fragile, subject to every fickle impulse and caprice of the human heart and will. Neither given nor earned, faith is chosen or refused, affirmed or denied. It is at once the supreme statement of human volition, and the guarantor of human destiny.

Jacob could have refused the cup. Locke could have shunned martyrdom. Jack could have rejected the call to believe. The history of the Island, microcosm of human history, is the story of human decisions and destinies centred on the attribute of humanity for which so many gave their lives: faith.

FAITH, NOT RELIGION

The word 'believe' occurs 275 times in LOST. This frequency is higher than the word 'love' (267 occurrences) or 'understand' (260 appearances) or even the word 'lost' itself (257 times). Yet Lostpedia contains no articles on 'belief' or 'faith.'

We will more easily find consensus on the theme of Faith in LOST by describing those things that it is not. Faith is not Science, for example. The clash between Faith and Science is a major theme in the series, and is strongly related to the conflict between Jack and Locke, and to Jack's inner conflict regarding his relationships and his Island destiny.

More important to our discussion is the fact that the concept of Faith as developed by LOST contains no necessary connection to religion. The major practitioners of faith were John Locke and the Season Five and Season Six versions of Jack Shephard, neither of whom was known to have affiliation with any established religion. The major theme of Faith versus Science only peripherally acknowledges contributions that might be made by established religion. For instance, Ben briefly discussed the story of the Doubting Thomas, a minor theme in Christianity.

BEN: Thomas the Apostle. When Jesus wanted to return to Judea, knowing that he would probably be murdered there, Thomas said to the others, "Let us also go, that we might die with him." But Thomas was not remembered for this bravery. His claim to fame came later... when he refused to acknowledge the resurrection. He just couldn't wrap his mind around it. The story goes... that he needed to touch Jesus' wounds to be convinced.
JACK: So was he?
BEN: Of course he was. We're all convinced sooner or later, Jack.

It is clear from context that Ben is not saying one must become convinced of the resurrection of Jesus of Nazareth. The only significance of the reference to the Doubting Thomas is in providing for us a glimpse into Jack's inner struggle. Jack needed to believe, even if he could not stick his fingers into the Island's wounds or see with his own eyes the wonders the Island had wrought.

LOST made frequent allusion to symbols, themes, and events of traditional religions. Flight 316 was a reference to John 3:16 ("For God so loved the world that he gave his only Son, that whoever believes in him should not perish but have eternal life."), a verse from one of the four Christian Gospels. Moriah Vineyards, the wine brand created by Desmond's monastery, was an allusion to the mountain where Abraham was called to sacrifice his son, Isaac (Genesis 22:1-24). As with every other instance of religious allusion in LOST, we are not being asked to believe in the veracity or efficacy of the Jewish or Christian faith. Rather, religious references are intended as a means of helping us understand ideas peculiar to the story.

DESMOND: Moriah. I find the name the brothers have chosen for the wine made here... interesting.
MONK: And why is that, brother?
DESMOND: Well, Moriah's the mountain where Abraham was asked to kill Isaac. It's not exactly the most... festive locale, is it?
MONK: And yet God spared Isaac.
DESMOND: Well one might argue then, God may not have asked Abraham to sacrifice his son in the first place.
MONK: Well then it wouldn't have been much of a test, would it, brother? Perhaps you underestimate the value of sacrifice.

Desmond was going to be asked to sacrifice much for the Island. The key players in the drama—Jack and Locke—would have to sacrifice their very lives. This is not the full significance of the Moriah allusion. However, if we were to exhaustively analyse the reference we would have to conclude that Moriah Vineyards is not part of any covert scheme on the part of LOST writers and producers to establish LOST as a twenty-first century Biblical allegory. Neither Jack nor Locke can be understood uniquely or even primarily as a sacrificial lamb in any religious sense. Desmond's sacrifices cannot be understood as being primarily related to Biblical themes or stories. In fact, the literary parallel to Desmond most frequently invoked by LOST analysts is the Greek hero, Odysseus.

LOST is a rich smorgasbord of religious allusion and themes. Religious references were sprinkled throughout the first four seasons, but in Seasons Five and Six the allusions became frequent and substantial, sometimes almost to the point of becoming oppressive. Flight 316, the frequent Canton-Rainier anagram for Reincarnation, the Dharma Initiative's rich Hindu allusions, and the heavy emphasis on themes of sacrifice, faith, and destiny worked in concert to provide a rich atmosphere of religious and spiritual sentiment. However, this atmosphere supported not the ideals of any particular religion, but rather the spirituality unique to the Island's purpose.

Mr. Eko, Charlie Pace, Sayid Jarrah, and Rose Nadler practiced the rituals and adhered to the tenets of their religious traditions. However, we understood very early in the story that these characters served as peripheral support to the great Faith Versus Science struggle between Jack and Locke, and the greater mystery of the Island's secrets. This small minority of religiously-observant characters could not have been intended to represent the main thrust of LOST's thesis. Based on the secondary or even tertiary importance of these characters, we are to understand their religious sensibilities as supporting the non-religious ideas central to the story.

BEHOLD THE LAMB

For Christian Shephard so loved the Island that he gave his only son, that whoever believes in him should not be killed by the Smoke Monster...

In the last two seasons, if we did not yet understand, it became clear that LOST was Jack's story. Jack was the final and most important sacrifice, the innocent, the lamb who was slain in order that the Island might live. In the end, he had the powers of a supernatural being. He conferred immortality on Hurley and transferred to him the full authority and perquisites of the office of Protector, including the ability to confer the same powers. He followed in the footsteps of one who had been compared to the most famous Jewish carpenter in history, and he bore one of the five wounds marking that carpenter's passing from this world to the next. He became the saviour of the Island, and the world.

There can be no question that the wound in Jack's abdomen, his spiritual transformation, and many of the particulars of his mission were intended to reference the life and works of Jesus of Nazareth. Neither can there be any question that Jack was intended as an example, not just to the survivors and the Others, but to everyone following the series. Some might claim, on the basis of the intentional parallels to the Christian Deity, that LOST must be understood as Christian allegory, that Jack's story is a symbolic retelling of the story of the Saviour, the Christ, Jesus of Nazareth.

Jack presents us with the strongest possible case for understanding LOST as Christian allegory. No reasonable analyst could construct arguments intended to deny the multiple references to the Jesus story in Jack's life. I will attempt no such argument here. Jack, son of Christian, accepted the sacrifice that the Island demanded. Christian Shephard so loved the Island that he gave his only son—a direct reference to John 3:16, which is embedded into the very fabric of the story.

These connections are strong, and intentionally so. Shouldn't we, then, accept the veracity of the allegory that LOST has apparently worked so hard to establish? I don't believe we should. I believe that to do so gives short shrift to the real intention of LOST, directs our attention away from consideration of the larger message, and takes from us much of the richness of the LOST story. In fact, I believe there is no allegory at all. LOST is its own story, though it has heavily borrowed from literature, history, and religion. Not only do I believe we lose much by considering LOST to be allegory, I believe we can demonstrate that there is in fact no allegory.

ALLUSION VERSUS ALLEGORY

The Lord of the Flies is allegorical throughout, a parable of the nuclear age lovingly crafted by Sir William Golding. Probably there are few in either the UK or the US who have not read the book and seen the 1963 film (I certainly hope no school systems are forcing children to see the deplorable 1990 version!). The novel is allegory because its plot is advanced through symbols, and the symbolism is unambiguous.

Allegory is "a story, play, poem, picture, etc., in which the meaning or message is represented symbolically" (Canadian Oxford). This is not a complete description of literary allegory, and we must turn to experts in literature to obtain an understanding suitable to this essay.

An excellent definition of allegory was devised by Dr. Ian Johnston, a Professor of Literature at Vancouver Island University. He spoke in November 1998.

"Simply put, an allegory is a fiction, almost invariably a story, which is designed, first and foremost, to illustrate a coherent doctrine which exists outside the fiction. Thus, the story and everything in it bear an immediate and point by point reference to a very specific aspect of the controlling doctrine which the fiction is illustrating. In that sense, allegories tend to be what we might call "philosophical" fictions, a term which means that they are to a large extent shaped and controlled by ideas or by a system of ideas which exists independently of the allegorical text." (Dr. Ian Johnston, quoted at http://records.viu.ca/~johnstoi/eng200/bunyan.htm, accessed November 26, 2010, used with permission.)

Notice Professor Johnston's insistence that allegory pervade the story: "The story and everything in it bear an immediate and point by point reference to a... controlling doctrine" This is important, because as Dr. Johnston says later in his lecture, "The purpose of the allegory is, first and foremost, to entertain, to engage the imagination of the reader so that the pleasure which arises from dealing with fictions can be put in the service of a particular belief system." (Ibid.) That is, the purpose of allegory is to assert a particular belief system, either for contemplation or for adoption by characters and readers.

William Golding's story is allegory because it asserts a belief system and it requires characters (and readers) to believe in the goodness and efficacy of the hero, Ralph. This cannot be said of LOST's hero, Jack. While LOST certainly asserts a set of principles, foremost among these being the concept of Faith, LOST does not require that all of the characters, or even most of them, believe in or act on the example established by Jack. We could find any number of characters who did not support Jack but nevertheless ended up enjoying unfettered access to the full range of benefits at the end of the story. For example, neither Rose nor Bernard supported Jack's work. In fact, they described his quest as constituting an effort to "find ways to shoot each other". Yet Rose and Bernard sat with Jack in the church at the end of the story. They were allowed to "move on" into the light with Jack and Kate and the other Constant-couples, even though they had not subscribed to Jack's vision of the Island's purpose.

LOST does not assert the utility or efficacy of the doctrines or practices of any religious tradition. It creates strong allusions to these traditions, just as it references literary works and pop culture, because the objective is to engage the participants' (viewers') imaginations and cognitive faculties. We are to understand that Jack's sacrifice is meaningful. There can be no better means of creating in our minds the idea that the sacrifice is imbued with significance than to compare his martyrdom in some way to the sacrifice of Jesus on the cross. So the writers created a situation in which Jack would be wounded in precisely the location in which Jesus was pierced by a spear during the crucifixion (John 19:34).

The writers may also have intended that Christian Shephard become the personification of the Island's call for Jack's sacrifice, to better mirror John 3:16. I don't know that this is the case, but evidence seems to support this conclusion. I suppose the only way we'll know with any certainty is if Darlton "break radio silence." But until Carlton Cuse or Damon Lindelof tell me I'm wrong, this is my explanation, and I'm stickin' to it. Either way, bolstering the connections to a verse from the Gospel of John does not constitute the establishment of an allegorical story, rather it serves merely as another instance of allusion, intended to stimulate our thinking about Jack's significance in the story. Regardless of any arguments we may wish to make, we cannot make the entirety of John 3:16 fit into the context of LOST. No one is obliged to "believe in Jack" in order that she might enjoy eternal life.

Certainly we can consider Jack's rescue of Desmond in the cave to mirror the Creator's instructions to Abraham as the man was raising the knife to slay his son, Isaac. Both Desmond and Isaac were spared. Jack, who would have to make the ultimate sacrifice, was not tied to the Mount Moriah imagery, but to the imagery of Christ; Jack would not be spared.

LOCKE'S FAITH: ISLAND, PURPOSE, DESTINY

In Episode 1.13, "Hearts and Minds", the only Boone-centric LOST episode, Locke took extreme measures to teach his protégé. He tied Boone to a stake in the ground and began mashing herbs. His methods and the result he expected tell us a great deal about John Locke's faith. Since Jack Shephard considered Locke 'was right about most everything', we will also appreciate Jack's understanding of faith by studying Locke's means and motivations.

Boone believed he would eventually divulge the secret of the hatch to his sister, Shannon. At this point in the series the hatch was a secret shared between Locke and his student, Boone. When it became clear that Boone would act on his threat, due to an inordinately strong emotional connection to his sister, Locke knocked him out, tied him up in such a way that he could barely move his hands, and applied an unknown but powerful herbal concoction to the wound on Boone's skull. Locke somehow knew the herbal mixture would suffice to make Boone open to suggestion. Locke threw a knife at Boone's feet, told him he'd be able to reach the knife when he had enough motivation, and left the young man in the jungle.

Locke trusted the Island to act in a positive way on Boone. It matters not at all whether one believes Locke was controlled at this point by the Smoke Monster. The important thing to keep in mind is that Locke considered that his visions were due not to the Monster, but to the Island.

LOCKE: Do you really think all this is an accident—that we, a group of strangers survived, many of us with just superficial injuries? Do you think we crashed on this place by coincidence—especially, this place? We were brought here for a purpose, for a reason, all of us. Each one of us was brought here for a reason.
JACK: Brought here? And who brought us here, John?
LOCKE: The Island. The Island brought us here. This is no ordinary place, you've seen that, I know you have. But the Island chose you, too, Jack. It's destiny.

The Island's purpose was so grand, so extraordinary, that extreme measures were justified. Locke didn't knock out Boone with a blow to the head because he was angry with the boy. He did it to allow Boone a vision of the Island, or at least a vision created and guided by the Island.

Faith for John Locke was faith in the Island. It was faith in a great purpose, not yet revealed at the time of Locke's death at Ben Linus' hands. The Island and its purpose for Locke, Jack, Kate, and the others was so important that even something as otherwise mean-spirited as knocking out Boone and tying him up bore little or no significance in comparison. The Island would teach Boone, and even a moderately high amount of discomfort for an afternoon was an acceptably low price to pay for enlightenment.

Faith for Locke was a surrender to destiny. The rigours of syllogistic reason, science, and medicine cannot explain destiny, can reveal nothing of the Island's purpose, and certainly cannot begin to make sense of the Island's supernatural abilities. Locke was paralysed for life, but on touching the Island's shore, he walked. Rose had terminal cancer, but it vanished when she reached the Island. Locke knew all the survivors were destined for the Island. Science only got in the way.

HIERARCHY OF VALUES: SACRIFICE

One of the most masterfully created scenes in cinema occurred in the 1972 film Brother Sun Sister Moon, about the early life of St. Francis of Assisi. In the fireplace scene, Bernardo di Quintavalle has just returned from the Crusades, finding his friend Francesco barefoot in the snow, working to restore the ruins of San Damiano church. The spoken portion of the scene is monopolised by Bernardo, but every other element of the scene points to something grander than anything Bernardo can identify in his rambling, stream-of-consciousness monologue before his old friend. At the end of Bernardo's meaningless rantings, Francesco straightens him out and reveals not only the answer to Bernardo's longings, but gives Bernardo a foundation for the rest of his life.

BERNARDO: Yet, it's too easy to blame the Crusades for this loss, this emptiness, this dissatisfaction that I feel. The horror of war, the destruction of our ideals, is part of it, I know. But there is something else. I feel stifled by my past, by my upbringing. None of it means anything to me anymore. You, Francesco, you know better than anyone else that I cannot live without an ideal, without something to believe in. Perhaps I'm wrong, perhaps one should be more cynical, and forget ideals. That's why I thought I had to come and talk to you.
ST. FRANCIS: [Pointing to a stone on the floor] That would make a worthy cornerstone. Strong... and true. Where did you get these? Some quarry near here?
BERNARDO: Yes. It's not far. I can take you there if you like.
ST. FRANCIS: O, come, and let yourself be built as living stones into a spiritual temple.

St. Francis no longer had a mind for the concerns that weighed human hearts. Bernardo used several hundred words basically to tell St. Francis something was missing in his life. St. Francis used just fourteen words to convey to his old friend the complete answer to all of his longings.

John Locke and St. Francis both had visions. In each case, the vision imparted a sure, irrational knowledge of something grand. Neither man had to worry any longer about fitting in, never again had to yell 'Don't tell me what I can't do!' The only possible response to the vision was surrender. Life had meaning only because of the truth of the vision, which brought purpose to the Saint's life, and to the future martyr's life. Locke and St. Francis gave up their former concerns and concentrated on serving their new masters. For St. Francis, this meant unswerving devotion to the Christian Deity. For John Locke, surrender meant applying himself to understanding and serving the needs of the Island.

Nothing was more important than the Island, its Purpose for the survivors, and their Destiny in serving that Purpose. Life itself was not as important as these three elements of John Locke's faith.

JACK: Did you talk with Boone about destiny, John?
LOCKE: Boone was a sacrifice that the Island demanded. What happened to him at that plane [the Nigerian plane, where Boone sustained the injuries that killed him] was a part of a chain of events that led us here—that led us down a path—that led you and me to this day, to right now.

The idea that service to the Island was worth any sacrifice, even the sacrifice of life, was foreign to the Season-One Jack. In the above discussion from the end of Season One, Jack clearly has contempt for Locke's interpretation of Boone's death as something ordained and approved by the Island. For Jack, Boone's death was accidental. Even if it were not a random event, Jack could not have accepted any presumption that the Island was worth anyone's life. As Jack said at the end of Season Four, "It's an island, John. No one needs to protect it."

JACK'S UNDERSTANDING OF FAITH

Some readers may shake their heads in disbelief when they read this, but "What Kate Does" (LOST 6.03) has become one of my favourite LOST episodes—more meaningful and entertaining than even "The Constant." It's not because of Kate, though I loved every episode that featured my favourite television heroine. No, the element of this episode that continually draws me is the deliberate construction of a philosophical framework for the endgame, and a demonstration of the fuller meaning of Faith and Trust as pivotal concepts in LOST. I will have more to say on Jack and the green pill. Before we take a second, deeper look, though, we're going to have to develop an understanding of nonlinear structures, which we will do in the next section of this book.

By the end of Episode 6.03 we knew Jack was willing to sacrifice himself, not for his friends, but for a concept—for the Island. Jack elevated trust and faith to heights of no lesser importance than those John Locke had claimed.

Faith, for both John Locke and Jack Shephard, was surrender to something greater, more meaningful, more enduring than oneself. Faith was worthy of any sacrifice, even the ultimate sacrifice of one's life.

VOLITION AND FAITH

There is neither blue pill nor red pill in LOST. We have only the green pill. If LOST were to draw a clear distinction between ignorant bliss and discomforting enlightenment, it is clear we would be expected to choose the red pill. In fact, I have to believe if Neo had chosen the blue pill, Morpheus would have insisted that he give back the sodding pill and take the red one. Did Neo really have a choice?

I believe there is choice in LOST. Jacob's early contemporaries had a saying: *Di immortales virtutem approbare, non adhibere debent*. Roughly translated, 'We may expect the gods to approve virtue, but not to endow us with it.' The significance, I feel, is simple. Destiny, for the ancient Romans and for the creators of LOST, is something chosen. Destiny is a matter of volition in the sense that at any moment an individual may choose to forego the rigours of acquiring virtues requisite to the fullest appreciation of enlightenment. Lacking that enlightenment, we have no opportunity to act in such a way as to fulfil our destiny.

I tend to think of Freedom in LOST as occupying one side of a coin. The other side of the coin is stamped with the word "Responsibility." This interdependence of freedom and responsibility is something all of us are taught as children. "If you want to go outside and play with your friends you need to wash the dishes." Responsibilities and freedoms go hand in hand. As the child acquires greater maturity, greater freedoms are bestowed, but they are always tied to higher degrees of responsibility. I tell my children that Paul of Tarsus, in chains, held under house arrest, waiting for his execution date, had greater freedom than anyone I have ever known in my life. In the same way, Jack Shephard, even knowing he is likely to die, enjoyed essentially infinite degrees of freedom, because he acted always in ways that would clarify the road ahead. Martyrdom was the path he was obliged to follow, but it was his true path, the most responsible path, and therefore the path of greatest freedom.

THE GREATEST VIRTUE

Faith is a bitter green pill. It called Locke and Jack to surrender themselves to a reality almost entirely hidden from their comprehension and to sacrifice health, happiness, and life to its maintenance and service.

Faith is certain knowledge, more certain than the shifting sands of logic and science, informing the soul of destiny and purpose, and instilling infinite capacities for trust, love, and devotion. It is the greatest of the LOST virtues, for when the survivors find it, they are no longer Lost, but instead find themselves, find each other, find the Island, discover their destiny, and exercise their freedom.

Faith, for LOST, is the most meaningful expression of our humanity. And it made the Island the most fascinating location ever depicted on television. It told us not only about our favourite characters. It told us about ourselves.

CHAPTER 5 LINEAR THEME III:
FAITH VERSUS SCIENCE

"Science" by Pearson Moore 2011

LOST was a war of ideas. Battle lines were drawn over concepts of destiny, faith, and trust. Fears and desires and the other usual motivators of the soul were usurped by beliefs and philosophies and modes of thought. Fierce struggles over concepts and creeds became paramount to every episode in the series and caused unrelenting turmoil in the minds and hearts of every major character. The longest, most furious battles were waged over the supreme ideas of LOST: Faith and Science.

Jack and Locke were the most visible proponents of the core ideas, but they were not the only two characters pitted against each other in the war of faith versus science. Stuart Radzinsky and Daniel Faraday can be seen as warriors in this series-long conflict, with Faraday becoming the original advocate of the idea of the Constant as a force of nature that superseded even the laws of physics, while Radzinsky adhered to the tenets of pure science. Even the battle between the Guardian ("Mother") and the Man in Black can be understood as primarily a conflict between her faith in the Island and his wheel-based light-and-water scientific studies.

LOST created a vast tapestry of ideas, but if we are to understand any of them we must begin here, at the central struggle between science and faith. We have already spent a good number of pages discussing the parameters of faith as they apply to LOST. If we are to understand the essentials of the conflict as LOST would have us approach them, we need to delve into a study of the facets of science important to the series. We are fortunate to have had lengthy exposure to the major proponent of science in LOST, the Dharma Initiative. We will begin our study of science here, with the group created by Magnus Hanso's great-grandson, Alvar Hanso.

THE DHARMA INITIATIVE

For the betterment of mankind and the advancement of world peace.

These were the stated goals of the Dharma Initiative. Dedicated scientists, conducting experiments and making breakthrough discoveries in six specific technical disciplines, and all of it carried out on a beautiful island with comfortable living spaces and tasteful decor. The Fifth Dimension could have sung its praises: Peace will guide this island, and love, love will steer the vans. This is the dawning of the Dharma Initiative...

The well-rehearsed propaganda must have been appealing to our grandparents. Here was an organisation that lived its values, and valued peace over war, love over death.

Except the organisation was funded by a munitions and arms merchant who became wealthier with every Vietnamese village incinerated to dust by napalm bombs. Except the DI was run by a mathematician whose primary aim was to build "security systems." And when Horace Goodspeed's bully tactics weren't aggressive enough, Stuart Radzinsky stepped in with handguns, rifles, and machine guns.

What was the Dharma Initiative? A band of peace-loving dropouts, or a group of power-hungry masterminds? Hippie utopia, or fascist nightmare? The Dharma Initiative is the story of happy image and harsh reality, idealists and schemers, the culmination of everything the Woodstock Generation believed in.

WELCOME TO THE ISLAND

The Dharma Initiative's mission, to improve conditions for mankind and to advance world peace, was focussed on six areas of scientific inquiry:

Meteorology
Psychology
Parapsychology
Zoology
Electromagnetism
Utopian Social Engineering

A research station was dedicated to each of the six technical endeavours. For example, zoological studies were conducted at the Hydra Station, electromagnetism was investigated at the Swan Station, and psychological observations were made at the Pearl Station.

The DI was founded by Gerald and Karen DeGroot, then graduate students at the University of Michigan, in 1970. The DeGroots, long-time associates of Alvar Hanso, were natural investigators with abiding curiosity in several far-flung scientific disciplines. They established the six major areas of inquiry to be pursued on the Island, and created an environment conducive to work centred on their vision of an ideal community.

Scientific work proceeded under tight security. "The Island has multiple research facilities, each with its own purpose and protocol. Throughout your day-to-day activities you may interact with Dharma personnel from these stations. We ask that you respect these team members' privacy, and do not inquire about their work, as they are not at liberty to discuss it. But remember, it is for the greater good of the community."

Unusual security measures were justified on the basis of the difficult environment. The barracks were surrounded by a sonar fence, to "protect us from the Island's abundant and diverse wildlife." A stray wild boar could inflict severe injury, after all. But boars were not the only security concern. Hostile natives could be found as close as five kilometres beyond the sonar fence. "Any encounters with the indigenous people of the Island should be reported to the closest security personnel immediately."

THE DHARMA INITIATIVE AFTER THE DEGROOTS

The realities of Island life conflicted immediately with the DeGroots' vision of a scientific paradise on Earth. Perhaps the DeGroots didn't even know about the Hostiles, but it wasn't long before Horace Goodspeed and Stuart Radzinsky realised they were not alone on the Island. Months or years later, they must have heard tales of a high authority, virtually a god, who controlled every move the Hostiles made.

Security concerns edged out the early ideal of a community focussed entirely on esoteric research. There was nothing at all esoteric about a Hostile levelling a Korean-War-era M-1 Garand Rifle at a scientist and shooting her dead. Radzinsky and Goodspeed had to revise the Initiative's preliminary plans. One of the DI's areas of research would have to be curtailed, and one of the stations would be devoted to security operations. The original intention of the Arrow Station was probably for meteorological or para-psychological studies, but it was hastily converted to a "mathematics" facility that was actually a security research bunker.

Horace may or may not have been a mathematician, but he would have had unique expertise in development of security systems. Security quickly became the number one concern as carpenters and contractors threw together the barracks housing. Goodspeed became the DI's leader on the Island because he was the best hope of protecting the scientists.

Horace and his team would have become quickly acquainted with their most dangerous adversary. Whatever the fast-moving black smoke was, it could be contained neither by concrete wall nor rope barrier. Neither bullets nor clubs inflicted any harm on the beast. But Goodspeed had a secret weapon, even before he was called to the Island. It was a weapon guaranteed to keep the Smoke Monster at bay. He received that weapon from the DeGroots, though they probably did not say how they knew of its efficacy. The weapon was dynamite, and Horace had literally tonnes of it.

Black Rock by Pearson Moore
contains elements of "Chesapeake"
by US Navy ca 1850 WMC PD

We do not know the precise circumstances of the Black Rock's arrival on the Island. We know that Jonas Whitfield, an officer on the Black Rock, paid hefty sums to a corrupt priest and prison officials on the Canary Islands to purchase Ricardo Alpert. Whitfield would have been paid for his troubles by the captain of the vessel, Magnus Hanso. Hanso, in turn, would have been richly rewarded by a patron.

The vessel was not on a trade mission to the Kingdom of Siam as advertised. We know this because we also know Magnus Hanso's patron: Jacob. Jacob confessed to his brother and to Richard that he had enticed the Black Rock to the Island. It was Jacob's plan to pay Magnus Hanso to bring several individuals of diverse background to the Island to determine their suitability as Candidates for the position of Protector.

It seems likely this last mission of the Black Rock was not its first. Developing strong rapport with a slave trader would require nothing more than a couple kilos of gold, and Jacob had stores of this metal in abundance. The difficulty for Jacob was not price but time. Mortals lived only so long, and getting on and off the Island was difficult. Quite likely, then, he would have arranged for several trips by a single ship. We can be relatively certain of this since Charles Widmore was willing to pay nearly half a million pounds for the Black Rock's first mate's log. It seems beyond belief that he would pay for pre-Island information on a non-descript sailing vessel. However, he would certainly pay any sum for unique information on the Island he planned to control. Therefore, the First Mate's log almost certainly contained detailed information on the Island, and that information would have been obtained during the course of voyages to and from the Island completed prior to the Black Rock's final voyage.

The wreck of the Black Rock contained information corroborating the view that Magnus Hanso was privy to unique Island information prior to his final voyage. Among the few items he carried were several cases of early nitroglycerin-embedded Kieselgur dynamite. It seems most likely that Jacob, intending to prevent his brother from killing everyone on board, would have advised Hanso to carry plenty of the explosive. It was the only nineteenth-century weapon capable of stopping the Man in Black. That Hanso did not use the weapon was probably the unfortunate result of being swept onto the Island. He had never had to use the dynamite before, because anchoring several hundred metres off the Island (during earlier voyages) he had never had to confront the Smoke Monster. Shipwrecked two kilometres inland, he was caught entirely off guard.

Information on the beneficial effects of dynamite likely made its way down the generations to Magnus' great-grandson, Alvar Hanso. Alvar would have known the stories of the Island, and his position as munitions and arms trader would have given him access to the highest echelons of the United States military. He would have learned of the Island's recent location from their failed test of Jughead in 1954. Or possibly he had earlier knowledge of the Island's location and led the military there, perhaps intent on using their presence to establish a foothold for his eventual control of the Island.

Alvar Hanso's pre-DI contribution was probably the Lamp Post. He knew of at least two and probably several historically accurate positions for the Island. To track its whereabouts would have been a relatively simple matter of hiring specialists in mathematics, geomagnetism, paleomagnetism, and early computers. He could hire the world's experts because he was a billionaire at a time when millionaires were considered the wealthiest people on Earth.

Horace Goodspeed's contribution was probably the one that earned him the position of Head Honcho. Goodspeed probably figured out that dynamite was effective not due to explosive force, but due to some other effect. After all, he would have received reports that dynamite had been used successfully, sometimes even catching the Smoke Monster off guard, but the beast seemed to sustain no injury, even when the dynamite was detonated in the middle of the smoke. But the dynamite was quite successful in deterring Smokey from continuing his attack. Intense sound waves were associated with explosions. The innovation of a sonic fence was almost certainly Horace Goodspeed's idea, and his ticket to appointment as Head of DI Operations.

ALVAR HANSO'S BIG ADVENTURE

Hanso Industries was one of the first companies to launch a space satellite into orbit. The primary objective of the satellite was to study "the geophysical properties of the Earth, and its region of influence in space. One of the most important scientific discoveries of the Space Age has been the Earth's magnetosphere, the region in space that is distorted by the Earth's internal magnetic field. The primary goal of the Hanso science team is to explore the shock wave and transition region on the sunward side of the magnetosphere and its extended tail, with its neutral magnetic sheet, on the night side of the magnetosphere. While in orbit, the satellite's secondary objective is to search for and observe any magnetic anomalies that may occur on the Earth's surface."

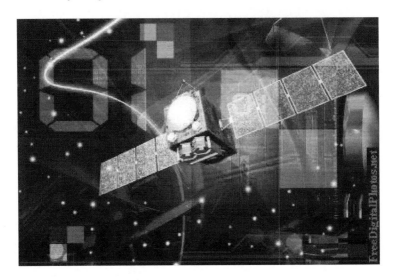

Geophysics was a hot topic in the late 1950s and early 1960s and was indelibly connected to the Space Race, being that the "Geophysical Year" took place in 1958 (only months after the launch of Sputnik in October 1957), and included some of the first major collaborations between Soviet and American physicists. Seven years later, in 1965, Hanso could cloak its satellite launch in the guise of a benign science project, using scientific jargon that would have been familiar to even lay people of that hyper-aware time. The "secondary objective" was of course its only objective, and it did not seek "any magnetic anomalies," but anomalies of a single, unique variety: The magnetic fluctuations caused by the invisible Island. Hanso's satellite could probably be considered the first and most important part of the Lamp Post Station.

We may never know Alvar Hanso's true intentions. Magnus Hanso was a slave trader. Alvar and his father before him dealt in munitions and arms, feeding humanity's hunger to destroy itself, growing wealthy beyond imagination from the destruction their products wrought.

Did Alvar Hanso have an epiphany? Did he turn away from a life and generations-long legacy of reaping rewards from others' suffering? Or, in establishing and funding the Dharma Initiative, was he hoping to geometrically increase his own wealth and power?

We know he accepted some blame. Not for seeking wealth and power, but for selecting Thomas Mittelwerk as his successor.

"I am to blame. For training Thomas Werner Mittelwerk. For grooming him to be my successor. For giving him all the tools he needed to do the awful things he has. He cannot kill me, but he can keep me locked up while he kills millions..."

Mittelwerk's genocidal plans were revealed near the end of the Sri Lanka video, while Mittelwerk's ability to manipulate public opinion became clear in his short "Reinvigorated Hanso Foundation" commercials.

Even if Alvar Hanso could conveniently blame Thomas Mittelwerk for his foundation's plan to kill millions of innocent people, we need to maintain some degree of neutrality in our thinking. After all, Mittelwerk did not wish to wipe out entire villages to establish himself as the greatest mass murderer of the twenty-first century. He was taking the final steps toward Alvar Hanso's goal of preventing the inevitable: the destruction of all human life as predicted by the Valenzetti Equation.

THE VALENZETTI EQUATION

Alvar Hanso himself explained the key importance of the Valenzetti Equation to the work of the Dharma Initiative.

"Why all the security, all the secrecy? The answer is simple: Your research is intended to do nothing less than save the world as we know it.

"In 1962, only thirteen years ago, the world came to the brink of nuclear war. The United States and the Soviet Union almost fulfilled the promise of mutual assured destruction.... After the Cuban Missile Crisis, both nations decided to find a solution. The result was the Valenzetti Equation. Commissioned under the highest secrecy, through the U.N. Security Council, the equation... predicts the exact number of years and months until humanity extinguishes itself. Whether through nuclear fire, chemical and biological warfare, conventional warfare, pandemic, over-population... The results are chilling..."

Valenzetti's work demonstrated that humanity's demise was inevitable. Nothing could be done to prevent the human race from being extinguished on the Earth.

"Valenzetti gave numerical values to the core environmental and human factors in his equation: 4, 8, 15, 16, 23 and 42." The entire work of the Dharma Initiative, according to Hanso in the 1975 Sri Lanka video, had the single goal of preventing the destruction of the human race.

PEACE, LOVE, AND CONTROL OF THE HUMAN RACE

"This station is being built here because of its proximity to what we believe to be an almost limitless energy. And that energy, once we can harness it correctly, is going to allow us to manipulate time." Unlimited energy and manipulation of time may not have been germane to a deeper understanding of the Valenzetti Equation, but they surely would be useful to anyone seeking control of the world.

While we may wish to believe that Alvar Hanso did in fact see the light, that the tens of millions of dollars he spent on the Dharma Initiative were the selfless investment of a man dedicated only to the advancement of humanity, we must consider the possibility that he had quite a different agenda. The historical record, and especially his family history, supports an initial hypothesis that Alvar Hanso was interested only in his own power, and not the preservation of humankind.

We cannot know what Hanso's intentions truly were. But we can make reasonable extrapolation to a viable hypothesis based on the outcome of certain events on the Island. We can know him by the fruit of his collaborators' work.

Security was not the primary objective of the Dharma Initiative. Whether for the advancement of humankind or the installation of Alvar Hanso as Emperor of the World, the DI had a single objective: manipulation of the Island's unique powers through scientific study. We should not be confused, then, when Horace Goodspeed, by title and right the Head of DI Operations, was superseded in authority by Stuart Radzinsky.

UNRESTRICTED MANDATE

Stuart Radzinsky, Ph.D., was the Director of Research of the Dharma Initiative. He was charged with the immediate development and exploitation of every one of the Island's unique powers. He was given carte blanche by the DI authorities in Ann Arbor, Michigan, to use any means necessary to achieve the Initiative's objectives.

Nothing, not even the lives of innocents, would thwart him in his single-minded pursuit of the Island's raw power. If Horace Goodspeed stood in his way, he was empowered to push Goodspeed to the side. If a high-ranking scientist was in danger of life or limb, the work could not stop, even for the moment that might be required to free Dr. Chang's hand from the crushing weight of metallic structures failing around him. If a worker died, Radzinsky knew he was authorised to bury the body in secret. The stakes were too high to ask this man to conform to social, moral, or legal constraint. Anything was permitted, as long as the action served the needs of the DI.

Radzinsky was not a maverick. Both he and Horace understood that Radzinsky was the de facto leader of DI operations, as was clearly revealed when Radzinsky used the threat of a call to Ann Arbor to clarify things for Horace. Radzinsky acted under clear and precise instruction, which certainly came not from the pot-smoking DeGroots, but from the ice-calm figure of Alvar Hanso.

SCIENCE VERSUS FAITH

The Dharma Initiative became a sad footnote in the long history of the Island. Benjamin Linus spoke for the writers when he offered his summary of the DI's greatest accomplishments:

LOCKE: Hey. Uh... was he talking about what I think he was talking about?
BEN: If you mean time-travelling bunnies, then yes.

LOCKE: You do know that he said specifically not to put anything metal in there.
[Ben stares at Locke for a second, then gives a curt, exasperated nod and resumes the work of loading metal objects into the time chamber.]

The Dharma Initiative's carefully planned experiments in the manipulation of Casimir space to realise object-specific time displacement were just so much nonsense to Benjamin Linus, who dismissed the work as "time-travelling bunnies." Science and logic, for Ben and for the writers of LOST, are inadequate to the full knowledge of our place in this world. The Dharma Initiative's limited understanding allowed a rabbit in a carefully controlled chamber to be transported one hundred milliseconds into the future. Ben's knowledge allowed an entire island to be transported halfway across the world and months into the past or future. In the same way, science in general illuminates only a miniscule fraction of the possible knowledge of the universe, while faith is the beneficiary of an infinitely more profound enlightenment.

The problem is the closed, self-referential nature of science and logic themselves. Science and logic are imperfect subsets of reality. If we rely on logic as revelation of reality we will discern only an incomplete, warped world far from true reality.

Science makes sensory observations, catalogues these data, uses the rules of mathematics and logic to create connections among the observations, and builds empirical findings into models of reality that we call hypotheses and theories. A scientist truly comfortable in her laboratory will never claim she is revealing reality, only a poor model for certain physical behaviours that seem to follow a reproducible pattern. There is no truth in science. Science is not a tool for illuminating the fullness of reality.

Science is confined by logic. If I expand the limits of research to any inquiry that might be included within the scope of logic, science, and mathematics, I must necessarily accept that certain limits nevertheless exist. Most importantly, I may not ever claim to investigate or to have discovered any facet of reality. The best I might hope to accomplish, even after a lifetime in the laboratory, is to establish the adherence of certain observed phenomena to models of reality that I create through inference, induction, and deduction. These models are most often referred to as theories, but they can never explain the real world. We rely on assumptions that negate any possible connection with reality.

OCKHAM'S RAZOR

One of the most important assumptions underlying science is Ockham's Razor. In plain language, Ockham's Razor insists the scientist must accept the simplest solution to a problem as being the correct solution. If I can imagine a chemical reaction as being the result of the collision of five molecules, but I can equally imagine that the reaction is the result of the collision of just two molecules, and if every observation I have made supports either of the fruits of my imagination, I must accept as valid and correct the imagined event that includes just two molecules. The reality may be that only one molecule is required, or seven molecules are required, or the event occurs only when there are sunspots on our solar system's star, but I can never know this. Even if the model I develop happens to support a theory that is close to reality, I may not ever claim to have elucidated even the slightest aspect of reality. I am allowed to conclude only that certain behaviours seem reproducible and that they also seem to adhere to a model consistent with Ockham's Razor and the other underlying assumptions of the scientific method.

I pick up a pen with the five fingers of my right hand. Science notes this fact, records the observations associated with the act. And that is all science can do. Science cannot tell us my motivation for picking up the pen, cannot predict what I will do with it, how I will do it, what the future outcomes will be, or how the ramifications of the simple act will ripple through the greater world, how the act will affect others.

Science cannot place even the simplest act within the continuum of reality. Complex interactions are so far outside the realm of pure science that they virtually defy adequate description. In fact, no interaction can be fully characterised. Science and logic must be forever partial, incomplete statements of certain events, and they can never claim to explain a basis in reality.

We say logic is "impartial." Even if logic cannot connect events to reality, we believe it is at least fair, in the sense that it applies the same syllogisms regardless of context. But every new, misleading application of logic is a fresh occasion for warped interpretations. Logic is, in every sense that has meaning, entirely partial, incomplete in every way. Logic can never, ever be considered impartial. It is, in its very nature, an instrument of partiality.

SCIENCE: INSTRUMENT OF DECEPTION

Logic serves dark objectives.

Benjamin Linus was the unequalled master of deception on the Island. He achieved this distinction through misdirection and the correct application of logic. He knew observation and syllogism are open to broadest interpretation, and he was ready at every turn to provide a self-serving explanation of anything those within his sphere of influence observed. He knew people are all too willing to believe their observations are the full revelation of truth. All Ben had to do was provide a few well-chosen words and he could lead dozens of people to believe in the integrity of his command decisions.

"Why do you let them talk to you that way, John?" Ben's words were simple and few, but they were perfectly placed to sow in Locke the seeds of doubt, fear, and anger. The implication of his words was that Jack and Sawyer, in telling Locke what to do, were treating him as they would a child. Jack's assumption of control over Locke was an affront not only to the elder Locke, but a perversion of the correct order of things. That Locke willingly participated

78

served to double the depths of this insidious subversion of the natural order. Locke's reaction to Ben's expertly-placed manipulation was predictable and served well Ben's growing control over Locke. In like manner, Ben controlled the thoughts and activities of dozens of Others over the course of nearly twenty years.

GROUNDED IN FAITH

Muslim Prayer Beads © Muhammad Rehan
2009 Creative Commons Share Alike 2.0

The heroes of LOST were grounded in faith. Sayid Jarrah and Charlie Pace were the two noblest examples of heroism in the six years of the series, and they were also the most observant of their respective religious traditions. In the great battle of faith between John Locke and Jack Shephard, faith won in a unanimous decision, with the former champion of science fully converted into the Island's leading practitioner of faith.

Those convicted in their faith are sure of their purpose and destiny. Science not only cannot fathom the possibility of anything associated with destiny, it rejects any notion of purpose. Science is built on the shifting sands of hypothesis, theory, and syllogism. Faith stands unshaken on the firm rock of truth.

DESMOND: This doesn't matter, you know.
JACK: Excuse me?
DESMOND: Him destroying the island, you destroying him. It doesn't matter. You know, you're gonna lower me into that light, and I'm gonna go somewhere else. A place where we can be with the ones we love, and not have to ever think about this damn island again. And you know the best part, Jack?
JACK: What?
DESMOND: You're in this place. You know, we sat next to each other on Oceanic 815. It never crashed. We spoke to each other. You seemed happy. You know, maybe I can find a way to bring you there, too.

JACK: Desmond, I tried that once. There are no shortcuts, no do-overs. What happened, happened. Trust me, I know. All of this matters.

Every action Jack took in that final episode mattered. From his prayer in the stream to his final instructions to the others, from his triumph over the Man in Black to his final embrace in his lover's arms, everything Jack did was imbued with purpose and significance. He was resolute, strong, and effective precisely because he had given up every last morsel of scientific scepticism. Replacing the Cork Stone into the Source was the final and most important action in the entire series. The Cork Stone, inscribed with the foundational truths of human civilisation, was the symbol of each of the characters' destinies, and witness and source of our own human dignity.

Faith, for LOST, is an expression of humility. It is the acceptance of a reality greater than one's ability to understand. It is trust in a power that exceeds any single person's abilities, and greater than even the most concerted and unified efforts of women and men. Faith asks "What can I give?" It is certain knowledge that hope abides, even in the most dire circumstance.

Science, for LOST, is a seeking of things. It is acquisitive, selfish, uncaring, and irresponsible. Science achieved its fullest expression in the Man in Black, working in his underground laboratory, endeavouring to discover ways to use the Light and the water. The Guardian had to stop him, because the Source was not something to be used, but something to be accepted, trusted. It was something to which one submitted, and never, ever was it to be considered an object of manipulation. Science asks "What can I get?" It is eternal desire, unrelenting selfishness.

CONCLUSION, PART I: INDICTMENT OF SCIENCE

The Dharma Initiative did not fail because of the Incident. It did not fail because of the Purge. It failed because it was inherently flawed. It could never have uncovered the true secrets of the Island because it relied on fundamentally incapable and irresponsible tools in seeking the Island's mysteries.

"Every question I answer will simply lead to another question." At some point we have to surrender scepticism and seductive "impartial" scientific inquiry and accept on faith things as they are and must be. If we can never accept that there are fundamental truths upon which we can base our lives, we will never be secure in who we are, we will never possess the unshakable knowledge of the foundational precepts of our humanity.

If we are not sure of our inherent dignity as human beings, we will be able to imagine experiments aimed at discovering alternative explanations. Josef Mengele was a great scientist whose work advanced theoretical knowledge. I will not list here any of the experiments he performed. They were of such a nature as to nauseate even those with strong stomachs (http://en.wikipedia.org/ wiki/Josef_Mengele). In some brave but misguided scientific circles debate continues to this day regarding the appropriateness of applying Mengele's data to "legitimate" science. From a strictly scientific point of view, data obtained from his experiments are as valid as any other technical information. From a human point of view, the reams of data are the worst imaginable form of pornography. The paper containing his records could serve us appropriately only as fuel for a fire.

LOST does not assert that scientists are misguided. Those of us who earn our living in the laboratory (I include myself) need not fear any comparison with Josef Mengele. LOST says simply that if science is to have any validity, it must be guided by the heart. If scientific endeavour is not informed by a firm reliance on the fundamental principles of human civility, it is not an activity worthy of our consideration or effort. The Dharma Initiative, guided by fear and lust for scientific power, was LOST's premiere example of humanity gone awry.

CONCLUSION, PART II:
INDICTMENT OF A GENERATION

The most recognisable saying of the late 1960s and early 1970s was "turn on, tune in, drop out."

Activate your mind, seek to understand yourself by looking inward, and disengage from all commitments to the outside world. Turn on, tune in, drop out was Timothy Leary's slogan, and it became my generation's mantra. The Vietnam War was, in hindsight, a stupid and pathetic response to the perceived threat of Marxism. The "Domino Theory" was flawed, for it was founded on the notion that human beings—selfish human beings—would voluntarily give up their self-centred desires in exchange for collectivism and social tyranny. Leaders in the Kremlin and in the White House had not the intellectual tools to understand that Adam Smith's capitalism and Karl Marx's communism were opposite sides of the same counterfeit eighteenth-century coin. The gold standard of human economics is neither laissez-faire free market nor centrally-imposed five-year plan, but the commitment of human beings, governments, and religions to full and harmonious engagement with the physical and spiritual worlds.

Your grandparents, children of the Greatest Generation, decided to disengage. We smoked pot and hash. We drank Sangria, Whiskey, and Budweiser. We shot cocaine, LSD, and heroin. We wore love beads, dressed in Nehru jackets, flashed the two-fingered peace sign, and thoughts ourselves advanced in every way. We were for women's rights (well, ah, to a point, anyway...) and we even thought Negroes should have equality. Most of all, we were opposed to that oppressive military action in Southeast Asia, the one we saw every night on the CBS Evening News with Walter Cronkite in the form of dead, maimed, and dying soldiers in red-earth ditches, on green army stretchers, on Huey helicopters. "Hell no, we won't go" and "All we are saying—is give peace a chance," on their own, are among the finest sentiments of the human heart. But my generation suborned the ideals of peace to the lusts of sex, drugs, and rock-and-roll.

We agitated and marched and chanted for peace in Vietnam not because we understood the war to be unjust, but because we saw no reason to die in a far-off jungle when the orgasmic pleasures of responsibility-free life beckoned. "I'm Okay, You're Okay" and "If It Feels Good Do It" were closer to the governing mantra of my generation than any pacifist or humanist or religious ideals. We temporarily adopted those ideals because they suited our true objectives, which in the end proved to share not a single point of reference with any of the nobility of our parents' hearts.

Timothy Leary made an appearance on Mittelos. We knew him as Stuart Radzinsky.

The inevitable outcome of a Lucy-in-the-Sky-with-Diamonds, navel-gazing approach to life is the imposition of one's will on others. If the only reality we know is the gut-based impulses of self, we will move to ensure that others secure for us the satisfaction of our urges and desires. We wake from LSD-induced stupor to find our taxes are too high, our government far too socialistic, our responsibilities too broad and too deep. No PTA and bowling league and civic duty for my generation, thank you. That was our parents' life, not ours. Just give me my remote, a few blow-em'-up action movies on the wide-screen TV, keep my taxes low, and stop telling me to participate, damn it. Life isn't about giving. It's about getting.

LOST is emphatic about few things, but this is one of them: The Baby Boomer generation's response to life is wrong-headed, inhuman, and uncivilised. As Russians say, it is некультурный. If we are to survive, if we are to make an enduring contribution to this world, if we are to realise Jacob's Progress, we must engage. We are compelled, by nature, by our truest selves, by everything holy and wise and good, to engage with this world and with each other in every dimension of life, spirit, and will. We all need each other, for the only way into the Church of the Holy Lamp Post is with a Constant at one's side, and the only way to move on into the warmth and light beyond is as a group, the congregation of all those who have interacted in harmony with each other to improve the human condition. Goodness is not singular, but collaborative. It is not a choice. It is our truest and only sustainable destiny.

THOUGHTS FOR THE JOURNEY:
THE HUMAN CONDITION

We are Lost until we find and recognise ourselves. We find ourselves through each other, through an unbroken commitment to a Constant, through a trust and faith in each other and in our common humanity, through happy adherence to the civilised values inscribed on the Cork Stone.

The Dharma Initiative represented an artificial, science-based civilisation founded in scepticism, fear, and thirst for power. There were no Constants, no equality, no fraternity, no liberty. Consensus was achieved through coercion, as in the "unanimous" vote to kill Sayid, or from the long barrel of a rifle. Dharma offered no means of reconciliation, redemption, or recognition.

In the end LOST does not assert faith over science, nor good over evil, but rather identity and certitude over incoherence and doubt. Lacking foundation in any of the enduring attributes of human identity, Dharma was doomed to fail. The Dharma Initiative was a rich, multi-layered creation that brought colour, depth, and focus to an already thought-provoking television drama. It is one of the key attributes of an inimitable series that will be forever cherished.

Our analysis of the conflict of science versus faith is not complete. We need to consider the opposing contributions that the Guardian and the Man in Black brought to this discussion, for their arguments are not only foundational, but they bring such clarity as to allow reconciliation of almost every plot point connected to the conflict. But to achieve this level of clarity we are going to have to engage in a bit of nonlinear analysis, a task we will take on in the coming chapters. Only by relating several story elements simultaneously will we understand why Jack Shephard and John Locke were pitted against each other from the first day on the Island. It was the battle of a lifetime, and it makes for one of the most fascinating studies in fiction.

CHAPTER 6
LINEAR THEME IV: LEADERSHIP

President Jimmy Carter, Press Conference, 1978 PD

"You are not on the list because you are flawed. Because you are angry, and weak, and frightened."

Mikhail enunciated these words with an air of finality and authority, as if proclaiming a truth etched in stone. The Gospel of Mittelos. He addressed his words to Kate, Sayid, and Locke, but he might as well have included in his dismissive assessment all of the survivors of Flight 815. All of them were angry, weak, and frightened—every one of them was Lost. Because they were Lost they could never be considered for inclusion in any task of significance. Their sorry lives merited not even a mention on a list, and none of them evinced even a shred of leadership potential.

We should have known then, by the twelfth episode of Season Three, that one person's opinion, or even one person's authoritative statement, had little relevance to the reality of the Island. Not even two-thousand-year-old Jacob could speak with authority on every subject bearing on the realm he was sworn to protect. In the end, the names Austen, Jarrah, and Locke were found on several lists. Far more than that, though, their leadership and sacrifice meant more to the Island than anything that had occurred in the two millennia of Jacob's reign.

The Island produced many leaders, each of them effective and capable in ways important to the resolution of the Island's greatest struggle. In fact, not only was Mikhail incorrect, but the greatest of the leaders were chosen specifically because they were flawed, because they needed the Island as much as it needed them. Let us consider these lost souls, these Candidates and Kings chosen to serve Mittelos.

THE MONARCH

King Edward VII by Sir Luke Fildes ca 1901 WMC PD

Jacob
Hugo Reyes

The Monarch rules from on high, aloof yet aware, acting always out of concern for her subjects and for the greater good of all.

We suppose a monarch such as Edward VII, or his great-granddaughter, Elizabeth II, to be apolitical, above the fray, untouched by the petty squabbles and posturings of those seeking the limelight. I don't know if Edward was. Perhaps Elizabeth is. I must admit, though, I harboured less than generous thoughts toward the Queen in 2008 and 2009, when she authorised the prorogation of the Canadian Parliament. Rather than allowing the democratic process to take its course—with the likely fall of Stephen Harper's Tory government—she, through her Governor General, shut down parliament so Harper would not have to face the voters. Her actions seemed political in the worst sense of that word.

In similar manner, Jacob isolated himself from the people of the Island. He established two layers of bureaucracy (Consigliere and Leader) between himself and the few residents of his realm. He deluded himself into believing that by forcibly bringing people to the Island he was somehow allowing them complete freedom of choice. Jacob saw himself as the eternal guardian of human progress and individual freedom, yet his actions ensured the deaths of hundreds—perhaps thousands—over the duration of his long reign.

We probably tend to think of Hurley as being somehow more benign than his long-lived predecessor. He seemed in touch with people's needs, perhaps even to the point of being overwhelmed by his responsibility toward those in his charge. He said as much to Ben when he invited the master manipulator to serve as his second. Yet Hurley began asserting the prerogatives of leadership long before his investiture as Protector. He assumed leadership in the critical days after the destruction of the Temple, insisting that Jacob had told him to seek out the Man in Black. He even convinced Jack to follow his lead. We blame the Smoke Monster for the deaths on the submarine, but I have to wonder whether the deaths might have been prevented, if someone had stood up to Hurley and argued against his plan to enter into close proximity with the Island's prince of darkness.

Monarchs enjoy privilege, but those that mean the most to their people work at the awareness and empathy and wisdom they need to perform their work well. Queen Elizabeth II provides an excellent example for Hurley.

Before she became queen, Princess Elizabeth served in World War II as a truck driver, a lowly Second Subaltern (roughly a second lieutenant), Number 230873. She saw with her own eyes what her people had to do to recover from the destruction wrought by the war. Forty years later, she was obliged to face political forces bent on undoing everything her generation had accomplished in rebuilding. The Iron Lady, Margaret Thatcher, had taken control of Queen Elizabeth's realm, and her libertarian vision of a world devoid of compassion was something the Queen would take no part in. At the height of the Iron Lady's stranglehold on the UK, the Queen delivered her annual Christmas message in December, 1983. "But in spite of all the progress that has been made the greatest problem in the world today remains the gap between rich and poor countries and we shall not begin to close this gap until we hear less about nationalism and more about interdependence." We might well imagine the Iron Lady fuming during this speech, perhaps even muttering curses under her breath.

Selfishness has its day, but the true nature of our humanity is never denied for long. Iron Maggie issued edicts from Parliament for a while, but now she's gone. Despite the best efforts of determined thugs and villains, humanity remains. Forces more noble than those possessed by any Iron Lady find quiet ways to confound their politics, frustrate their knavish tricks. The Queen still reigns. Thy choicest gifts in store, on her be pleased to pour.

Born on the Western shore of the Atlantic, I am not supposed to find anything worthy in the words and acts of a monarch. But I do believe Queen Elizabeth serves with the best interests of her people in mind. And even though Jacob committed deeds that might be considered thoughtless or even cruel, I believe he, too, served the Island with the interests of people in his heart. "It only ends once. Anything that happens before that is just progress." I don't consider these were empty words. He believed in them. And whenever Hurley said, "Hey, that's not cool, dude," he was speaking on behalf of those not able to speak for themselves. Hugo Reyes (the name means "Kings") was cut from royal cloth, exemplifying the best traditions of human leadership. Send him victorious, happy and glorious.

THE DICTATOR

The Man in Black
Benjamin Linus
Charles Widmore

All Adolf Hitler ever wanted was for Germans to have their own country, without the interference of foreigners. He was at heart a peaceful man.

If you believe this, you might also be inclined to consider the Man in Black a saint who never wished for anything more than the right to return to the land of his ancestors. You might not even have to be persuaded to believe that Benjamin Linus almost always spoke the truth and fabricated the occasional lie only for the good of those in his charge. And if anyone were to tell you that Charles Widmore authorised the execution of an infant girl, your only response might be to question the sanity of the person delivering this unlikely message.

Even the worst among us, those universally considered to have no redeeming qualities, are not motivated by anything they would recognise as evil intent. I believe Adolf Hitler truly felt a strong communion with the German people. The Man in Black was wronged by the woman who adopted him, and by his own brother, and really did wish to return to Rome. The Dharma Initiative sought to exploit the Island's powers. Ben Linus and Charles Widmore knew that, and they did everything they could to protect the Island. All four of these men had pure motivations.

The problem for these leaders is that others stood in the way of achieving their objectives, and they felt empowered to commit any act—even genocide—to force the world to bend to their will. They were never the servants of anything we would recognise as the common good. They served their own selfish desires. It is selfishness that leads to the atrocities that we recognise as the outcome of an evil heart. Adolf Hitler, the Man in Black, Benjamin Linus, and Charles Widmore were selfish men. It necessarily follows, since they took the initiative to serve their selfish desires, that they were evil men. Perhaps there is no sin in a selfish heart. But when the will acts to satisfy selfish ends, others necessarily suffer; the word 'evil' must be applied in such cases. Hitler killed tens of millions. The Man in Black killed hundreds or thousands. Benjamin Linus filled a trench with the rotting bodies of the dozens he killed.

"We have to kill him." These were Kate's words, delivered not with emotion, not out of a sense of retribution. She was simply forming into words a truth that she and the other survivors should have recognised long before that awful morning after the submarine explosion. There is no sin in doing away with people like Hitler, the Man in Black, and Benjamin Linus. In fact, those in Queen Elizabeth's generation believed not to take action against evil was morally indefensible. The Greatest Generation lived up to great responsibilities. The heroes of LOST fought the good fight again, demonstrating that valour, courage, and commitment need not die with our parents and grandparents.

THE VOLUNTEER

Peace Corp Togo Secondary Science Induction 1983
Peace Corps USA PD

Kate Austen

We were told it would be the toughest job we would ever love. I think the television ads were correct in that assessment. During our two years serving as Peace Corps Volunteers in Togo, West Africa, we learned to live with amoebic dysentery, intestinal worms, and the occasional bout of malaria. We buried two of our own, and many of us won the "TWA Prize," returning to the States too injured, too diseased, or too worn out to function anymore. But I imagine even those who were forced home before the end of service would agree it was the toughest job they ever loved.

Kate Austen was the first to volunteer for any mission. Even when Jack or Sawyer or another of the men sought to exclude her, she found a way to get in on the action. Her restless spirit was not her only motivation, but rather the sign of a deeper source of angst. Her mother had chosen a man who beat and abused her over the man who truly loved her. How could Kate know that any choices she made would not be as bad—or worse—than the ones her own mother had made? Kate could never commit herself to a single man, or a single course of action. She could never settle in one place.

But then she fell into the Island world. Two men competed for her, but neither was able to tame her spirit. She found herself, and her lifelong vocation, in the helpless form of an infant boy, and she tried to become his mother. The three years with Aaron demonstrated the giving nature of her heart, but they also served as proof that she could never be Aaron's mother. Somewhere in dense jungle, on an island appearing on no map, the boy's mother lived in daily agony, separated from her own flesh and blood.

Kate Austen was no ordinary volunteer. In her tenacity, in her unwillingness to remain thwarted by any obstacle, regardless of its difficulty, Kate gave of herself to an extent unrivaled in the series. In reuniting Claire and Aaron and committing her life to the boy's upbringing, Kate repaired the damage to her soul, filled the enormous void, and became the person she was meant to be. She was the supreme example of the good that can be accomplished in devoting energy and passion to a worthy objective.

THE HOLY MARTYR

Mural Oscar Romero by Pedro Nonualco 2007 Univ. de El Salvador CC SA 3.0

Jack Shephard
John Locke

They not only died for a cause greater than themselves. They knew they had to sacrifice their lives for the Island. They might have tried running from their fate, but all four of them instead embraced death as the final and most meaningful act of their lives.

What causes a man in the prime of life, in relationship with his truest soul mate and her infant son, to relinquish all he has, even life itself? Why did Jack Shephard struggle for years against forces that nearly killed him, only to give his life willingly short days after his spiritual torments ended? Their selfless act was testament not only to their limitless courage and boundless commitment; it was proof of the greater glory to which they commended their lives, and their deaths.

It is said that there is no greater love than to give one's life for one's friends. But these men did find a love of even greater and more enduring significance.

[Sawyer pulls all the wires from the timer - timer pauses at 1:31 and then countdown accelerates.]
SAYID [to Jack]: Listen carefully. There's a well on the main island, half mile south from the camp we just left. Desmond's inside it. Locke wants him dead, which means you're going to need him. Do you understand me?
JACK: Why are you telling me this?
SAYID: Because it's going to be you, Jack.
[Sayid grabs bomb and runs off.]

Jack and Sayid had a solid relationship based in trust, to the point that their trust in each other became more important to both of them than their own lives (see Chapter 3, "Linear Theme I: Trust"). I believe it was in the moment that Jack swallowed the green pill intended to kill Sayid that Jack embraced the true, unbounded nature of his calling and set himself on a course that could only lead to his vanquishing of the Smoke Monster.

Sayid knew, when he seized the bomb, he had only seconds to live. If all he wished to accomplish was saving his friends' lives, he would have managed a noble and memorable deed, worthy of being recounted for all time. But he accomplished more than this great act. In the few seconds remaining in his life, he succeeded in conveying the single thought weighing heaviest on his mind. At the moment of his death, the fate of the Island had greatest importance to Sayid Jarrah. "It's going to be you, Jack." The idea he was expressing to his most trusted friend was more than a guess about Jack's future job assignment. It was not a guess or a hope or an expression intended to boost morale or any such fluff. One does not express shallow sentiment at the hour of death. No, Sayid's statement was the most important expression he could make, for it contained the martyr's fullest understanding of Jack's need to defeat the Smoke Monster ("Locke wants him dead, which means you're going to need him.") and serve the Island ("It's going to be you, Jack.").

Surely these four men proved themselves the most valiant and noble of leaders, willing to give everything for an objective possessing greater value and significance than life itself.

THE PHILOSOPHER

The School of Athens by Raffaello Sanzio 1509
Stanza della Segnatura, The Vatican WMC PD

John Locke
James Ford

Two leaders' counsels were informed by truths far beyond their own experience.

JACK: So where do we go from here?
SAWYER: I'm working on it.
JACK: Really? Because it looked to me like you were reading a book.
SAWYER: [Chuckles] I heard once Winston Churchill read a book every night, even during the Blitz. He said it made him think better. It's how I like to run things. I think. I'm sure that doesn't mean that much to you, 'cause back when you were calling the shots, you pretty much just reacted. See, you didn't think, Jack, and as I recall, a lot of people ended up dead.
JACK: I got us off the Island.
SAWYER: But here you are... [sighs] right back where you started. So I'm gonna go back to reading my book, and I'm gonna think, 'cause that's how I saved your ass today. And that's how I'm gonna save Sayid's tomorrow. All you gotta do is go home, get a good night's rest. Let me do what I do.

Sawyer's words, ground rough and unvarnished into the wounds of Jack's soul, must have stung, but they were conveyed with a force of authenticity. Sawyer not only recognised his responsibility as leader and defender of the survivors, he made every effort to acquire the intellectual tools that would allow him to face any situation, regardless of difficulty.

John Locke was the supreme source of philosophical perspective. We know him as the one chosen by the Island to become Jack's mentor. And what a mentor he was. His first teaching act was not to demonstrate for Jack the inadequacy—in fact, the illusion—of science and logic. Rather, Locke pointed Jack's psyche toward the single objective that would have to become his passion.

"I'm an ordinary man, Jack, meat and potatoes, I live in the real world. I'm not a big believer in magic. But this place is different. Special. The others don't want to talk about it because it scares them. But we all know it. We all feel it. Is your white rabbit a hallucination? Probably. But what if everything that happened here, happened for a reason? What if this person that you're chasing is really here?... I've looked into the eye of this island. And what I saw was beautiful."

This speech became the basis for the fan-made video I consider the best ever put together:

http://www.youtube.com/watch?v=swHST-s0s3E

If you search the entire LOST transcript using the string "for a reason" you will find a single instance of Hurley using the phrase in Season Two (Lost 2.18 "Dave"), but every other occurrence prior to Season Five is due to a single character: John Locke. Locke provided the philosophical basis for understanding the entire series. He was chosen for the most important project the Island had ever conceived: the teaching and reorientation of Jack Shephard.

Locke continued to orient Jack as best he could toward the Island, leading to the most memorable speech at the end of Season One.

LOCKE: I believe that I was being tested.
JACK: Tested?
LOCKE: Yeah, tested.
JACK: I think...
LOCKE: That's why you and I don't see eye-to-eye sometimes, Jack—because you're a man of science.
JACK: Yeah, and what does that make you?
LOCKE: Me, well, I'm a man of faith. Do you really think all this is an accident -- that we, a group of strangers survived, many of us with just superficial injuries? Do you think we crashed on this place by coincidence—especially, this place? We were brought here for a purpose, for a reason, all of us. Each one of us was brought here for a reason.
JACK: Brought here? And who brought us here, John?
LOCKE: The Island. The Island brought us here. This is no ordinary place,

you've seen that, I know you have. But the Island chose you, too, Jack. It's destiny.

This pivotal speech became the foundation for another timeless fan-made video:
http://www.youtube.com/watch?v=msS5uXGjTgQ
In John Locke's world, no task was so mundane as to be beyond careful deliberation. He cited historical or philosophical precedent for everything he did on the Island.

BOONE: So, not to be too difficult, but we've been coming here for two days just staring at this thing. I'm not really sure what we're supposed to be doing.
LOCKE: Ludovico Buonarrati, Michelangelo's father. He was a wealthy man. He had no understanding of the divinity in his son, so he beat him. No child of his was going to use his hands for a living. So, Michelangelo learned not to use his hands. Years later a visiting prince came into Michelangelo's studio and found the master staring at a single 18 foot block of marble. Then he knew that the rumors were true -- that Michelangelo had come in every day for the last four months, stared at the marble, and gone home for his supper. So the prince asked the obvious -- what are you doing? And Michelangelo turned around and looked at him, and whispered, sto lavorando, I'm working. Three years later that block of marble was the statue of David.

John Locke, philosopher, was the very heart of LOST. The hallmark of LOST was not adventure or mystery or drama or any other characteristic shared with every other television programme before it. What distinguished LOST was not its characters or the island atmosphere or the unique interpretation of the rules of time travel. LOST was special because of these elements, but it was unique in asking—demanding—that we think. How appropriate, then, that we were led by a philosopher.

THE MOTHER

Kate Austen
Claire Littleton
The Guardian ("Mother")

The mark of the philosopher is the insistence that some principle independent of one's highest yearnings must guide one's actions. Yet, at some point the philosopher must act based on her own flawed understanding of the hierarchy of principles she has fitted into her philosophical system. She must act of her own accord. It is in this respect that mothers outshine the most gifted philosopher. A mother never acts of her own accord. Every action she takes is oriented toward the needs of someone outside herself. The mother gives herself—heart, body, and soul—to another human being. She gives herself for her child.

We saw many examples of mothers compromised in their values, women who would not give everything for their children. Perhaps the most obvious example of this false type of mother was the one whose charges came to call her "Mother"—the first Protector of the Island, who killed Jacob's mother and claimed him and his twin brother as her own. Her agenda, her warped interpretation of her role as Protector, carried in her mind an importance far greater than a mother's life, far greater than the needs of Jacob and the Boy in Black. It was more important for her to believe that people are "greedy, manipulative, untrustworthy, and selfish," that human beings "come, they fight, they destroy, they corrupt... and it always ends the same."

We should not be surprised at the outcome of parental disposition that gives greater gravity to pessimistic philosophies than to the nurturing of children. A parent's first obligation is to love and imbue in children a sense of love, of wonder, of openness to others and to the world. When a mother considers the instilling of distrust, hatred, and scorn as her primary objective, we can be quite certain of the result.

The Boy in Black became the Man in Black long before Jacob threw his brother into the Cave of Light. The Man in Black's pessimism and selfishness were the consequence of careful preparation over a period of forty years by a woman who cared not at all about the two boys in her care, but about her position on the Island. The Monster who brought death, destruction, hatred, and darkness was the inevitable result of a guardian devoid of the single element that bonds a real mother to her children: Love.

Claire's love for Aaron and her desire to meet every one of the baby's needs were greater than even her love for Charlie. When Charlie lied to Claire about the heroin in the Virgin Mary statues, Claire's first thought was Aaron's welfare.

CLAIRE: You lied to me, Charlie.
CHARLIE: I know I did. I'm sorry. I just -- it made me safer to have it around.
CLAIRE: Look, I can't have you around my baby, okay?
CHARLIE: Claire, I...
CLAIRE: Charlie, I don't want you sleeping anywhere near us, okay? Just go.

Claire's behaviour after the departure of the Oceanic Six was no different than that of the Island's most famous mother, Danielle Rousseau. Neither Claire nor Rousseau was influenced in her behaviour by the Smoke Monster. Everything the two women did was motivated entirely by the need to find and ensure the safety of Alex and Aaron.

I believe there must be in heaven a place set aside for adoptive parents. Their call to parenthood is so strong that not even a blood tie is required to bond with a child. These are parents possessed of purest motivation, whose selflessness is beyond anyone's sense of doubt or reproach. We witnessed in Kate Austen such a love in the last three seasons of LOST. In fact, so great was this woman's love, that she recognised her own inadequacy to the child's wellbeing, and pledged every resource she could muster to finding the mother, and reuniting her with her child.

Some months ago I wrote that Aaron would likely return to the Island as Walt's second, and that the boy would certainly make arrangements for "Aunt Kate" to visit from time to time. A reader pointed out something important in his comments. He said Aaron would not think of Kate as "Aunt"—Kate Austen would forever remain "Mom" in Aaron's mind. The reader was certainly correct. Kate Austen conceived no child in her womb. But her position as mother, the fact that she put a child's welfare ahead of her own, cannot be questioned. Kate Austen was the most selfless example of motherhood the Island ever experienced.

THE PROPHET

"The Prophet" by Miika Ahvenjärvi. Used with permission. © Miika Ahvenjärvi 2007

John Locke
Desmond Hume

Prophets do not foresee. Rather, they bring coherence out of chaos. Prophets bring order to our lives by reminding us of values that transcend our limited view of reality.

Eloise Hawking was a seer. She knew the certainty of the future, because her son's notebook, completed through 2004, fell into her hands in 1977. But she was no prophet. She told Desmond that his life was already worked out in full, that he would never marry Penny because that was not his destiny. Pushing the button in the Swan Station every 108 minutes would become the greatest accomplishment in his life.

[Suddenly, there is a loud crash behind the bench Ms. Hawking and Desmond have been sitting on. Some scaffolding has fallen and killed the man with red shoes.]
DESMOND: Oh, my God. You knew that was going to happen, didn't you? [she nods] Then why didn't you stop it? Why didn't you do anything?
MS. HAWKING: Because it wouldn't matter. Had I warned him about the scaffolding tomorrow he'd be hit by a taxi. If I warned him about the taxi, he'd fall in the shower and break his neck. The universe, unfortunately, has a way of course correcting. That man was supposed to die. That was his path just as it's your path to go to the island. You don't do it because you choose to, Desmond. You do it because you're supposed to.
DESMOND: I'm going to meet Penny in an hour. I've got the ring; she'll say yes; I can choose whatever I want.
MS. HAWKING: You may not like your path, Desmond, but pushing that button is the only truly great thing that you will ever do.

Desmond saw the future as well as Mrs. Hawking, but his vision was not clouded by the petty fatalisms that guided Ms. Hawking's view of reality. Desmond was not a seer. He was a prophet. Regardless of the content of his visions, he knew his walks into past and future had a greater significance, that his visions could only be interpreted from a position of absolute faith in their beneficent outcome. Not only would he achieve things much greater than pushing a button, but he would be united forever with Penny. In the end, the seer was entirely wrong, and the prophet was proven correct in every particular. The difference between Desmond and Eloise was not merely one of outlook or philosophy. Desmond made himself aware of the principles underlying the Island and the world. With complete openness to these truths, he could never be led astray.

John Locke was usually alone in seeing the importance of the Island and his and Jack Shephard's connection to it. His prophesy was more profound and more complete than any other. By the end of the story, one man was willing to risk himself and the fate of the world on the truth of John Locke's vision.

[Jack and the Man in Black lower Desmond with a rope into the cave.]
MAN IN BLACK: This remind you of anything, Jack?
JACK: What?
MAN IN BLACK: Desmond...going down into a hole in the ground. If there was a button down there to push, we could fight about whether or not to push it. It'd be just like old times.
JACK: You're not John Locke. You disrespect his memory by wearing his face, but you're nothing like him. Turns out he was right about most everything. I just wish I could've told him that while he was still alive.
MAN IN BLACK: He wasn't right about anything, Jack. And when this island drops into the ocean, and you drop with it, you're finally gonna realize that.
JACK: Well, we'll just have to see which one of us is right, then.

The result was, of course, something the real John Locke could have predicted. Jack Shephard saved the Island—saved humanity—because he believed in the prophesy of John Locke.

THE FATHER

Christian Shephard
Michael Dawson
John Locke

All the best cowboys have daddy issues.

Every character in LOST had a poor relationship with her father. Even Jin, whose father was virtually a saint, had such a poor image of his father's social standing that he told his father-in-law and his own wife that his father was dead. The most important father in the series, Christian Shephard, was so flawed that he performed a surgical operation under the influence of a few too many martinis, and his patient died because of it. He told his son, Jack, that the boy didn't have what it takes to make decisions of any kind, and certainly not the life or death decisions that Christian was called upon to make every day. Such a man as this—flawed, diseased, inconsiderate—became the most frequent apparition and representative of higher authority during the survivors' tenure on the Island.

Despite all his foibles and flaws, father knows best. Sixty years ago we learned the lesson from an immaculately dressed Robert Young. During the six years of LOST, we came to appreciate the same lesson from a greying man addicted to alcohol who had so little confidence in his son that his major contribution to the boy's upbringing was telling the young man that he was a failure, that he would never measure up.

We all have daddy issues. The closest relationships we have are with people who have done the most to hurt us, to make us question our own worth, our place in this world. LOST was truer than fiction in this regard, in its unrestrained, reckless opening of these wounds in every one of our lives.

Christian Shephard was, like Jack, a wounded man. The wound at the sideways Jack's neck can be looked at literally as the manifestation of his final duel in the Island world with his nemesis, the Man in Black. However, we can equally consider the wound at his neck as the physical representation of his state of spiritual woundedness. He was wounded to his very core by the harsh words of his father, by his own rejection of John Locke, by the slings and arrows he suffered through his broken relationship with Sarah.

But Christian, with Jack, was a healer. Henri Nouwen, the famous Dutch spiritual writer, spoke forty years ago of The Wounded Healer. Those who wish to heal, Nouwen told us, must carry deep inside themselves the unhealed wounds of their own suffering. There is no balm for the wounded healer. But in accepting the full intensity of her deepest pain, the shepherd becomes the most effective healer of those in her care.

In our childhood we believe ourselves the only ones made to suffer. Parents inflict hardships of every kind. Making matters worse, we learn as teenagers that our parents are not perfect. They are flawed and carry within themselves pessimistic and selfish and even dangerous attitudes and behaviours. And yet they and society insist that we not only obey, but respect and even revere them. Society asks too much. We rebel, and most often in our rebellions, discover our own ways of inflicting on others our own pessimism and selfishness, taking dangerous chances that usually far exceed any unhealthy tendencies we see in our own parents.

Jack was certainly no different from us in this regard. His father was addicted to alcohol. Jack went beyond his father's imperfections, becoming addicted to booze and opioid narcotics. But by far Jack's greatest addiction was to his own ego. He needed to fix everything. Not because anything needed fixing, but he had to prove his own worth at every turn.

There is no perfection in this world. Parents are no less flawed than children. If we grow out of adolescence it is because we recognise our parents' faults and sins, and love them anyway. Making Robert Young into the Island's representative would have been cheating. Putting Christian Shephard—hung-over, inconsiderate Christian Shephard—in charge of the Island was as honest as it was profound. There were no instances of cheating in LOST, and certainly not when it came to the most important relationships in the series.

Jack had to swallow his pride, learn to stop worshipping at the altar of his unquenchable ego, and accept his father as-is, alcoholism and all the rest of it, looking to him not only as father, but as guide and shepherd. The Island asked too much. Far too much. But with the help of his Constant, Kate, his mentor, Locke, and his shepherd—the resurrected image of his father—Jack did overcome himself, learned to grant the respect and reverence his father deserved, and learned to trust the Island. It was the greatest story ever told on television.

THE DISCIPLE

Jack Shephard

LOST is not the story of monarchs or dictators, mothers or fathers, volunteers, prophets, or shepherds. It is the story of many who overcame themselves to find each other, to find their Constants, to bring an end to lives Lost in the wilderness. But LOST is also the story of one human being, a great hero, who went beyond his own salvation to save humanity itself.

The greatest leader in LOST is neither Candidate nor King, neither Philosopher nor Martyr, but the one among us who can give up every shred of self interest to serve the needs of others. This is the one who becomes the great hero, the saviour of all that marks us as human beings.

Jack Shephard is Joseph Campbell's hero, but he lives and moves and has his being far beyond the archetype. He is not one of a thousand faces, he is unique. Different. Special. He is not his own person, or the person others would like him to be. He is the one who most truly adheres to the happy path of his destiny, who surpasses every understanding of fate and freedom, who alone is worthy to approach the fullness of light that emanates from the Source.

Most of all, Jack Shephard is the Disciple. He recognises his own inadequacy ("you just don't have what it takes"), but he recognises, too, that he shares that inadequacy with everyone, even with his own father—but he is not stifled by this recognition, and moves beyond it, to embrace his connection with mentor (Locke), disciple (Hurley), father (Christian), and Island. He comes to respect and revere all of them in their connection to him and in their connection to the world and each other. And if he didn't know before the lava cliffs that

Kate was his one-and-only, he certainly understood then, without a single question in his mind.

The greatest hero is one who makes herself disciple to the needs of humanity. Jack Shephard did this, and defined a new, nearly unattainable category of heroism.

Jack was on the list. He was there because he was flawed. Because he was angry, and weak, and frightened. In fact, these are the only kinds of people who can appear on any list of Candidates. Only the flawed among us can recognise their imperfections, overcome them, and become the greatest among us. The greatest know that they are flawed, they are dependent, they are mere followers—disciples to those greater than themselves. Jack Shephard was all of these things, Candidate and King, disciple to the Island, to his father, to all of us. We shed tears at the end of LOST, not for an aloof leader, but for one of us, for our brother, Jack Shephard.

CHAPTER 7 LINEAR THEME V:
THE ISLAND

Oahu From Space 2005 NASA WMC PD

A single question fascinated us for six years.

One question, posed over six seasons, in each of 121 episodes, in thousands of scenes, the query was always the same. Thirty-five characters tried to answer the question; twenty-one of them died in the attempt.

The scope was measured not in years but in millennia, not in lives lost but in the hundreds of souls sacrificed. Time itself had no meaning, for those asking the question and seeking the answer could move about unrestrained by the forward march of the clock. Each character formed the question into unique words. For Pierre Chang, the question centred around the origin of exotic matter. Charles Widmore wondered how the place might be exploited. The question in its most essential form was simple:

What is this Island?

PARADISE

Life is what we make of it. One couple witnessed the anger and fights and bloodshed and decided none of it made any sense. Rose and Bernard found a quiet corner of the Island and built a hut. Occasionally one of the zealots would happen upon their camp, trying to talk sense into these contented people. The visitor would prattle on about this or that imminent catastrophe. Rose and Bernard listened patiently, even if the visitor really had nothing to say.

JULIET: Rose, we just need to know which way the Dharma Barracks are from here so we can stop Jack, or you're gonna be dead. We all will.
BERNARD: So we die. We just care about being together. That's all that matters in the end.

The wise old couple knew more about the Island than Juliet and all of the Others combined. Not one of the almost daily fights on the Island required their presence. No one anywhere suffered injustice because these two gentle souls refused to raise a hand in violence. And when their time came, they found out they had held the secret of life all along. What would have happened if everyone else, or even a small handful of them, had adopted the Nadler attitude toward life and the Island? Could Ben, living in such a blissful state as theirs, ever have plunged a knife into Jacob's chest? Would the Island ever have known discord or death?

Rose was never a candidate for any position of authority, and yet the Island cured her of cancer. Jacob had the power to bestow eternal life. Could it be that Richard Alpert was not the only resident of this Pacific paradise who had been granted immortality?

HELL

"This place is death."

Rose and Bernard knew the secret of life, but this was not the only facet of their character that allowed them to enjoy paradise on earth. Others, not as fortunate, paid with their emotions and their psychological well-being. Some ended up paying for the Island's unique powers with their very lives.

The Island had the ability to heal, but it could also induce suffering and death. Charlotte Lewis was among the unfortunates who could not physically endure the Island. Hers was not an unusual case. Only a small percentage of those brought to the Island survived more than a few weeks. Danielle Rousseau and Claire Littleton outlasted their contemporaries, but gave up their sanity to do so. Of those who arrived on the freighter, only Miles Straum and Frank Lapidus survived. Everyone from the tail section of Flight 815 ended up dying, with the notable exception of Bernard Nadler.

The Island was a living hell for almost everyone. By the time Daniel Faraday returned from Ann Arbor with a plan for re-setting all of their lives to a time before the Island, most of them were immediately receptive to the idea. After the leaders of the Dharma Initiative revealed their true allegiances to power and exploitation, every one of the survivors joined the plan to drop the nuclear bomb on top of the electromagnetic anomaly.

A GAME

"Two players. Two sides. One is light … one is dark."

Life is what we make of it. Some players in the game of life have the power to make vital decisions about not only for themselves, but for anyone in the vicinity. Jacob didn't wait for people to accidentally make their way to the Island. Sometimes they just needed a bit of encouragement, and no matter where they were on the globe, Jacob appeared and gave the little push that would send them to the Island.

The Game was more important than life. Hundreds of people died in the game, but Jacob continued to look into the lives of thousands around the world, seeking individuals he deemed strong enough, with depth of character sufficient to endure the travails of the Game. He valued human life, but he valued the well-lived life even more.

Senet Game 1 © Pearson Moore 2011

SAWYER: Tell me something, Jacob. Why do I gotta be punished for your mistake? What made you think you could mess with my life? I was doin' just fine 'til you dragged my ass to this damn rock.

JACOB: No, you weren't. None of you were. I didn't pluck any of you out of a happy existence. You were all flawed. I chose you because you were like me. You were all alone. You were all looking for something that you couldn't find out there. I chose you because you needed this place as much as it needed you.

Sawyer didn't protest enough in his only conversation with the backgammon master. It was his last chance to get answers, but for some reason he chose not to ask. The important question was finally asked and answered, but this event had to wait until a conversation between the new Protector and his freshly-appointed "Number Two." The question is simple:

How is anyone on earth different from the Candidates?

Very few people on earth would ever claim they are not flawed, that they are not "looking for something". An unbiased scrutiny of any life would find the person lacking in the way she had decided to respond to the crises and unjust events and ordinary turns of life. All of us at one time or another—and most of us on a daily basis—make judgments and take actions we consider favourable to ourselves, regardless of the way our personal biases and actions affect those around us. We hurt others so as to come out ahead. We are all selfish. We are all flawed. We are all "looking for something."

THE RULES OF THE GAME

I believe it is essential to point out that the Man in Black had no name, and he was given no name by design. At the very least, even if he had a name, this knowledge was intentionally withheld from us. A year and a half ago, in audition scripts for the character that eventually came to be called the Man in Black, the character was referred to as Samuel. We might reasonably ask why such an important character was never given a name.

This is no small matter, and I believe this conscious decision on the part of the writers goes a long way toward understanding the way in which we are meant to look at the series as a whole.

The creators of the series elevated the importance of the character by plucking the show's first Emmy winner from the role he had given award-winning depth and substance. I intend no offence to any of the other actors, but polls over the years have shown Terry O'Quinn the favourite actor on the show. The role of the nameless man was assigned to the series' most capable actor, but even then the character was never given a name.

I cannot tell you why Benjamin Linus was dispatched to kill the suicidal John Locke in a Los Angeles hotel room. I cannot tell you why Aaron and Walt were deemed critical to the story, but by the end of the story were almost-forgotten details. I can make a few guesses here, but the fact is we were not told, and we do have to guess. I can tell you that some of these unresolved details have contributed to a certain level of dissatisfaction, even disappointment, in the way the series ended. But I realise now some of that dissatisfaction was intentional. The writers intended a certain level of dissatisfaction. They wanted us to seek answers.

ANSWERS

What are the true Rules of the Game? Many answers apply, most of them are similar or identical, but the only answers that have any enduring value are those provided by faith, or by grace through faith, or by trusting in the Tanakh, or by surrendering to the Creator and His Prophet, Mohammed, may peace and blessings be upon him. The terminology and rubrics of dialogue and faith vary from one religious tradition to another, but they are all surprisingly similar.

Darlton are not telling us that we must launch into immediate studies of any of the world's great religions, or that we must experience spiritual epiphany and conversion of the heart in order to understand LOST. But they have imbedded into the very fabric of the series critical markers that guide us in our understanding. A hierarchy of values has been created in these six years. The systemic placement of values gives us a route to questions and responses otherwise obscure. This hierarchy can be applied to ferret important answers out of critical scenes. I intend to illuminate some of these markers on the road to understanding. The questions remain, but our responses do not constitute guesses. Rather, they constitute the hopes of our heart, the desires of our soul. Our response is not the stuff of guesswork or theories. Our answers are the response to John Locke, stretching out his arms and lifting his face to the rain come down from heaven. Our answers are the response to Jack Shephard, standing ankle-deep in sacred waters, hands clasped in humility, lips chanting words of invocation. Our answers are the response to faith.

A PLACE BEYOND SCIENCE

Perhaps no one among us can speak with authority on a subject as broad as "science." The only exception might be "Dr. Science":

"Ask Dr. Science. He knows more than you do."

Dan Coffey of Duck's Breath Mystery Theatre took the ludicrous notion that any one person could speak on behalf of "science" and turned this impossible conceit into one of the most amusing series on radio. No one can speak for the diverse set of logic-based disciplines to which we apply the broad term "science."

We should have no expectation that Dr. Science or even Albert Einstein could explain for us the true nature of the Island from a scientific perspective. As I wrote in earlier chapters, science can do nothing more than offer hypotheses and models of physical, chemical, and biological behaviour. When science confronts something such as electromagnetic energy ten thousand times more powerful than any other magnetic source on Earth, it has no theoretical precedent—no model—to allow even a valid hypothesis. Something like the unearthly light emanating from the Source is entirely beyond the capacities of science to comprehend.

We had some idea of the impotence of science in Season Four when Ben and Locke descended to the Orchid Station. The difference in the way they understood the Orchid orientation video was an indication of the utility of scientific knowledge to an understanding of Island phenomena.

TIME-TRAVELING BUNNIES

PIERRE CHANG: In our first demonstration, we will attempt to shift the test subject 100 milliseconds ahead in four-dimensional space. For the briefest... of moments, the animal will seem to disappear...

LOCKE: Hey. Uh... was he talking about what I think he was talking about?

BEN: If you mean time-travelling bunnies, then yes.

LOCKE: You do know that he said specifically not to put anything metal in here.

[Ben stares at Locke for a second, then gives an exasperated nod and turns back to the task of filling the chamber with metal objects]

Benjamin Linus is no man of science, but he does understand quite well the limitations inherent to science. He ignores the prohibitions regarding the placement of metallic objects inside the time chamber because he knows the injunction is based on nothing more than a feeble understanding of the nature of the phenomenon the Dharma scientists studied. Pierre Chang dared approach no closer than his time chamber. He had seen x-ray images of what lay beneath the Orchid Station. He knew civilisations from ancient times had manipulated space and time to extents he would never be able to duplicate.

FOREMAN: There's something in there. And the only way to get to it is to lay charges here and here and blast through it and take a look—

CHANG: Under no circumstances! This station is being built here because of its proximity to what we believe to be an almost limitless energy. And that energy, once we can harness it correctly, it's going to allow us to manipulate time.

FOREMAN: [Chuckles] Right. Okay, so, what? We're gonna go back and kill Hitler?

CHANG: Don't be absurd. There are rules, rules that can't be broken.

FOREMAN: So what do you want me to do?

CHANG: You're gonna do nothing. If you drill even one centimeter further, you risk releasing that energy. If that were to happen... [Chang looks at the fallen workman and the blood all over his face.]...God help us all.

For twenty years the Dharma Initiative controlled most of the Island. But never during that time did even the most adventurous among the scientists attempt to unravel the full mystery of the Island's underworld. Stuart Radzinsky, using the full force of the science at his disposal, came closest to unlocking the Island's mysteries, but his experiment aimed at unlocking the secrets of the Swan Station site failed in a most spectacular manner, illustrating again the limitations of science.

Science is limited in the behaviour it is allowed to posit and explore. Since logic is a small, man-made, artificial construct, it follows that science is unable to study and develop models for most of the reality we interact with on a daily basis. Pierre Chang would not go within fifty metres of the Light, could not go within fifty metres of the Light, because not a single observation in the history of science could explain for him the true nature of the Light. Benjamin

Linus could approach the Light, not fearlessly, but with a proper attitude of humility. He knew of the Light's power, and he knew that power was not anything that would ever be catalogued or studied or rendered as model by any discipline within science.

Ben Linus knew the experiments at the Orchid Station could only scratch the surface of the Island's capabilities. The Dharma Initiative made bunnies travel hundredths of a second through time. With the ancient wheel far underneath the Orchid, Ben could travel across the globe and across months, years, or even centuries, far exceeding the feeble capabilities of Alvar Hanso's scientific corps. But time travel, too, barely scratched the surface of the Island's capabilities. Ben knew Jacob's Number Two, Richard, was ageless, made that way by Jacob, whose powers were in turn granted by the Island.

Most of reality is unknowable to science. The person most fitted for life on the Island was the one who understood this intuitively. John Locke was a man of faith, and because of his deep trust in the Island, he understood her better than anyone, better even than Jacob or the Man in Black.

A CORK

The Island knew no greater authority than Jacob, son of a Roman shipwreck survivor named Claudia. Jacob was given Protector status by the Island's former Protector, the woman who raised Jacob and his brother. Jacob knew the Smoke Monster obtained its power from the mixture of water and light in the illuminated cave. As long as the Light shone in the cave, the Smoke Monster would be unable to leave the Island. Jacob understood the position of Protector as more than anything the Guardian of the Cork. He explained this to Richard and to Jack and impressed upon them the absolute necessity of preventing the Monster from ever leaving the Island. He was, in Temple Master Dogen's words, "evil incarnate." Allowing him free reign in the outside world would lead to more than an exponential increase in suffering. The consequences were nothing less than the complete destruction of all human life. This was because the only way for the Monster to leave the Island was by snuffing out the Light. But the Light was the very stuff of life and death and rebirth; its destruction would lead to the end of life, the end of death, the end of rebirth, the end of all events and conditions making up the cycles of existence.

A SANCTUARY

Life is what we make of it. Jack inherited the Island from Jacob, but he was no disciple of Smokey's brother. From his epiphany off-Island to the detonation of Jughead and the sharing of Communion with Jacob to his final breath in this life, Jack Shephard was the unapologetic disciple of John Locke.

For Jack, the Island was not a "cork," not the Monster's leash, not an abode of evil. The Island was, in the words of his master, "a place where miracles happen." Jack understood something Jacob never did. The Island had a multi-dimensional character that went far beyond acting along the narrow constraints of anything that might be understood through logic and science. There was no logic to the Island, for nothing so joyous could be crammed into the narrow etiologies of human understanding. There was no science capable of modeling her abilities and powers, for nothing so terrible could be forced into a syllogistic stream.

It was Jack's more mature understanding of the Island that allowed him to plot and execute the Smoke Monster's destruction. Jacob knew the Smoke Monster originated in the terrible power of the Light, but he seemed not to understand, as Jack did, that the Monster was a child fed by the Light. If the Light went out, the Smoke Monster's powers would go out with it. Jack, man of faith, trusted his understanding of the true nature of the Island, trusted in something Jacob never imagined.

THE SOURCE OF LIFE AND DEATH

The Light has the power to create and destroy, heal and wound. It is the source of life and death and rebirth. Jacob's adoptive guardian expressed her limited understanding of the Light in these terms because they were the only words suitable, because the full reality of the Light is ineffable. Here there can be no logic, no science, no words to compare, contrast, or describe. The Light is at once terrible and glorious, life-giving and deadly.

It is the Source, which means it is not of this world. That which is the Source of life and death and all things cannot possibly have physical residence in the created world. We experience the Source as Light, but it is of course entirely beyond our understanding. It is the only visible sign of the Alpha, the Omega, that which was and is and will be.

The Source is the umbilical, the connection between the natural world and whatever lies beyond the realm of the senses. It is through the Source that we live and move and have our being. Each of us carries a bit of the Light inside our hearts, as Jacob's guardian told us. When the Light goes out, we lose our identity, our connection to reality, we lose any possibility of life, death, or rebirth.

FOUR THEORIES OF LIFE

Life is what we make of it.

During the last 150 minutes of LOST we witnessed four distinct theories of life. The proponents were the Man in Black, Rose and Bernard

Nadler, Desmond Hume, and Jack Shephard. I'm going to begin the discussion with the Man in Black.

CARPE DIEM

Life is tough, and no one has suffered more in this life than the Man in Black. Even before he lost his body and his soul, he was trying to find ways to rectify the injustices of life. He knew the Light to be sacred, but he knew his objective--leaving the Island--to be more important than something as simple as a light shining from underground. When did the Light ever suffer anything? The Man in Black had to live every day with the knowledge that his people were far away, somewhere across the sea. [Oh! Accidental pop culture reference! And I don't even like Bobby Darin! Taking "La Mer" and turning it into "Somewhere Across the Sea" must be one of the worst musical perversions of the twentieth century]

After he came thundering out of the Cave of Light he knew he was even more tightly tethered to the Island than ever before. Extreme measures were called for. Jacob was preventing his escape and guarding the Source. Anyone aiding and abetting Jacob would be dealt with in a most severe manner. Those he killed were just ordinary, mortal human beings. And hadn't Mother told him people were selfish and untrustworthy? They come, they fight, they destroy, they corrupt. It always ends the same. People are vermin. The only suitable way to lead one's life is to take what one can get. If a few people—or even hundreds of people die so one's life goals might be attained, well, so be it. Take what you can get. Fulfill your dreams, and to hell with everyone else.

"We don't get involved," Rose said. It's a common enough sentiment. Who among us would not want to settle down in a little cabin by the sea, catch enough fish to live, steal enough Dharma tea to enjoy breakfast. They have their dog... and their walking stick to protect them. Entire songs have been written about this way of life.

Rose and Bernard are not exactly the hermit of Simon and Garfunkel's classic song. They certainly had much greater things to worry about than the pain of broken friendships. Of course I'm assuming here that neither Paul Simon nor Art Garfunkel was ever ruthlessly hunted through a Pacific island jungle by an unstoppable, immortal cloud of smoke that travelled faster than an F16 fighter jet, or stalked by a band of evil mercenaries carrying grenades, bazookas, and 300-round-per-minute machine guns. And as for the final verse of the song, I'm not so sure. Every time something bad happened on the Island, it rained. Sure seems to me like the raindrops might constitute tears.

Rose and Bernard made a good choice. It is not merely a matter of having adopted the philosophy of "live and let live." The plane crash threw them into an unhealthy environment. The people of Mittelos were much more likely to draw guns on each other than engage one another in pleasant conversation. The Island was reeling and swaying and moving about the ocean and zooming first back in time then forward in time, all of this incomprehensible movement hither and yon accompanied by calamities and catastrophes that literally took six years to catalogue. Rose and Bernard made a sane choice in the face of their fellow survivors' uncontrolled, irrational, and patently insane lifestyles. Given a choice between peaceful days and nights in a hut, and being hunted by Stuart Radzinsky and his henchmen, who among us would choose to be on the receiving end of rifle fire?

GET YE TO A NUNNERY

Desmond Hume had a well-defined mission. Both in Mittelos and off the Island he took upon himself the difficult task of enlightening everyone. It was a holy task, a mission aimed at bringing people together at a spiritual level. The ultimate goal was to get everyone into a church--Eloise Hawking's Church of the Holy Lamp Post (or was it more properly called Our Lady of the Perpetual Pendulum?), but getting them there would be a complicated endeavour. Desmond would have to choose an appropriate way for all of them to recognise their spiritual connections, their Constants. He would have to provide enough enlightenment that each one could discern her connection to her Constant in both life and death.

In "The Seven Storey Mountain", Trappist monk Thomas Merton's autobiography, he referred to the Abbey of Gethsemane in Kentucky as the centre of the world. It was monasteries like his that held the world together, he thought. Desmond was not only helping to hold the world together, he was bringing people together spiritually, helping them see the Light.

Just outside the Cave of Light, Desmond gave Jack the good news.

DESMOND: This doesn't matter, you know.
JACK: Excuse me?
DESMOND: Him destroying the island, you destroying him. It doesn't matter. You know, you're gonna lower me into that light, and I'm gonna go somewhere else. A place where we can be with the ones we love, and not have to ever think about this damn island again. And you know the best part, Jack?
JACK: What?
DESMOND: You're in this place. You know, we sat next to each other on Oceanic 815. It never crashed. We spoke to each other. You seemed happy. You know, maybe I can find a way to bring you there, too.

FOR THE COMMON GOOD

Desmond believed Jack could just leave the Island, forget about what may or may not happen, and settle down to a happy life with Kate. It was not to be. Jack had a calling, a responsibility he could not forsake.

"Desmond, I tried that once. There are no shortcuts, no do-overs. What happened, happened. Trust me, I know. All of this matters."

Jack had to kill the Smoke Monster. He had to protect the Light. He knew these things from the certainty of faith and no talk of happiness and being with the ones he loved was going to sway him. If he left the Island only bad things could result. If he faced his responsibilities he at least had a chance of making things right again, and preserving the Source for the sake of the entire world.

Living life the Jack Shephard way is difficult, challenging, and at times dangerous. LOST would have us believe that this is the best life one might choose. Life is not just about enjoying good times in a hut by the sea, or spending time with those we love in a church pew. Life is about our responsibility to each other, the human need to work with others toward the Common Good.

LIVING AND WORKING TOGETHER

I loved Kate's return atop the lava cliffs, delivering the bullet she saved for the Smoke Monster. Kate was back where she belonged, a full and equal participant in the struggle to free the Island from the Man in Black. Jack would never have been able to kill him on his own. As Christian said, "Nobody does it alone, Jack. You needed all of them, and they needed you."

LOST gave us much to consider over six years. The series went to greater depths in the philosophical, cultural, and social realm than any other television programme I can think of, and created some of the most detailed and complicated and human characters ever to appear on the small or large screen. Jack Shephard, in particular, was a masterful artistic creation, a kind of hero we can all believe in and have faith in.

My favourites remain Locke and Kate. Who would have thought Kate Austen would redeem herself by taking a rifle in her arms and putting a bullet in a man's back? Both the character and the actress were under-utilised in the series, but when Kate did what she had to do, the series was better for it. John Locke ended in a way I never would have guessed. But the other characters, and especially Jack, honoured his memory and revered his wisdom. In this way John Locke's story ended in the proper place, not hanging by a cord in a third-rate hotel, but living as mentor and example in the minds of those who protected the Island, and those who saw in Jack the fulfillment of Locke's faith.

A PLACE WHERE MIRACLES HAPPEN

A 5600-word chapter in a book cannot delineate every nuance, or even every major facet of the Island. The questions that most fascinate us remain to be asked: Why did Hurley need to become the final Protector? What did the apparitions of Christian Shephard signify? How is the sideways world tied into the main themes of the story? Why was the Man in Black never given a name, and what did his state of namelessness mean to the larger story? Why did Locke sit alone in the final scene before "moving on," and what is the significance to the thesis of LOST?

We have much to consider in the coming chapters. I invite you to continue the journey!

Senet Game #2
© Pearson Moore 2011

Rules are illogical.

If rules flow directly out of logic, there can be no need for rules, since they are the self-evident results of elementary logical axioms and mathematical principles of identity, syllogism, and substitution. LOST bent logic almost to the breaking point in its exposition of the rules of the Island, candidacy, and physical behaviour.

While the rules formally obeyed the strictures of logic, the intention of the rules was to demand an appreciation for harmonies that exist outside the bounds of scientific reason. The idea that a green pill filled with poison should become symbol of both life and death ought to strike everyone reading this as preposterous. That is precisely the intention of the rules. We are to see them as pointing to a reality that is not moored to the limits of logic.

When we dig into the nitty-gritty of the rules we begin to see apparent inconsistencies. More often than not, though, the perception of inconsistency seems to be a function of a narrowly interpretive mindset. If we demand that the rule be applied in a physical sense, we may deprive ourselves of a more harmonious understanding derived of a psychological or metaphysical or time-dependent interpretation. Moreover, we will arrive at rules, like the ones governing the green pill, that will be understood in full only if we apply two or more sets of syllogistic templates.

If we approach LOST in a conventional manner we will never understand the series. The story was presented in nonlinear fashion, and understanding any single piece of the puzzle requires intimate knowledge of every other piece. But we need to know much more than this. We have to understand the most important character in the series and its connection to the rules.

The story focussed on a single character, present in every one of the 121 episodes. This character had a back story and a culture all her own. She was strong-willed, always on the move, responsible for not one but several murders. No one could control her. This character made her own rules, and everyone, even the Protector, was obliged to obey her.

The most important character in LOST, the one whom all obeyed, was the Island. LOST was not the story of isolated, unrelated rules. It was the story of a struggle to surrender the ordinary precepts of human logic, to submit to the Island's metalogic, to work toward a common destiny. LOST was the story of the survivors' relationship with a living, breathing, illogical Island.

THE PROTECTOR

At Jacob's meeting with the final four Candidates in 2007 we learned much about the structure and history of the Island and its rules. The Island was defended by a Protector, who was empowered by the Island to train and approve the next Protector. The Guardian (usually called "Mother"; see Lostpedia) trained the Boy in Black for this most important position, but when he made choices rendering him unsuitable to the office, she appointed Jacob. Two thousand years later Jacob appointed Jack after the doctor volunteered. After Jacob did his best to offer a choice, Jack gave Hurley no option to decline leadership. "It needs to be you, Hugo," Jack told him, in spite of his protests.

The means of recruiting, training, and installing the new Protector was left entirely to the former Protector. The only apparent formal requirement was the ritual drinking of fresh Island water at the request of the former Protector. The formal Latin invocation ("Nam non accipimus hoc quasi vulgarem potionem, sed ut ille sit quasi unus mecum") was not required, since Jack did not use these words during transfer of authority to Hurley. The words of installation were simple: " Now you and I...are the same," or "Now you're like me."

More than one person could be in training for the position. The Guardian had two Candidates that we know of. Over the following two thousand years Jacob considered at least 360 Candidates, if not more (see the lighthouse wheel). He did not seek their consent. The last round of Candidates was drawn from among the survivors of Oceanic Flight 815, and consisted of individuals Jacob had touched and spoken with over the thirty years before the crash, the first being James Ford during the summer of 1976.

THE WILL OF MITTELOS

We are used to thinking of land as being a passive entity subject to the whims of the organisation or government claiming control over its borders. We don't normally think of land as possessing a personality or a will. At most, we might think of land as having a kind of symbolic consciousness, as in the expression "The king and the land are one." Possibly we could even imagine the land as expressing a reaction to historical events. For example, Arthur is destined to become king, so the land allows him and only him to free Excalibur from the stone. We might even think of land as enjoying a kind of collective consciousness, responding to stresses and strains with corrective actions, as with versions of the Gaia Hypothesis.

It is much more difficult for us to understand an island with an agenda, planned over millennia, executed by agents accountable to and controlled by the land, in response to specific needs. But this is the full reality of the Island. In this awareness of the Island's volition we understand some of the folly associated with a rational belief in "rules." We can think of the Island as conferring immortality, or we can understand the Protector's longevity as a natural outcome of the Island's need (desire) to survive. Since the Island had no way of protecting itself, it had to employ at least one agent able to physically protect it from harm. But the Protector was not the only agent falling under the Island's control.

Michael committed unthinkable murders. His wife divorced him, his son hated him, his mother wanted nothing to do with him. Living a life without meaning, enduring nightmares every night, Michael sought to end his life with a bullet to the brain. But when he pulled the trigger, the gun barely clicked. He had already tried crashing his car into a wall. He might as well have tried electrocution, poisoning, or stabbing himself. Every attempt at suicide failed and would have failed.

TOM: I got some bad news for you, amigo. You can't kill yourself. The Island won't let you.
MICHAEL: (Panting) What'd you say?
TOM: No matter how bad you want to, no matter how many different ways you try, it won't happen.
[Tom hands the revolver back to Michael.]
TOM: Give it a shot if you don't believe me. You got more work to do, Mike. When you figure that out, I'm in the penthouse at the Hotel Earle.

Michael was not a Candidate. Jacob never touched him. He had the Island's protection, but unlike the Candidates, he was given an immediate task: he had to return to the Island to blow up the Kahana. In carrying out his mission he would have to give up his own life, after which he was consigned to indefinite detention as one of the Island whisperers. This might have seemed unfair punishment. Wasn't the execution of the mission and the sacrifice of his own life sufficient redemption? Not quite, as it turns out. In the epilogue we learned Michael had two enormous tasks waiting for him in the whispering afterlife: Enticing his son, Walter, back to the Island, and then reconciling with him.

In Michael's mission we begin to see the truth of the Island's personality and deviation from logical rules. There is no general rule stating that a 34-year-old man accompanied on the Island by an eight-year-old boy must be recalled to

119

the Island every time a 184-tonne freighter shows up in its waters so that he can destroy it. The Island doesn't have rules. It has needs. The freighter had to be destroyed, and someone had to do it. What better choice than the man whose son would ultimately become the Protector of Mittelos?

THE REPRESENTATIVE

Man in Stripes: "You can go now, Michael."
Michael: "Who are you?"

The man in striped shirt didn't get the opportunity to respond to Michael's inquiry; as the explosion interrupted all conversations on the Kahana. We should consider ourselves fortunate in not having heard his answer, because the words he chose would have confused us more than anything our ears had picked up in the previous four years.

Christian Shephard spoke with authority in the five words he uttered to Michael. The possibility that he was speaking on his own behalf seems remote. Not only was he dead, but he had never previously been to the Island. If he had been acting on his own behalf we would also have to wonder how he knew where the freighter was, how he boarded the ship, and why he felt the destruction of the Kahana to be necessary. Much more likely, it seems to me, is the possibility that Christian's form was inhabited or projected by some other entity.

That Christian's body went missing from his coffin was no indication he had been taken over by any particular being. The Smoke Monster is most often invoked when discussing the apparitions of Christian Shephard, but we must resist the temptation to immediately assign a causal relation. We know the Man in Black didn't need a body--all he required was the impression of a form of someone's body. The body didn't even have to be on the Island. From Richard's memories the Smoke Monster was able to copy Isabella's form exactly, for example. He took Yemi's form from Eko's memories. No, the disappearance of Christian's body had nothing to do with the Smoke Monster. Rather, it was the sign of a much greater mystery, and too big a topic to cover in a chapter dealing with the rules.

I will mention the Christian Shephard apparitions from time to time but I defer the complete analysis of his appearances until the end of the book. For now it is sufficient to ponder Christian's place on the Island, and the forces that may have been responsible for manipulating his apparitions. Jack's father is yet another sign of a set of "rules" that transcends logical assignment.

THE CANDIDATES

The Valenzetti Equation contained six integer coefficients: 4, 8, 15, 16, 23, and 42, corresponding to John Locke, Hugo Reyes, James Ford, Sayid Jarrah, Jack Shephard, and Jin-Soo Kwon respectively. The "odd man out" was

Jack Shephard; he was unique in being assigned the only prime number among the Velenzetti coefficients.

Some of you are wondering how I was able to assert that Jin-Soo Kwon was one of the Six but not Sun-Hwa. Wasn't Sun-Hwa Kwon one of the Oceanic Six? True enough, but the Oceanic Six were not connected to Jacob's Six. The Oceanic Six included Aaron, who was never touched by Jacob. Sun-Hwa was touched, but she didn't time travel. Recall that the Ajira 316 passengers were divided into two groups: those who traveled through time to the 1977 Island and those who crash landed in 2007. Sun Hwa was among the large group who did not leave the plane in a brilliant flash of light. The Candidates, though—Jack, Hurley, and Sayid—were sucked into the time vortex. The Candidates all traveled through time at one point or another, and it is this commonality that can be applied as criterion of candidacy. Jacob's Six shared three crucial characteristics: They were on Jacob's long list of candidates, they were touched by Jacob, and they traveled backwards through time.

Time travel should not be considered a criterion of candidacy, but rather a natural and necessary outcome of formal consideration for installation as Protector. Time travel was merely a proof that the person touched had also been granted candidacy. Touch alone was not a sufficient proof. We know of several instances in which Jacob touched a person who was not a candidate. Jacob touched Richard on many occasions, for instance, but never conferred candidacy. Jacob also touched Ben, just before the former leader drove a knife through his chest. Note, too, that several individuals who were not candidates traveled through time. Miles Straum, Charlotte Lewis, and several others traveled through time without the benefit of formal candidacy.

RULES OF TIME TRAVEL

In fact, we can understand the selective nature of the time travel phenomenon in the light of Candidacy. Not everyone on the Island traveled back and forth in time. Daniel Faraday, Charlotte Lewis, Miles Straume, and Juliet Burke were neither Candidates nor were they 815 survivors, but they moved to and fro through time with Sawyer and Locke. I believe Daniel Faraday and Miles Straum, like Michael Dawson, were the unwitting agents of the Island. Faraday had to time travel because his incorrect notion of the Time Boulder would not reset events as he imagined, but his idea would serve to collect the Candidates into a single location immediately above the Swan at the time of the Incident. That location would allow all of them to be catapulted forward in time thirty years, to the precise moment of Jacob's death. The abrupt forward time travel was necessary because it became the only way to enforce the cardinal rule of the Island, that a Protector or Candidates must be on the Island and able to serve as Protector at all times. Miles had to be there to assist Sawyer in integrating into Dharma culture. Sawyer was essential to the whole effort because he would provide for safe housing and transport of the two most important players in the Island's history: Jack Shephard and Kate Austen.

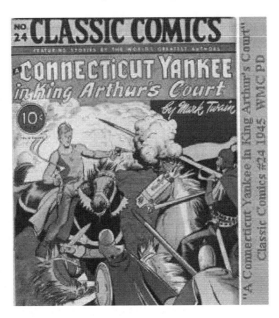

Charlotte Lewis and Juliet Burke time traveled even though they were not among Flight 815 survivors. If time travel was Candidate-centric, their time travel is explained as a privilege of Constancy: Juliet was Sawyer's Constant, and Charlotte became Daniel's Constant.

This idea goes only so far. This Candidate-centric model doesn't explain the necessity of time travel for such apparently useless individuals as Neil Frogurt and Rose and Bernard Nadler. Rose and Bernard may have been the only mechanism for getting Desmond Hume to the Source. As for Neil and the other minor time-traveling characters, they may have been included due to their proximity to the Flight 815 Candidates. Perhaps almost everyone who crashed and who stayed on the Island was obliged to travel through time. We might think of the Island's ability to segregate individuals for time travel as having limitations. If the Island selects an individual for time travel (or for some other distinction that includes proclivity to time travel as intended or unintended consequence), perhaps everyone within a certain physical radius of that person must also be imbued with whatever qualities render that person amenable to time travel. But this idea doesn't allow easy reconciliation of selective time travel from Ajira Flight 316.

The irrational nature of time travel selection again seems to point to a metalogic controlled by the Island. Perhaps if we dig deeper into other facets of Island behaviour we will gain more insight into these "rules."

Jacob touched nine individuals, not six. Two of the nine were not Candidates, leaving seven. Of the several passengers on Ajira Flight 316, only four were selected for travel back to 1977: Jack Shephard, Hugo Reyes, Sayid Jarrah, and one not found on the list of the final six Candidates: Katherine Anne Austen.

Jacob supplemented the six most visible Candidates with one who was always the first to volunteer for any difficult mission. The urge to run had been her supreme weakness in the outside world, but on the Island it became Kate's strongest virtue. She was always first in line, always ready to explore an unknown hatch or lead a rescue mission.

Kate was number 51 on Jacob's lighthouse list. An unremarkable number for a most remarkable woman. Only Kate would have had the reckless courage to pick up a rifle and fire it at the Smoke Monster. This psychological tendency would have been understood as undisciplined foolishness before the struggle on the cliffs, but after she put a bullet in the MIB's back, only seconds before he would have killed Jack, the true nature of her courage and the reason for her selection became clear.

The number on first glance did not appear to have any deeper significance. But it was paired with the very significant 108. The number 108 is sacred in the Hindu religion because it represents perfection. It is said each of the Hindu gods has 108 names. The Hindu rosary, called a japa mala, has 108 beads. Shiva takes 108 poses during his cosmic dance. If number 51 has any deeper meaning, we are likely find it by way of a consideration of Hindu tradition.

Shiva had a bride, a goddess he loved above all other women. Her name was Shakti, the consort-wife of Shiva. Early in their marriage she was insulted by one of the gods and took her own life. To end Shiva's grief, Vishnu cut Shakti's corpse into 51 pieces and they fell all across India. For centuries, Hindu women have visited the 51 shrines (pithas) in hopes of being healed.

Kate's number was the perfect complement to 108, and it brought a consideration of place and purpose to the fore. The Island transported Kate from Ajira Flight 316 to the same waterfall-fed pool she and Sawyer discovered in Season One, for example. Even without the benefit of clear retrospective, it is obvious that the Island recognised Kate's connection to that place.

We know of her affinity for trees. At the age of twelve, she and her sweetheart, Tommy, buried their "time capsule" under a big tree. When she woke from the blast at the Swan Station, she was high in the branches of a tree. Twice she has sought shelter from the Smoke Monster in the strange circular centre of banyan trees. Was protection afforded her because of some natural or acquired power of the banyan tree, or because she was Number 51, a reincarnation of the most beloved goddess in the cosmos who by her very presence brings sanctity and purpose to a place?

A DEVOUT MEDITATION IN MEMORY OF STUART RADZINSKY

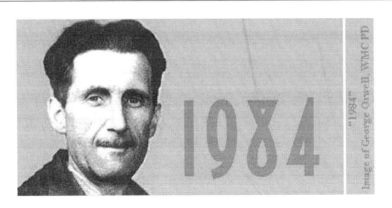

"1984" Image of George Orwell, WMC PD

As we have seen in this chapter, the Island asserted the value of the irrational over any system of rational thought. This may seem a perplexing, anarchistic position to take regarding the value of logic. We would certainly be correct in assuming that rational processing of ideas is the basis for sanity. If we give up logic, aren't we giving up on the entire notion of sanity? And if we are willing to part with a comfortable reliance on sanity, is this not tantamount to saying we are giving up our very humanity?

The contemplative writer Thomas Merton wrote possibly the most famous essay on rational thought—what we call sanity—some fifty years ago, just after the trial of the Nazi war criminal and mass murderer, Adolf Eichmann. His essay was called "A Devout Meditation in Memory of Adolf Eichmann." In the essay, Merton comments on the fact that Eichmann was found to be sane.

"One of the most disturbing facts that came out in the Eichmann trial was that a psychiatrist examined him and pronounced him perfectly sane. I do not doubt it all, and that is precisely why I find it disturbing.

"If all the Nazis had been psychotics, as some of their leaders probably were, their appalling cruelty would have been in some sense easier to understand. It is much worse to consider this calm, "well-balanced," unperturbed official conscientiously going about his desk work, his administrative job which happened to be the supervision of mass murder. He was thoughtful, orderly, unimaginative. He had a profound respect for system, for law and order....

"The sanity of Eichmann is disturbing. We equate sanity with a sense of justice, with humaneness, with prudence, with the capacity to love and understand other people. We rely on the sane people of the world to preserve it from barbarism, madness, destruction. And now it begins to dawn on us that it is precisely the sane ones who are the most dangerous."

Logic constitutes a small and dangerous sub-set of reality. Those who wish to experience the full range of human reality, according to the Island, must be willing to assert the ascendency of irrational optimism even in the face of the most rational proof of pessimistic outlooks.

The sane thinkers of the world are the ones who believe Winston would at some point be obliged to pour acid on a child's face in order to advance the precepts of rebellion against control by the Inner Party (George Orwell, "1984"). That is to say, rebellion is pointless because those who rebel are only going to assert their power with the same tyranny demonstrated by the Inner Party.

The irrational thinkers, those who assert the primacy of humanity and believe in the principles of the Island, proclaim that there is no Goldstein, there is no inevitable tendency toward self-destruction. George Orwell had it wrong, Darlton tell us. The fall of Winston is not inevitable, because there are always Kate Austens among us—or as Steve Jobs and Ridley Scott would have us imagine, there are always sledgehammer-wielding freedom fighters ready to destroy the instruments of rational control.

DHARMA INITIATIVE

The Dharma Initiative was doomed.

The Dharma Initiative was based on the rules of rational science. The Initiative's top scientist at the time, Stuart Radzinsky, used the time-tested principles of science to devise a plan for study of the electromagnetism that was to become the focus of the Swan Station. The catastrophic release of electromagnetic energy, referred to as "The Incident," was inevitable because rational science does not map reality, and therefore cannot predict events outside the narrow constraints of rationality.

The scientists running the Deepwater Horizon in early 2010 used sound scientific principles and models in developing drilling and capping equipment and procedures. The models had been tested for several decades and were found to be not only adequate, but accurately predictive of oil, sedimentary rock, and ocean behaviour, even at depths of several thousand metres. No one could have imagined an explosion aboard the Deepwater Horizon, or that the blowout preventer would fail, or that the well would spew oil into the Gulf of Mexico without restraint for over three months before finally being shut down after around-the-clock, heroic measures were taken. Here was a real-life "Incident" that perfectly mirrored the events on Mittelos, and demonstrated the folly of placing trust in science.

For the purposes of this survey of Island rules, it will suffice to point out that the Dharma Initiative contained within itself the potent seeds of its own destruction. If the Initiative had been based on the core principles of civilisation it would have prospered. But since it was based on the narrow-minded limitations of scientific rules, it could only fail.

THE CONSIGLIERE

The positions of Protector and Candidate were the only etched-in-stone requirements of the Island. The Island conferred special powers on the Protector, as already discussed. The Protector conferred Candidate status and had the discretion to grant immortality.

The position of Consigliere was probably created by Jacob. The Island had vested him with authority to grant immortality, which until 1867 had probably been used exclusively to protect Candidates from the Smoke Monster. But Jacob, who had never experienced love, did not relate well to people. Richard, who had known love all his life, and especially with Isabella, not only related well, but he had been steeped in the best traditions of humanity--the very traditions that Jacob was sworn to protect.

At some point after 1867 the position of Leader was probably created. Richard had been successful in harnessing the people's desire to serve the Island's needs, as expressed by Jacob, and a more formal structure must have seemed useful. The Protector, in collaboration with the Consigliere, appointed a Leader who would be responsible for executing the Protector's commands. So it was that Richard, Jacob's right hand man, came to carry considerable authority.

In 1954 Richard faced what was likely the first major test of his authority and discretion when he was approached by a bald man who claimed to be his leader, from the future:

LOCKE:... tell me how to get off the Island.
RICHARD: That's very privileged information. Why would I share it with you?
LOCKE: Because you told me that I had something very important to do once I get there. And because I'm your leader.
RICHARD: You're my leader?
LOCKE: That's what you told me [in the future].

Richard took no action on Locke's request at their 1954 meeting, but the brief encounter did cause him to wonder about John Locke, and probably also made him aware of the need to develop strong bases for the selection of a Leader. Were their selection criteria even useful at all?

Richard exercised discretion in 1961 and again in 1972, contacting Locke to determine his suitability for leadership. The 1961 meeting caused Richard to doubt Locke's leadership capacity, and in 1972, when Locke didn't even bother to inquire about the Mittelos Laboratories summer camp, Richard became apprehensive about Locke. Careful not to draw hasty conclusions, though, Richard asked Jack about Locke five years later, in 1977.

RICHARD: Over, uh, twenty years ago, a man named John Locke, he walked right into our camp. And he told me that he was going to be our leader. Now I've gone off the Island three times, to visit him. But he never seemed particularly special to me.
JACK: You said you had a question.
RICHARD: You know him? Locke?
JACK: [chuckles] Yeah. Yeah, I know him. And if I were you, I wouldn't give up on him.

Here was yet another instance of the Island's assertion of desire over rules. Through the teaching of John Locke and the direct experience of events after the crash, the Island was molding Jack Shephard into a committed man of faith. Three years before this 1977 meeting with Richard, in 2004, Jack would have labeled Locke a lunatic. Now he was teacher, mentor, and leader in Jack's opinion. Thanks to the Island, working through Jack, Locke briefly occupied the office of Leader.

The most experienced Protector in the Island's history had some strange notions about the Island's significance. In 1867 Jacob explained the nature of the Island to Ricardo Alpert, newly arrived from the Canary Islands.

JACOB: [picks up the bottle of wine] Think of this wine as what you keep calling hell. There's many other names for it too: malevolence, evil, darkness. And here it is, swirling around in the bottle, unable to get out because if it did, it would spread. The cork [raises cork] is this island and it's the only thing keeping the darkness where it belongs.

Jacob was more than a little out of touch with the outside world. He had probably already been a frequent traveler, but it seems unlikely he ever attended Sunday mass. Ricardo had attended mass, of course. Probably every Sunday of his life. Every week he heard that wine symbolised the divinity of Christ. Now this strange man who lived in a shoe was telling him wine was a symbol of evil?

Jacob inverted many conventions of the outside world, the most fascinating of which, I believe, was his "baptism" of Richard. Jacob dunked Richard four times. I counted. Why would I do such a thing? Why would the number of dunkings have any significance?

In the Christian tradition we are baptised "In the name of the Father, and of the Son, and of the Holy Spirit." Most of us are baptised with the gentle passing of a few drops of water over our foreheads. Some of us, like my son, are fully immersed in water. In a few Christian denominations there is a single dunking. But in most traditions, including the one I try to follow, the candidate is immersed three times, once for each Person of the Trinity. Jacob's four-fold baptism was intentionally devised so as to prevent any religious interpretation.

At this point we could move on and admit that Jacob's baptism was not intended to have Christian or generally religious undertones of any kind. However, I think it may be important to consider the wider context of Jacob's action.

Baptism, in Christian theology, is a sharing in Jesus' passion and death. We are forced under water--into death. It is only after the third time under water (mirroring the third day in the tomb) that we finally rise to new life. Baptism is not a denial of death, but an embracing of death. It is not a continuation of life, but the beginning of an entirely new life. It marks a turning point.

Richard's baptism was no turning point. The only goal of Jacob's violent exercise was to point out that Richard was not physically dead. "Still think you're dead?" Jacob kept dunking Richard until he admitted, shouted, that he was not dead, that he lived, that he wished to live. I found the entire scene fascinating. Far from a baptism, this was an anti-baptism. Jacob forced Richard to say he was not dead. The "baptism" was not an acceptance of death—literal or figurative, physical or spiritual. It was, rather, a violent continuation of life as it had been. Richard remained among the damned of the earth—or at least he continued among those who considered themselves beyond redemption. The only change in Richard was the psychological awareness that he was not physically dead. Nothing truly important changed.

This "baptism" became a means of gaining control of Richard's soul. Richard would forever look to Jacob as the man who made him aware of being alive, but he enjoyed no more spiritual or physical freedom after the dunking than he had known before. The change in Richard was not for his benefit, but for Jacob's.

Jacob's philosophy was weird, fragmented, and in many ways just plain incorrect. The beauty of the Island's power is that it was able to overcome Jacob's fragmented leadership. Thanks to the Island's influence on history neither Jacob nor the Man in Black had the final word. A common sense beyond logic prevailed.

ANCIENT RULES

The Guardian, the first Protector, was bound by the rules. She had wide latitude in protecting the Island. She was immortal. The only thing that could end her life, that we know of, was a ferromagnetic knife thrust into her chest or abdomen. With her touch, she had the power to grant immortality. Her Candidates could not take their own lives, and they had limited or full immunity from death by natural causes. All of this power was directed toward a single end: She had to protect the Light.

The Guardian was tired of Protector duties. She looked worn out, and she was. She probably stayed at her post for centuries, perhaps thousands of years. When the Man in Black thrust the pugio into her abdomen, the greatest sensation she experienced was gratitude. "Thank you," she told him. It was as if an enormous burden had been lifted from her. The responsibility of guarding the Light was no longer hers.

Why hadn't she just walked away, centuries ago? I believe she did. She walked away, but found she could not leave. She brought ships to the Island and found out about limited access to and from Mittelos. But even when she had the master of the vessel point the ship on the narrow course with proper bearing, she could not leave. The ship and its crew could make their way out, but she was captive to the invisible sphere engulfing the Island.

She tried killing herself. We know how that ended. She could try to poison herself, but she'd just vomit the poison back up. She could try to jump from a high cliff, but the vegetation below would break her fall. She could swim far out in the ocean, inhale sea water, lose consciousness and think herself successful, only to wake minutes later on the beach, coughing the water out of her lungs. If she cut off her arm she'd see blood spurting everywhere, and she'd again think herself successful as she lost consciousness, only to wake hours later, her arm restored, her ruddy complexion a proof that she had lost no blood.

I have to believe she was more determined than this. After several Groundhog's Day-style suicide attempts she must have understood that engineering her own death was pointless. She would have recruited others to design her demise. I wonder if she felt shock at living after an arrow pierced her chest?

"The land and the king are one," was not an empty phrase on Mittelos. Without a Protector there could be no Light. Therefore, there has always been a Protector. Until she designated Candidates or had selected a replacement, the Protector could neither leave nor die. So the Island decreed. So it was.

Any rules we might wish to attribute to the Island can be understood only in the context of the Island's personality and ambitions. This is especially evident in the case of fertility and pregnancy issues.

PREGNANCY, CANCER, AND IMMORTALITY

The Source was the guarantor of the cycles of life. The severe cyclic regulation imposed by the close proximity of the Source meant that any bodily process—and especially cellular processes—would be subject to more than the normal level of control. Any cellular process that would normally proceed unchecked was kept in complete balance so close to the Source. Thus, disease cells, which normally spread quickly, were forced to spread slowly. Because they multiply slowly, the body's defence mechanisms were able to kill the disease much more easily on the Island. So it is that wounds healed quickly in Mittelos, and disease was uncommon.

In general, any type of cellular activity that occurred rapidly was slowed or even arrested on the Island, due to the regulation of life cycles through the Source. In this special place, women and men could live forever. In scientific terms, we can understand Island immortality as an inhibition of the normal processes of aging and apoptosis—cellular death. Apoptosis, like the spread of disease, is a rapid process of cellular death. The Source, with its ability to regulate life processes, slowed apoptosis and led to a kind of reinvigorating of the cell. Thanks to this dampening of cellular processes, people could and did live forever in this place.

Cancer cells multiply much faster than the surrounding tissue. The Source again forced the cancer to slow and eventually the body killed the foreign cells. Cancer was virtually unknown on the Island.

When a human egg is fertilised it undergoes rapid mitosis into a zygote and then into the differentiated tissues of a fetus. Like cancer cells, the cells of the fetus multiply quickly. The Source sought to slow this process, but the mother's body, primed for new life, fought the unnatural dampening effect of the Source. After several months of fighting the Source—an essentially unopposable force—mother and baby were overwhelmed. The mother, her hormonal system entirely out of whack, went into shock, and within minutes, both mother and baby were dead.

The earliest inhabitants of Mittelos were grateful to the gods that none of their loved ones ever had to suffer disease or cancer. Human nature being what it is, though, there were no statues of thanksgiving on the Island. No days set aside to celebrate another cancer-free year. One quite prominent statue greeted every visitor to the Island. This statue was the islanders' grand attempt at appeasing the very angry goddess of fertility, Taweret. This ancient Egyptian goddess was so angry, in fact, that many woman who became pregnant died several weeks before the baby was due. The unusual state of the Island that prevented disease and cured cancer was the same state that interfered with pregnancy and eventually caused the death of mother and child. The problem was especially severe after the Incident. Electromagnetic energy was at such a high level that between the birth of Ethan Rom in 1977 and Aaron's birth on November 1, 2004, neither pregnant women nor their babies survived.

I must point out that the preceding explanations are all based in science. The observations of lack of disease, lack of cancer, and death of women during pregnancy are consistent with the hyper-regulation of cellular function by some entity on the Island. Since we knew the Source to be a regulator of life, death, and rebirth, a hypothesis stating that the Source was the entity responsible for all these observed phenomena is entirely valid, and draws support from a wide variety of repeating events on the Island.

I don't know that this is the type of explanation of Darlton had in mind. This is a nitty-gritty science-based theory, and in the end, science proves inadequate to the elucidation of most phenomena on the Island. The fact that the Man in Black was not given a name, the fact that faith was demonstrated to be far superior to logic, and the fact that the Source and the Light and the Island itself were shown to be multi-dimensional entities I believe points us toward an inevitable conclusion: Some of the mysteries will forever remain veiled to human logic.

I believe this was Darlton's intention. If they had wanted us to believe all the mysteries were subject to rational understanding, that A causes B causes

C therefore A causes C, they would have shown us the superiority of Dharma science, rather than belittling the hippie-scientists. If they wanted us to treat this story as a linear unfolding of black and white, good versus evil, they would not have made Jacob a flawed man, and they would have made sure every character addressed the Man in Black as "Samuel," rather than flagrantly leaving him without appellation of any kind.

The most compelling mysteries of the Island cannot be unravelled by science or logic. Most of this book is aimed at a nonlinear, non-scientific interpretation of events because I feel this is truly the only way to understand the full depth of LOST.

FOUNDATION

circa 4000 B.C.

We don't know when the Island came to be, or when the Cork Stone was first used to supply the Light of the Island to the world. We don't even know the duration of the Guardian's tenure as Protector. Claudia began asking the question, but the Guardian cut her off before she could finish.

CLAUDIA: How long have you—
GUARDIAN: Every question I answer will simply lead to another question.

We know that the Cork Stone was inscribed with cuneiform symbols. According to Lostpedia, "The stone cork and the hole that it stoppered have markings on them. The clearest are cuneiform script, some of the earliest known forms or writing, used by Akkadians and Sumerians in ancient Iraq circa 5000– 1000 BC."

The Cork Stone might have been carved as late as 50 A.D., according to information supplied by Damon and Carlton, but the symbols etched into the stone were considerably older. What shall we make of this? Have we discovered an inconsistency?

I don't think so. There is nothing new under the sun. Jacob was averse to modern technology because it was a distraction from the elements of life that have real bearing on our survival: Trust, Love, Faith, Honesty, Hope, Charity. I don't think the placement of the Cork Stone was a first statement of humankind's commitment to the greater truths of our humanity. It certainly was not a temporary or interim measure. But the upholding of the truths carved into the Cork Stone, according to Lost, may turn out to be the best action humanity could ever take.

When did the words defining our humanity come into our lexicon? Certainly not in 50 A.D. They are at least as old as Gilgamesh, and probably older than Gilgamesh's oldest contemporaries' most distant memories of their grandmothers' and great-grandmothers' stories of ancient times. People trust each other. We love each other. These are the crucial elements of our humanity, carved into the Cork Stone, guarded by Hurley, carried in our hearts.

The Cork Stone was inscribed with script that even two thousand years ago was more ancient than the pyramids, more enduring than the mountains, more meaningful than any scroll or book of wisdom. This is the stuff of which we are made, a firm foundation without beginning, more valuable than gold, worthy of our vigilant protection.

LOST is not the story of rules and regulations. It is the story of our struggle to protect our dignity and our humanity, our status as people of the Light.

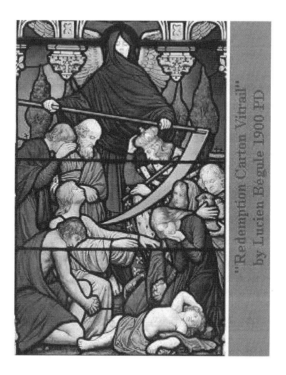

"Redemption Carton Vitrail"
by Lucien Begule 1900 PD

The sideways world was purgatory, nothing more. Cheap and artificial redemption.

After all the writers' denials, their insistence that the Island was real, that there would be no St. Elsewhere snow globe, no purgatory, the best thing they could come up with for Season Six was... Purgatory. Its only connection to the greater story was artificial and contrived, a means of resolving a plethora of questions that could never be explained on the Island in a single season.

Perhaps. We enter this cinematic Starbucks expecting Darlton to pick up the tab. I think we do this to our detriment, and to a much diminished appreciation of Lost. I prefer to accompany Damon and Carlton to the coffee shop, dollar (or loonie or pound coin) in hand. Perhaps I don't need to give anything, but this is my desire. With Juliet, I prefer to go Dutch, recognising the multiple and essential connections between the sideways world and the Island world, realising that I get out of Lost only those riches that reflect the effort I bring in trying to understand this most complex but most rewarding and most fascinating television series.

The heart of Lost is not the Island. The heart of Lost is a mirror, reflecting Jack's wounded body, Locke's unhandicapped courage in a wheelchair, Sawyer's fragmented soul. The heart of Lost is our own reflection, the stark image of our own wounds, our fragmented selves, our rare acts of courage, the mirror in which we find redemption. The heart of Lost is the sideways world.

RESOLUTION

Many have marveled at the expertly edited five-minute ending sequence of Lost. This was no ordinary editing accomplishment; its perfect beauty and symmetry earned the editors the greatest honour in television: an Emmy for Outstanding Editing. As Jack took his final walk through the bamboo forest, he entered the sanctuary of the church. Locke was the first one to greet Jack, and breaking from Locke's handshake, Jack greeted Penny and Desmond, took Boone's hand—and grasped a green bamboo shoot just as he passed the decaying shoe, hanging by its laces in the bamboo, that was the portal to his final resting place. Grasping Boone's hand in the sideways world at the moment he passed the shoe on the Island is of course no coincidence. The awkwardly placed shoe was a symbol of the apparent chaos of the Island, among other things, just as Boone was the first of many incomprehensible "sacrifices the Island demands."

More importantly, the recurring juxtaposition of the sideways world in the church and the death walk on the Island was meant to convey the intimate connections between the two worlds.

The shoe and Boone and the chaos they represented are now understood in a new light: they are the symbols of a grand plan, the one initiated six years ago, when the mysteriously resurrected Christian Shephard whistled to the yellow Labrador Retriever, Vincent, calling the dog to the second-most important assignment he would ever perform. "I need you to go find my son. He's over there in that bamboo forest, unconscious. I need you to go wake him up.... He has work to do."

When Vincent rushed toward Jack, the noise of his forward motion awakened the unconscious man. Even before he reached this most important disoriented crash survivor, the dog had accomplished his mission. I said earlier this was only Vincent's second greatest assignment. The task of greatest moment was the one he carried out three years later, when he took his place at Jack's side, comforting the great hero in his last two minutes on Earth.

The comfort he provided was symbolic in many ways, not only as a way of ensuring the one who had given his life so that others could live together would not himself have to die alone. There was much more than that to the dog's act of compassion to a dying man. In fact, the entire five-minute sequence chosen to bring closure to the episode perfectly resolved the entire six-year series.

TRIUNE SYMBOLISM

The actions and images in the final five minutes on the Island paralleled not only the events in the sideways world, but those that occurred in the first five minutes of the series' beginning. In fact, all three scenes—the opening minutes of Lost, Jack's walk to his death, and the last moments in the church sanctuary—point to each other, demonstrating a triune parallelism of images that complements the deeper conceptual symmetry of the series as a whole.

The series began with Christian (Lost Missing Pieces M.13, "So It Begins"), apparently acting as an agent of some greater power. Many believe, and there is a good amount of evidence to support the idea, that Christian's form was inhabited by the Smoke Monster. My take on Christian and Vincent, which I believe is more consonant with the continuity of events over six years, is that Jack's father and the dog were messengers. Christian, acting on behalf of—or perhaps as the embodiment of—a powerful entity, dispatched his agent, Vincent, to wake his son. Jack's task completed, the messenger in the sideways world (Christian) patted Jack's shoulder just before he opened the double doors to the brilliant white light. In that same moment on the Island, Christian's agent (Vincent) barked and took his place next to Jack.

Christian began the series with instructions to Vincent to wake Jack, who "has work to do." When Jack's work was done, Christian (in the sideways world) and Vincent (on the Island) were the last two individuals he interacted with, other than Kate, who would forever remain a part of him as his Constant. The presence of Christian and Vincent—messenger and agent—at both beginning and end, on the Island and sideways worlds, symbolised the momentous importance of Jack to the Island, acted as bookends to the Island's most important story, and demonstrated the dependence of both Island and sideways realities on each other.

CONFLUENCE OF VIRTUES

Trust is the centre of the philosophical underpinnings of the series. Without trust Jack could not have grown into a man of faith. He would never have entered the Cave of Light to replace the Cork Stone. But trust is not limited in scope to unifying the events on the Island. It is the attractor for every other virtue, both on the Island and in the sideways purgatory.

Trust and love are the stuff of which our physical existence in the world is based. Without a Constant, Desmond would succumb to time-travel-induced confusion, unstoppable nosebleeds, massive internal haemorrhaging, unconsciousness, and death.

It may be true that most characters in Lost did not travel through time, and therefore never suffered nosebleeds. We might be tempted to conclude that Lost considers love of the type that requires a Constant to be a good and noble part of the well-lived life, but in the end not essential to human existence. If you adhere to the faith principles of your religion, regardless of the religious tradition you follow, you probably are not required to seek and find a soul mate. The religion I attempt to practice teaches that all people, whether single or married, in relationship or not, are eligible for any of the benefits that might accrue from having lived a good life.

This is not the teaching of Lost.

The Constant relationship is not an expression of love. It is one of the human expressions of the need to belong. As we will see later in this book, the need to belong is itself the natural result of an even deeper need to express human identity. The Constant relationship, and its mirror-image counterpart, the Strange Attractor relationship, are expressions of our identity. The only way we can assert our identity as individuals, according to LOST, is to express our identity as personally and socially connected beings; we are independent because we are dependent. We have freedom and independence only because we have connection and destiny.

If you do not have a Constant, you will not receive a ticket admitting you to Our Lady of the Foucault Pendulum. You will never sit in a pew, waiting for the light to carry you to Shambala. For all eternity, you will be among the unhappy, whispering ones on the Island, forever cursing your lonely existence. Live together, die alone.

This may seem a harsh statement, but we can rely on the integrity of very clear statements in Season Six to provide guidance and understanding.

Martin Keamy not only did not have a Constant, he had no concept of civil behaviour. For some reason (perhaps a bookkeeping error, possibly an extreme example of what some religions call "undeserved grace"), the uncivilised mercenary was granted a place among those in the sideways reality. But there he died, his existence forevermore expunged from reality. There would be no redemption, no afterlife of any kind for Martin Keamy.

Michael never connected with his ex-wife. He loved his son, Walt, but not to the extent of being able to call him his Constant. To his eternal regret, he was to be forever marooned on the Island, never even granted a chance to redeem himself in the land of sideways souls.

Ben Linus was granted a place in the sideways world, but without a Constant at his side he could not enter the Church of the Holy Lamp Post. As we saw in the Season Six episode "Dr. Linus," Ben was working on a serious relationship with Danielle Rousseau, giving his all to ensure Alex's safe passage to adulthood—something he failed to do on the Island, a fact that shook him to the core and changed his outlook on everything. No doubt upon the successful completion of his relationship-building efforts in the sideways world he would be granted a ticket to a moving-on party inside Our Lady of the Perpetual Pendulum, but it would be with a group clustered around the Rousseau family, and not with the Island group led by the Shephard dynasty.

But, you argue, what about Locke? He had no Constant. How did he end up with a first-class ticket with front-row seating? I think in this case you'd find Jack Shephard vigorously disagreeing with you. Locke had a Constant alright. His Constant was the Island itself.

The case of John Locke indicates those who devote themselves whole-heartedly to a noble cause might also experience redemption, even without a visible Constant. Boone was the only other person in the church without a significant other at his side. I attributed this to his close relationship with his step-sister, Shannon, thinking perhaps she was Constant to both Sayid and Boone. But possibly Boone's case was similar to Locke's. Perhaps martyrdom to the Island was sufficient to ensure oneself a place in the pews. Certainly there was never any question that both Charlie and Sayid, arguably the greatest of the Saints of Mittelos, would have honoured positions at any banquet celebrating the redemption of lost souls.

CASCADE OF VALUES

Anyone could become eligible for a chance at redemption during life or after death--even murderers like Kate Austen, James Ford, and Martin Keamy and his henchmen. Earning the opportunity for redemption was as easy as escaping a polar bear cage. But actually achieving redemption was considerably more difficult--maybe akin to beating the polar bears' fish biscuit challenge. The bar was set high, and not everyone would make it. Even the greatest of the heroes, Jack, had to end the Shephard legacy of psychological abuse of the family's sons before he was allowed a glimpse of nirvana with Kate. In fact, getting the Shephard family affairs in order carried such importance that an imaginary son, David, was created for Jack so he could work on the requisite parenting skills. Even after righting the wrongs in his family, though, he still had to find his Constant. Fortunately for Jack, that pre-requisite was taken care of on the Island.

Redemption in Lost is the end result of a cascade of values that begins with human civilisation. Civilisation is founded on trust, which leads to faith, which leads to love, which leads to a soul-mate Constant, which leads to redemption. Without the proper placement of the Cork Stone over the Source, there is no Light in the human heart, no civility between people, no trust, no collaboration. Everything begins with the energy of the Source, modulated by humanity's pledge of civility (carved into the Cork Stone), which converts the fierce, red energy to soft yellow Light, converts hardness of heart to lightness of spirit, opens our eyes to the Light in everyone around us.

Until the Cork Stone was replaced at the Source, there could be no warm and fuzzy hug-fest in the pews. There could have been no light to see, no light to share. The events in the sideways after-world were entirely dependent upon the continuity of human civilisation in the physical world. But the nobility of the human spirit that takes earthly form in civilised behaviour finds its most enduring expression in the faith, hope, and love of the sideways reality. Just as Desmond could not physically endure the trials of this world without his Constant, the physical world itself cannot exist without the unbroken continuity of the sideways world. It is truly in this sideways reality that we live and move and have our being.

The sideways world was not purgatory. It was LOST's final and best statement of who we are. We are women and men of trust, people of faith, enduring Constants, children of the Light.

"RCMP Officer On a Horse"
© Robert Thivierge 2008 CC SA 3.0

Her politicians are unknown outside her borders. Her history is subdued; even the most jarring social movement of the last two hundred years is called the "Quiet" Revolution. But her culture?

Hockey. Mounties. Maple Syrup. Molson Dry. We know her culture.

If we know Canada's culture, we must know her citizens. Constable Benton Fraser, Dudley Do-Right, Sergeant Bruce, and Sam Steele taught us. Canadians are decent, polite, trustworthy. When Australian farmer Ray Mullen found a vagabond woman sleeping in his sheep barn he was understandably suspicious. "You're an American." Not a question, but a statement. Only Americans could be so disrespectful. The woman shook her head. "Canadian," she said, correcting him. "I graduated from college and figured I'd see the world."

Her declaration of Canadian citizenship changed everything. Now she was a good neighbour, fellow citizen of a Commonwealth country. She was Canadian. She was decent, polite, trustworthy. He believed her immediately. How could he not? Annie was a fine young woman from a fine country. Ray knew he could trust her with his money, with his farm, with his very life. What could possibly go wrong?

Deception, lies, and psychological manipulation occurred in every episode of LOST. They formed the backbone of a larger scheme of disorientation that was a major facet of the programme. At times the extent of deceit and disorientation was overwhelming, even frustrating. I found myself thinking on at least one occasion that a particular instance of trickery in Season Five was mean-spirited and unfair—not to any of the characters, but to me as a viewer-participant.

As unwelcome as the layers of deception were at times, they were integral to the story and necessary to us as the active recipients of the drama. We had to be able to accept the self-centred James Ford as leader. We had to be willing to stay with the series after the deaths of beloved characters. We were expected to understand that the great battles of Mittelos were not fought by the good guys in white and the bad guys in black. In fact, we were obliged to contend not only with moral shades of grey, but with every colourbust and pastel and shade and hue of the Island rainbow. Those exhibiting faults of character saw their shortcomings become virtues, while virtuous people failed and died.

Mittelos turned our expectations upside down because the series had to accomplish major readjustments of our value systems. We saw already, in the last chapter, that redemption could be achieved only by the surrender of self to another (as a Constant) or to a great project of the common good (e.g., Locke's sacrifice of himself to the Island). As I pointed out, I am not aware that any major philosophical or theological system requires this level of commitment from its adherents. The LOST state of redemption is far more rigorous and difficult to achieve than the similar state held to be an ideal in the religious traditions that the majority of us follow.

The Constant was among the innovative ideas expressed in the series, but it was not the final one, and it was not the most important concept. The purpose of the next few chapters is to provide a basis for understanding the topsy-turvy complexities that LOST brought into our living rooms every week. We will see that the Constant is only the most visible of a new set of virtues created by the show. To open our eyes to the others, we need to examine LOST's connections to the literary world, which we will do in the next chapter. We must also take a close look at the unique ways in which characters were related to each other, and we need to consider our own relationship to the series as metadrama. But we begin our nonlinear analysis here, with disorientation. Our first stop is the Canada Deception, which was a minor plot thread through the entire series.

ETHAN ROM - FROM ONTARIO

Hurley called him "Lance," until the soft-spoken man corrected him. "I'm Ethan—Ethan Rom. From Ontario." Hurley's response was in line with our own thoughts, and in keeping with Ethan's hope: "Right on, love Canada, great." Who could not love Canada? Therefore, who could not love Ethan Rom?

Anthony Cooper also said he was from Ontario. Ben traveled with a Canadian passport identifying him as Dean Moriarty. When some of the Others asked about Greta and Bonnie, Ben told them they were "on assignment in Canada." Charles Widmore gave John Locke a new identity as Jeremy Bentham and new citizenship—in Canada. Sawyer told the woman he was trying to con that he had a business partner "in Toronto." Kate, just before she stole Ray Mullen's money and nearly killed him, said she was Annie, from Canada (Kate Austen was from Iowa. Confusingly, the actress who played Kate, Evangeline Lilly, is from Fort Saskatchewan, Alberta, a western province of Canada).

Canada was referenced ten times in the span of 121 episodes. Not a single character--even a minor character among the otherwise international dramatis personae—was actually Canadian. So notorious were Ethan and Kate's fabricated citizenship that by the time Nathan claimed in "The Other 48 Days" to be from Canada, we were immediately suspicious. Even in Season Two we knew a claim of Canadian citizenship meant the character was almost certainly lying. When Ben told everyone that Greta and Bonnie were "on assignment in Canada," we knew this meant they were anywhere but Canada, and they would be found in a location Ben wished to keep secret. This turned out to be precisely the case: Greta and Bonnie were in the semi-secret Looking Glass Station, awaiting Ben's confidential command.

The deception was effective. But why?

I blame Sam Steele, and with him, the entire tradition of the NWMP and the Royal Canadian Mounted Police.

CONSTABLE BENTON FRASER, RCMP

Benton Fraser, Royal Canadian Mounted Police, played by Alberta-born actor Paul Gross, was a fixture in American living rooms in the 1990s on the CBS television series "Due South." Fraser was a Mountie very much in the tradition of Sam Steele and a sympathetic but over-the-top caricature of the polite, trustworthy, and self-sacrificing Canadian.

Stationed at the Canadian Consulate in Chicago, Fraser and sidekick Chicago cop Ray Vecchio solved the most difficult of the Windy City's crimes. In four years on U.S. television, Constable Fraser fired a weapon only once— when the Great Lakes freighter he boarded sailed into Canadian waters, meaning his sidearm was (finally!) legal and he could disable the bad guy's equipment with a perfectly-aimed shot.

Always-polite Constable Fraser is not the only reason for the success of the LOST deception. If a confidence man has his way with us, it is not because of some independently verifiable fact of life in Canada, but due rather to something internal, something askew in our understanding of the world. The confidence artist plays to that incorrect understanding, exploits it, and achieves her nefarious ends.

APPEARANCES AND UNDERLYING TRUTH

The mysterious man at Jin and Sun's wedding should not have been able to speak Korean, but here he was, not only wishing them well in their marriage, but doing so in flawless, perfectly fluent Korean. Jin and Sun were amazed. They thought they understood the world and the way it worked. A man of

European ancestry—a man who should have had no understanding of Korean—broke through the bonds of appearance and gave them a glimpse into the underlying truth of his mission.

We need to break through to that underlying truth if we are to understand the con artist's game. It is not enough to laugh and say, "I know Constable Fraser is a caricature; Canadians are not always polite." True enough. But as I said above, the problem does not derive of some independently verifiable fact of Canadian culture—it derives of a deficit in our understanding of the world. It's internal, not external.

I served in the Peace Corps in Togo, West Africa, for two years. The culture of West Africa, the way people speak, understand, and carry themselves is very different from what I experienced growing up in the Midwestern United States. One day toward the end of my service I was in a crowd of people in Lomé. Everyone was walking with me in the same direction, and I saw only the backs of people's heads. One man stood out from the crowd. He was wearing African clothes, wore his hair close to the scalp as the other black men around him. He was of average height and build. I could not see his face. But something in the way he carried himself, in the way he held his head high, shoulders back, moved arms and legs with purpose—gave me confidence, inner knowledge, that he was not Togolese. He was American, maybe European. When he and his friends stopped to purchase some Ghanaian chocolate from a little girl, my curiosity forced me to quicken my stride. "Cent francs," the girl informed him. Twenty-five cents. I looked at the man. "It's the going rate for Ghanaian chocolate," I told him. "You live here?" he asked with a heavy British accent. I tried not to smile. He was from Charlie's city, Manchester. Two years in West Africa had given me the ability to understand mannerisms, even to the point of pulling a black man from the UK out of a sea of black men from Togo.

I knew the man was from England, but did I know anything else? His motivations? His ideals?

I visited Munich in the summer of 2006. It was a time when Americans were becoming less welcome around the world and some travel experts were advocating a bit of deception: try to make people believe you're Canadian. As I returned from my one-week stay I gave up my seat on the subway to a woman just boarding. The man in the seat in front of me asked where I was from. "North America," I said. It was not deception--it was the way I was thinking. But my response could mean only one thing to the German fellow: I was Canadian. Americans simply don't identify themselves as being from "North America." He turned to his girlfriend and said something to the effect that he didn't like Canadians.

What were my motivations for saying "North America"? I was born and raised in Minnesota, I carry an American passport. But I speak and write using Canadian rhythms and norms. I did this for many years before my visit to Germany, and I will be doing it for the remainder of my life. Can anyone say they understand the rationale for my adoption of Canadian sensibilities? Does it even matter that I have U.S. citizenship? Does it matter that I might be able to write my name as Pearson Moore, U.E. (United Empire Loyalist; my great-great-great-great-great-great-grandfather, Daniel Smith (Smith #1 in the New Brunswick Provincial Archives), was a resident of Connecticut, fighting for King and Country in 1775 when hostilities broke out.)? We need to look deeper if we are to understand the Canada deception invented by Damon and Carlton.

I'M HENRY GALE, FROM MINNESOTA

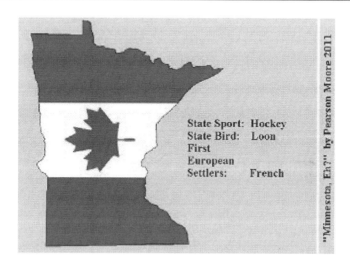

He said the words with a wondrous combination of conviction and fear: "I'm Henry Gale, from Minnesota." Henry Gale, probably much better known as uncle and legal guardian to Dorothy in the Wizard of Oz. But we're not in Kansas anymore, Vincent. This Henry Gale was from Wayzata, western suburb of Minneapolis. Wayzata's only claim to fame, as far as I know, is that it is the city in which Greg Lemond, three-time winner of the Tour de France, decided to raise his family.

If Sayid hadn't found that Minnesota driver's licence, the deception might have worked longer than it did. The discovery of this first of many lies was the beginning of what must have been five dozen or more beatings of the Dharmaville master of manipulation.

Why Minnesota? The original Henry Gale was doing just fine from his home in Kansas. Why did Darlton make the conscious decision to change his domicile to a location in the Land of Ten Thousand Lakes?

The state sport in Minnesota is hockey. The state bird is the loon. The first Europeans to visit its shores were French fur traders in the 17th century. If you replace the word "Minnesota" with "Canada" and "state" with "national," the truth of the first three sentences of this paragraph remains unaffected. Canada and Minnesota share history, languages, culture, and social institutions.

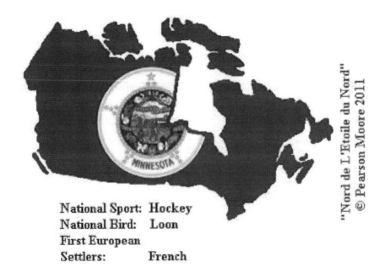

National Sport: Hockey
National Bird: Loon
First European
Settlers: French

The ties between Minnesota and Canada are commonly recognised. Rick Mercer, maybe the best-known comedian in Canada, a few years ago gave his humorous take on the placement of professional hockey teams in southern U.S. cities. "Now teams from cold places, like Québec, Winnipeg, and Minnesota, are moving to warm places, like Carolina, Tampa Bay, and Nashville. These are places where hockey is about as popular as bull riding, or women's bowling. People who live in the desert don't like hockey. They'd rather shoot rats at the dump." The video is hilarious.

Darlton recognised, with Rick Mercer, that Minnesota and the provinces north of its border share more than five-month-long winters. There are deep cultural connections affecting the way people in these places think, behave, and interact with one another. Kansas wasn't going to cut it as a credible fabrication on the Island of Mittelos. The Island's most notorious deception artist would have to hail from a location indicating decency, politeness, and trustworthiness, but it would have to be a location not as blatantly obvious as Ethan Rom's Ontario. It had to be Minnesota. And the way Michael Emerson said it—I could almost smell the air.

KNOWLEDGE, TRUTH, AND UNDERSTANDING

Cerberus (The Smoke Monster) knew even the master manipulator could be made to act on incomplete knowledge, that he could plant in Ben's mind the idea that Jacob was not sympathetic friend but ruthless and uncaring enemy. Cerberus' plan worked perfectly, and Ben ended Jacob's life with very little prodding in their first and only confrontation.

The Canada Deception shares much in common with the MIB's fabrications about Jacob. Smokey told Ben the truth, but only those truths that would support his goal of building Ben into the willing and eager assassin of the MIB's arch enemy. The last two sentences pose a juxtaposition of thought you may not have anticipated. After less than a few seconds of reflection the careful reader will take exception with the first statement in this paragraph. Kate was from Iowa, not from Canada. John Locke was not "Jeremy Bentham," and he was from California, not from Vancouver. So how could the Canada deceptions in LOST be anything other than the most blatant of lies? How can I say any truth is contained in these deceptions?

If we consider only the obvious aspects of the deception, we will see only the lie. But every good deception contains solid truth, or the deception would not hold its own weight.

We must endeavour to think about the deception in new terms to grasp the reason for its success.

What is deception if not a manipulation of the assumptions and norms we hold to be reasonable? If I tell you the sky is green I have fabricated a falsehood, but there is no deception. On the other hand, if I run into your office, eyes wide open in sheer terror, and say, "Shannon needs her inhaler," and when you ask, "What about the one on the night stand," and I say, "It isn't there," you believe me. You have good reason to believe me, because I was speaking the truth. The inhaler wasn't on the table—because I stuffed it in my pants pocket (note I didn't say "I didn't see it"). That she asked for her inhaler is also true, and that further strengthens the efficacy of my deception. I'm using against you the reasonable assumptions you made regarding the significance of the deeply-etched concern on my face and my apparent desire to help. If you discover in the future that I had the inhaler in my pocket the whole time, you will be shocked at my lack of humanity, but your anger will not be limited to indignation over my dishonesty. More than anything, your rage will be fueled by having been taken advantage of—by having been disoriented.

Disorientation was not limited to the frequent occasions of deception engineered by Ben or the Smoke Monster. We were witness to important instances of cultural and situational disorientation as well. As an example, consider the depiction of the meeting of Anubis and the Smoke Monster under the wall of the Temple, the image Ben saw when he went to be judged.

"Anubis and Pan" by Pearson Moore 2011

The depiction of the Smoke Monster's horned head is familiar to us. We heard Dogen refer to the Man in Black as "evil incarnate." In our culture we understand Satan, or the Devil, to be the purest form of evil. That the Smoke Monster would be depicted as the Devil is consonant with our understanding of his identity and purpose.

I wish to argue that the depiction of these two entities would have been understood quite differently during the days of Jacob's childhood. For one thing, the concept of "Satan" had not been fully developed by 50 A.D., the likely period in which Jacob grew up. Educated people of the time would have immediately recognised the above images, though, and they would have assigned significance very different from the meaning we would apply.

Let us consider, then, an imaginary meeting between a Greek scholar, Socrates, and an Egyptian philosopher, Ptah-Hotep, the Governor of Memphis and first lieutenant to Pharoah. The meeting takes place around 50 A.D. in Ptah-Hotep's home, with his twelve-year-old niece, Sekhet, waiting on them. [Note: The Egyptian philosopher Ptah-Hotep reigned as Governor of Memphis during the Fifth Dynasty (2465 B.C. to 2323 B.C.). Socrates lived in and around Athens from approximately 469 B.C. to his execution in 400 B.C. I've changed the time period of their imaginary meeting since... it's imaginary]

CERBERUS VERSUS ANUBIS

Vizier Ptah-Hotep says, "We are like the gods in bearing, but not in essence. We carry ourselves on two legs, as the Greats are wont to do, but the gods who control our fate govern desert wind, river current, ocean tide, sun and moon. They are Taweret, the hippopotamus-god of the fertile Nile; Khnum, the ram-god of the yearly inundation; Anubis, the jackal-god of the desert underworld—"

Socrates, no longer in control of his amusement, bursts into unrestrained laughter. Ptah-Hotep frowns in contempt of the toga-clad barbarian's insulting behaviour.

Ptah-Hotep takes a deep breath. "I do not belittle the Great Ones of Mount Olympus. Why do you—"

"I respect your culture." Socrates has pulled himself together, reclining again on the governor's guest couch. A mischievous grin crosses his face. "But is it any wonder Alexander the Great conquered your nation in the course of two short battles? You and your menagerie of farm yard animal-gods! We train hawks to do our bidding on the hunting field. Our kings keep jackals as house pets at their feet. True gods bear human faces, for we are like unto the gods in essence and in—"

"Stop!" Ptah-Hotep's stern eyes drill into Socrates. "Stop this blasphemy at once! Human faces, perhaps. Full likeness of the gods? Never! This is sheer blasphemy, and gods like your Pan, with horns and the body and genitals of a goat—why, it's blasphemy, pornography, an affront to everything civilised, a—"

Roman depiction of Pan pursuing the nymph, Pitys ca.50 AD PD

"An affront!" Socrates' eyes grow big, his jaw drops open. "I tell you, Pan is the most noble of the gods, he—"

"He's a goat, nothing more. Sticking his staff into anything that moves, raping any woman who tries to cross his—"

"Not a goat, Mister!" Socrates rises to his feet, hands on hips. "I'll tell you about affronts to civility, Governor! I'll tell you. On the island of Mittelos, near Atlantis, your people erected a statue to your ridiculous hippo-god, Taweret. And worse! In your silly temple you carved a depiction of Cerberus, not with three heads, but with a single head—with the countenance of Pan himself! As if that weren't bad enough, you gave him not a proper goat's body, but the body of a snake!"

Ptah-Hotep's anger disappears, replaced by a single raised eyebrow, pursed lips and eyes betraying deep concern. "Pan's visage, yes. But that is no snake's body, my philosopher friend. And this Cerberus, this three-headed dog of Mittelos, does not protect, but destroys. And it is not man, but woman. A she-goat who expresses only contempt for human beings. 'They come, they fight, they destroy, they corrupt,' she says."

"A woman?"

Ptah-Hotep nods. "She's inhabited the Island for thousands of years." He takes a deep breath. "Our people say she calls herself 'Protector,' but she takes the form of smoke. Black Death, they call her. She-goat of the Greeks."

Socrates frowns. "That hardly seems fair."

"Oh?"

"We only came to the island of Mittelos four hundred years ago, about the time Alexander conquered your nation. How could your artists possibly depict her as a Greek god? It's not fair."

Ptah-Hotep shrugs. "What is fair? You barbarians came and took over the island, proclaimed yourselves our people's masters. Would you say that's 'fair'? Our priests carved the image of this ancient she-goat with the likeness of Pan, with a body of smoke, bowing down to the jackal-god, Anubis, bowing down to our superior Egyptian culture, bowing to—"

"This is preposterous!"

"You may think what you wish, my Hellenic friend. But I speak the truth. This she-goat, this Black Death, destroyed an entire Roman village on—"

"The Romans are on Mittelos now, too?" Socrates returns to the visitor couch.

Ptah-Hotep reclines on his own ornately-carved couch and faces the Greek visitor. "Yes. They arrived forty years ago. Shipwreck, I'm told." A sly smile crosses his face. "They speak Latin."

Socrates' knit brow shows his disbelief. "Not Greek? Even after the village was destroyed?"

"Not everyone speaks Greek, my friend."

"Pfah." Socrates wrinkles his nose. "Everyone in the world speaks Greek—except the Romans. Even the people they conquered."

Ptah-Hotep exhales and shrugs. "Like it or not, a few survived the Black Smoke's rampage, after she killed them, burned down their village, filled in their deep underground diggings--all in a single afternoon [Lost 6.15, "Across the Sea," end of Act Five]. And they all speak Latin. Even the she-goat."

Socrates frowns, looks down at the floor, shakes his head. "It is a sad day when an entire island adopts the language of a murderous, conquering hoard like the blood-thirsty Romans. A sad day, indeed."

Ptah-Hotep nods. "On that we can certainly agree, my friend. The Romans are most uncivilised."

"Indeed." The bearded philosopher's lips move into a contented smile. "Thousands of years hence, the world will have forgotten the barbarous Romans. They will remember ours as the two greatest civilisations."

Ptah-Hotep grins. "My sister, Beset, has said as much."

"She looks well, for a woman with child."

"Thank you. It will be our first. A boy we hope. Beset and I prayed fervently to Taweret on our wedding night."

"A boy..."

"Yes." Ptah-Hotep opens his mouth wide. "Oh, I'm sorry! I forgot my earlier promise. Where are my manners?" He rises to his feet, turns to the servant girl. "Sekhet, summon your young brother, Ammon."

The girl bows and turns around, takes quick steps through the doorway to the courtyard.

"I trust you will find our accommodations satisfactory , Socrates."

Socrates nods and smiles with genuine warmth. "Thank you. Your hospitality has already made me forget the uncivilised Romans."

The carved image of the Smoke Monster confronting Anubis, the ancient Egyptian god of the dead, portrayed not only a clash between gods, but a clash of cultures. The image was carved in the manner of the ancient Egyptians, indicating Egyptians were the artists responsible for the rendering. The face of the Smoke Monster was not drawn from any Egyptian source, though. The Monster was represented as Greek or Roman, most likely with the face of the Greek god, Pan.

The interpretation of the image is critical to our understanding of LOST. I presented an imagined meeting between an educated ancient Greek and an educated ancient Egyptian to illustrate the point that interpretation of the image is a product of cultural background. The Greeks would understand Pan in quite a different way from the Egyptians, while the Egyptians would have a very firm understanding of the major god, Anubis that would have been incomprehensible to Greeks.

If we wish to understand the image through the eyes of the people who created it, we need to abandon our preconceived notions of the significance of a ruddy-faced man with horns and a goatee. But the difficulties associated with this task are enormous. Indeed, the most common way of referring to horns of the style used in images of Pan is "devil horns." Even when we attempt to describe the imagery we must forget, we are obliged to use words and images and histories that bring us back to the point we wish to depart from.

The fact that we are so narrow-minded and culture-bound as to assume the Temple image of the Smoke Monster represented the Devil is strong indication of the titanic effort that must be undertaken to move beyond these unhelpful and misleading associations. Cultural disorientation is not something the writers did for the sake of confusion. They didn't gather together saying, "Hey, let's make it look like the Monster is Satan, just for laughs." The objective was not our confusion or torture, but the destruction of stereotypes and cultural and logical associations so that we would be able to understand the deeper ideas of the series.

What was the Smoke Monster, then, from the point of view of an ancient Egyptian living in a culture heavily influenced by the invading Greek and Roman overlords? What was the significance of Anubis' raised arms? Was Anubis merely greeting the Greek god? Was he claiming mastery of the invader? Was he bowing in obeisance to a new master? We need to come to terms with the significance of the image, but we will not be able to do this until we have gained a better understanding of the other storytelling novelties of LOST. We will return to a consideration of the relationship between Cerberus and Anubis in the final chapters of this book.

The lesson at this point is more than enough for us to ponder. Whenever we confront an aspect of LOST we do not fully understand, we must first of all remember that our logical, analytical skills are inextricably intertwined with our cultural heritage, and that this co-mingling of assumption and logic will cause us, in most cases, to misunderstand connections or remain blind to otherwise obvious connections. We need to discard our cultural biases. As this is beyond the capabilities of almost all of us, those telling the story needed to disorient us, shake us loose from the cultural forces that bind us to incorrect interpretation. This is precisely what Darlton and the other writers did.

THE OTHER 48 DAYS

If we require any convincing of the need for reorientation of our values and understanding, we have several rich examples from which to make our choice. To my mind, the best of these is the story of Ana Lucia and the survivors of the tail section of Flight 815.

Within hours of their violent crash into the water off the northern coast of the Island the survivors were infiltrated by one of the Others, Goodwin Stanhope, but no one among the Flight 815 passengers knew they had been compromised. Within a few days the Others had killed several survivors and kidnapped many others, including at least two of the children. No one could be trusted, not even their own members, because details of location, names, and even backgrounds of the survivors were ending up in the hands of the unseen enemy. The fact that the enemy knew so much about them had to mean the enemy was in their midst, but they didn't know which of their number was the spy. When Nathan disappeared for several hours he became Suspect Number One in Ana Lucia's mind.

We don't know with certainty that Nathan was one of the Others, though particulars of circumstance indicate he was. We do know that both he and Goodwin were murdered—Nathan by Goodwin, and Goodwin by Ana Lucia. We know that because of the high level of paranoia within Ana Lucia's group, Shannon Rutherford was shot in the abdomen and died from her wound. Even before the tail section survivors left the beach, their every move was governed by a supreme distrust of everything around them. With their numbers dwindling through inexplicable murders and kidnappings, with the enemy apparently aware of their every move and even their pre-flight histories and occupations, we can perhaps understand their justifiable state of anxiety-bordering-alarm. When Jin, Michael, and Sawyer washed up on the beach near the tail section survivors, the only reasonable assumption must have been to consider them hostile until proven otherwise. Indeed, even after Ana Lucia learned from Michael and Sawyer that they had survived the crash, that the gunshot wound at Sawyer's shoulder was due to his attempt to prevent the Others from kidnapping Walter, she still distrusted them and kept them in the underground cage.

Ana Lucia was not a good leader. Her own background rendered her unsuitable for leadership, but she was most especially unsuited for leadership in such a hostile environment. Barely surviving a shooting several months before, she hunted down the perpetrator and murdered him rather than allow justice to run its course. She drew a gun on an unarmed petty criminal who presented a risk to no one. She came to hate the public and the police force she served, and despised her own mother. Even before boarding the Oceanic flight she understood the world as oriented against her, and she brought this unhealthy bias to her role as leader of the tail section survivors.

A good leader would have recognised that an unknown, deadly environment required deep understanding, not a "shoot first, ask questions later" mentality. A good leader would never have succumbed to paranoia, as much as this would have been the default disposition of any ordinary person. A good leader would have resisted the temptation to see the entire world as evil, and would have instilled productive survival attitudes and skills in her people. Ana Lucia had neither temperament nor training for such leadership, and the result was several unnecessary deaths and much suffering among those who survived her unenlightened command of ambiguous and deadly situations.

Even in the midst of the most severe disorientation, LOST told us to retain our faith and trust. When the light inside the Swan Station came on during the early morning of November 1, 2004, Locke at first believed it was a sign that the Island had heard his pleas. Later, when he learned that Desmond was the only occupant of the hatch, he became disillusioned. "The light was probably just you, Desmond, going to the bathroom." But there were no coincidences in LOST. The light was Desmond's response to Locke's plea, and the response had deep significance to both of them. For Locke, it meant the Island heard him. For Desmond, who held a gun in his hand, contemplating suicide, not even a beautiful letter from his beloved Penny could lift him out of despondency. He ran to the bookshelf, threw the books to the floor, then pushed the long-play record albums off their shelves. What good was a letter from his beloved when there was no way to touch her, or even see her? He was alone on the Island... but then he heard Locke's cries of anguish, and he knew he was not alone. Locke saved Desmond, Desmond saved Locke. LOST teaches that Ana Lucia's loss of faith and trust was not the favoured approach to her predicament.

In the midst of severe disorientation, a good leader would have questioned the validity and utility of her decisions rather than plowing ahead with strategies and tactics that were useless in a deadly environment. Ana Lucia did not do this. She did not reorient her values and understanding. Because of this, many died. She died, too. There are no coincidences. Her death was not merely the result of Michael's depravity; it was Island karma.

ASCENT TO ENLIGHTENMENT

We can look at the six years of LOST as attempting an ascent to enlightenment. At each stage of the journey we were obliged to rid ourselves of cultural, scientific, and logical associations that interfered with our understanding of the Island. In many ways, we had to become as kindergarteners, as children able to absorb radical, new ideas, without the incorrect and misleading assumptions we learned later in life. We began in kindergarten with knowledge of a few simple rules. These were the same rules we needed to bring to the Island:

Play fair.
Don't hit anyone.
Share with everyone.
Clean up after yourself.
Don't take things that belong to others.
Put things back where they came from.

The supreme adherent of the Rules of Life was Dr. Jack Shephard. But once on the Island, Jack's boy-scout mentality seemed no longer to apply. Jack had to trade science and rules for faith and hope, and in the process he lost his poise, lost his sanity, nearly lost his life. He was obliged to surrender the certitude and safety of his society's privilege for chaos and danger as his Island's Protector. He discovered the irony of his journey at the Source; that which he believed he had surrendered in the end he was sworn to protect: the founding precepts of civilisation. Everything he learned in kindergarten.

The Island's purpose was to serve as repository and guardian of the rules of humanity. The survivors' purpose was to protect the Island and its precious, life-giving cultural treasure. Our purpose was to make sense of it all, to distil enduring kindergarten sensibilities from the post-graduate chaos of the Casimir Effect, the Valenzetti Equation, the tropical polar bears, the malevolent masses of sentient smoke. And to do all that we had to keep our thoughts focussed on the one sure truth spanning six years: Destiny. Purpose. The final objective. Res qui nos omnes servabit (The thing that will save us all).

THE NINE LEVELS OF UNDERSTANDING

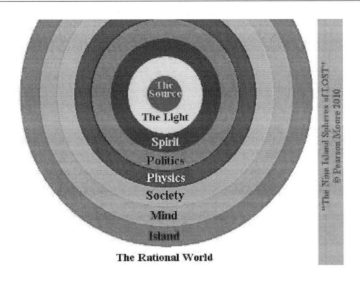

The Rational World

154

LOST is a journey. We began that journey in the first sphere, in the rational world, at twelve thousand metres, just a bit higher than the tallest mountains, sipping vodka on the rocks courtesy of Flight Attendant Cindy Chandler. This mountaintop view of the rational world was an appropriate, Dantesque location from which to begin an arduous journey through eight more spheres that would bring us to the Source.

Surviving the crash was the introduction to a strange Island world that brought life and death by means unknown and unimaginable. The crippled and dying were instantly cured, while the innocent were hunted down and killed by a formless black death. The Island (Season One) was the second sphere. It was in this sphere that we learned why the crash occurred.

LOCKE: Do you really think all this is an accident—that we, a group of strangers survived, many of us with just superficial injuries? Do you think we crashed on this place by coincidence—especially, this place? We were brought here for a purpose, for a reason, all of us. Each one of us was brought here for a reason.
JACK: Brought here? And who brought us here, John?
LOCKE: The Island.

The survivors had a purpose. That purpose was to be found on the Island, and somehow in service to the Island.

Confusing as it was, this introduction to the second sphere was not nearly as disorienting as the third sphere, the realm of the mind, explored in Season Two. It was in the third sphere, in the Swan Station, that Jack was forced to confront the limitations of his scientifically rigid mind. Faith, not science, was the surest and most powerful guide to understanding Island phenomena. By the end of Season Two, no one, not even Locke, had faith enough to prevent the implosion of the Swan Station. Desmond alone knew the action that was required, and he turned the reset key, preventing the Island's destruction.

The lessons of Season Two are absolutely essential to our full enjoyment and understanding of LOST. Reality cannot be understood through logic. Logic and science are inherently flawed tools, useful only in proving models (artificial, simplified, imaginary constructs) of reality, not reality itself. It is the failure to accept this truth that has prevented millions around the world from appreciating the last 150 minutes of the series.

A lack of logic does not imply lack of sure destination or purpose. In fact, if the essential premise of destiny is not employed as firm anchor, the events of the subsequent four seasons will seem entirely disconnected from each other. We must go into Season Three with faith and purpose as our sure guides.

In the fourth sphere (Season Three) we began to appreciate the social ramifications of Island life. The Hostiles believed the Dharma Initiative's activities so contrary to Jacob's plan that they murdered all of them—women, men, and children—en masse. The social aspect of Island life was essential to long-term survival.

WE'RE THE GOOD GUYS, MICHAEL

The Others kidnapped, imprisoned, enslaved, executed, and murdered according to their own unposted rules. They connived, collaborated, and conspired in schemes elaborate and bold or simple and quick to turn events in their favour. Having experienced their treachery first-hand, Michael was shocked when their leader, Ben, honoured his agreement to reunite him with his son and gave him a boat to escape the Island. Was this an instance of honour among thieves and murderous criminals, or did it represent the sterling adherence to virtue that Ben claimed? Many of the activities of the Others seemed entirely at odds with any reasonable understanding of behaviour that could be accounted "good." Our disorientation as viewer-participants was profound. This was not confusion merely at the level of syllogism or causality, but at a moral and spiritual level. One simply does not conspire to murder and enshrine the deed as hallowed activity.

One of the accepted activities of the Others was the kidnapping of children. Ben Linus was an early practitioner, but by the time Oceanic 815 crashed in 2004, the practice was institutionalised among the Others, and they quickly moved to extract all of the children from among the survivors. Abduction of the children from the tail section was relatively easy, since that part of the plane crashed near the Others' camp in the Dharmaville barracks ("New Otherton"). Walter's abduction required significantly more planning, though Michael's insistence that Walter accompany him on the raft made the Others' work easier, since a water abduction would allow a faster getaway.

"Kidnapped" by John Mix Stanley 1853 PD

I cannot imagine a civilised culture in which kidnapping is deemed virtuous activity by the state. But the Others practiced and perfected this crime, and seemed to consider it necessary. That there was apparent unanimity of opinion regarding the need to extract young ones indicates that reorientation of values was possible for those among the Others, like Juliet, who had been raised in traditional societies outside the Island. The implication is that we ought to be able to understand the Others' strange behaviour, and at some level consider the activity morally justified and beneficial to both the children and the Others.

If we are to understand, we must know the facts. Only one child that we know of—Walter—was held at Dharmaville. The other children, including Emma and Zach, became residents of the Temple in Cindy Chandler's care. Walter underwent testing for "special" abilities, while the other children, as far as we know, were left alone. Walter was returned to his father after sixteen or more dead birds were found on the steps outside the room where he was being held (Episode M.06, "Room 23"). Ben told Michael, "we got more than we bargained for when Walt joined us," indicating that Ben no longer considered Walter's presence useful or beneficial to his group.

We need to apply reasonable interpolation to the situation. We know Richard had spoken several times with the Man in Black, and he was aware of the man's ruthless nature and ability to coerce. Even if Richard did not warn the Others of this particular aspect of the Man in Black's character, he almost certainly would have communicated to them the fact that there were harmful forces on the Island. After all, he considered the Island to be "Hell," and not in a figurative sense (Episode 6.09, "Ab Aeterno"). Children would be especially vulnerable to these forces, and they could become agents of the evil one.

That the Others would have aligned their activities to account for the presence of an evil entity in their midst is not an unreasonable assumption. Unrelated behaviours indicated an awareness of the need to prevent an evil force from overcoming the Island. For example, Cindy Pickett's Viking-style burial at sea could be taken as "the normal method by which The Others dispose of their dead" (Lostpedia). Many analysts have concluded that the Others' practice of burial at sea was adopted out of necessity; those who were buried on land tended to "appear" after they had died. The Smoke Monster, as we have known at least since Season Three, made a habit of appearing to others in the form of dead loved ones.

Taking into consideration these reasonable assumptions, we arrive at a point of understanding the Others' strange practice of child abduction. The peculiar conditions of the Island forced them to employ tactics that would otherwise be unthinkable. If they had not abducted the children, the Smoke Monster would have used them to support his dark objectives. He would have used them to force compliance to his will, or he would have killed them and used their apparitions to advance his agenda. In the end, the Others were acting out of a concern for the children and out of the need to preserve their own lives. Bringing to bear other facts of Island life, and using appropriate interpolation when required, most if not all of the other "uncivilised" behaviours of the Others can be reconciled with the activity of a healthy society adapted to a hostile environment.

The problem of child abduction is an excellent example of the need for disorientation followed by reorientation of assumptions and values in the LOST world. In coming chapters we will see even more spectacular examples of reorientation that will allow piercing insight into LOST's view of the world.

PHYSICAL AND POLITICAL SPHERES

With the fifth sphere, physics (Season Four), we began to appreciate the effect of Island phenomena on the behaviours of the physical world. The Island bent space and light and time itself. The Rules of the Island had greater effect than any law; they were the expressions of a supernatural will to which even the "laws" of physics were obliged to yield. Daniel Faraday's experiments not only confirmed the counter-intuitive nature of Island phenomena, but deepened our awareness of the Island as possessing powers beyond human comprehension.

"Cassini Science Br"
Artist's rendering of a general relativity expt.
NASA 2006 PD

In the sixth sphere (Season Five) we confronted political reality. Who was in charge of the Island? Ben Linus? Alvar Hanso? Richard Alpert? Stuart Radzinsky? Charles Widmore? Or was it ille qui nos omnes servabit, Jacob?

Lack of guidance regarding the identity of the Island's ruler mirrored the dearth of information about the antagonist. Who was the bad guy? Ben Linus? The Smoke Monster? Eloise Hawking? Ambiguity surrounding both of these important matters was not accidental but intentionally and emphatically built into the underlying structure of the series. Darlton went to great lengths to suppress any idea that the Smoke Monster had a name. He remained nameless.

Arriving at the identity of LOST's antagonist is the subject for a very long essay. However, we know who made the rules on the Island. The most important of the Island's Rules are literally etched in stone, and remain unchanged regardless of the identity of the person holding the title of Protector. The Island itself made the Rules.

More importantly, we know what was necessary in order to make that determination. At this point in the story our active participation, in ways we are not used to providing for entertainment we believe should be feeding us, is essential. We must string together the disparate parts of LOST on our own. In fact, as I will argue later in this book, we, the participant-audience, must supply the narrative structure. LOST is not drama, but metadrama. We are not "viewers," but participants.

THE INNERMOST SPHERES

Season Six threw us into the seventh sphere, a realm of pure spirit. Those called to defend the Cork Stone—the physical vessel bearing the cuneiform inscriptions of humankind's most ancient and enduring precepts of civilisation—had to be transformed at every level of their being, and most especially in the spiritual dimension.

The Cork Stone was the ninth sphere. What lay beyond the stone was a tenth plane of existence, referred to as the Source. We have no words to describe the Source. There is no name, no reliable point of reference. We have no means of becoming oriented toward it. When Moses put the question in the third chapter of the Hebrew book of Exodus, the response he received was, "I AM WHO AM." There is no reference for the Source. The Source is the point of contact with the Divine. We might think of it as something akin to the Burning Bush, but the comparison is feeble. The Burning Bush was a divine apparition in a form suitable to Moses' human understanding. The Source is raw, unfiltered divine power. It is the Burning Bush, but it burns not only with bright light, but with heat, with angry red judgment, with the full majesty and fury and terror of a million suns, with the complete force of divine will.

Much as the gaseous atmosphere surrounding our planet prevents deadly solar radiation from frying our bodies and disfiguring our nucleic acids, and transforms the cosmic energy into life-giving heat and light, so too the Cork Stone, properly placed over the Source, transforms raw energy into the Light that makes civilisation possible.

There is but one way to meet the Source, and that is through an eternal commitment. Theology expresses this commitment as something called "Covenant." In Judeo-Christian-Muslim tradition, one of the most important covenants was expressed as a set of Ten Commandments etched on stone tablets. The physical instrument of Covenant in LOST was the Cork Stone, inscribed in ancient cuneiform script with the most important lessons of human civilisation. We meet the Source by coming into Covenant with the Source. The Cork Stone was humanity's statement of commitment to the ideals of civilisation. By dropping the Cork Stone into the centre of the Source, Jacob and then Jack maintained the only possible connection between that which is human and that which is pure power beyond our comprehension, a connection that was both basis and consequence of the unceasing propagation of human civilisation. This pledge of civility was the Protector's covenant with the Divine.

The Cork Stone is the final statement of reorientation of values and understanding in the face of irreconcilable disorientation. We have no means of understanding the Source. But we do have the ability to maintain the kindergarten values—the Cork Stone values.

SAM STEELE, NORTHWEST MOUNTED POLICE

What truth in deception?

I wrote at the beginning of this chapter that I blamed Sam Steele for the effectiveness of Darlton's Canada deception. Unlike the other Mounties I have invoked, however, Sam Steele—Superintendant Sir Samuel Benfield Steele—is not a fictional creation. He was, for fifty years, the flesh-and-blood leader of the Canadian Mounties. In order to understand why the Canada deception worked, you need to understand Sam Steele, his attitude about police work, and the tradition that flowed from his example.

Sir Samuel Benfield Steele ca. 1900 PD

The most striking truth—possibly outside of the realm of belief, even for Canadians, was this simple fact: In his fifty years of police work, Sam Steele did not draw his service revolver. Not once. I trust historian Pierre Berton (Canada's most widely-read authority on Canadian history, frequent television personality, and author of roughly fifty tomes) to have researched the facts surrounding this most famous of Mounties. Steele believed police work was accomplished by force of character. Modern-day RCMP officers who go about tazering people—literally to death sometimes—could learn deep truths from this man. He faced greater challenges (e.g., the Klondike gold rush) to peace, order, and good government than any of his successors.

Sir Sam Steele is real. His life is stranger than fiction, beyond even the over-the-top perfection of Constable Benton Fraser.

We have to move beyond caricatures to truth. Sam Steele is real, stands for something real, something that has endured even longer than the 144 years that have passed since Sir John A. MacDonald became the first Prime Minister of the Dominion of Canada. Benjamin Linus and Ethan Rom and "Jeremy Bentham" stood for something, too. They did not make deception their goal. It was a means to an end. Occasionally even Ben would speak the truth. "Everything I did, I did for the Island," Ben said into his walkie-talkie. Ben and Ethan and Locke served something greater than themselves, something real, something that endured even longer than the 140 years of Richard Alpert's immortality. They served the Island.

SERVICE TO KING AND COUNTRY

Even those we considered for many years to be human refuse, the putrid vessels of all that is and can be corrupted, turned out instead to be fighting for the existence of the one thing above all others on this planet that must be protected. They fought for the idea inscribed on the cork stone, that human civilisation, the work of human hands and joy of human hearts, labouring for the good of all humankind, shall not perish from the earth. Peace, order, and good Island government. It's a new idea, born in the land of hockey, Mounties, Timbits, and Bombardier. But it's as old as Samuel de Champlain's handshake with Grand Sagamo Anadabijou in 1603, as old as the hieroglyphs at the time wheel, as old as Jacob and the Man in Black, as old as the values that drove Sir Samuel Benfield Steele, Superintendant of the Mounties.

"Ulysses and the Sirens"
Herbert James Draper 1909 PD

The journey's the thing.

You know the details of Odysseus' journey: You recall the nymph Calypso, the lotus eaters, Scylla and Circe. You remember how Odysseus inebriated the cyclops, Polyphemus, waited until the giant was fast asleep, then blinded him with a stake. You recall the story of the sirens, and how Odysseus resisted their bewitching song by having his men, their ears plugged with beeswax, tie him to the mast. The story has an ending, too, and it resolved the themes of the Odyssey. But do you remember the conclusion of Odysseus' story?

The journey's the thing because the adventure itself, not its resolution, conveys the ideas that broaden our minds, the sentiments that stir our hearts, the awe and wonder and majesty that fill our souls.

LITERARY CONNECTIONS

Although Lostpedia cites nearly one hundred literary works mentioned in dialogue, featured in a scene, alluded to indirectly, or used as the basis for events, conditions, or actions, not all of the works have the same degree of influence. Some well-known authors, such as Stephen King and Charles Dickens, were frequently and prominently mentioned. Certain works, such as the Bible, "Lord of the Flies," and King's "The Dark Tower" series played a central role in the development of themes and plotlines. Some lesser-known works, such as Abraham Merritt's "The Moon Pool" share striking similarities with major plot points or characters. Most of the featured works are available at little or no cost through major booksellers. "The Moon Pool," for instance, was available in a free Kindle edition as of February 14, 2011.

Literary References in Lost

Title	First Name	Surname	References
		Author of the work	
Bible, The		several	20
Alice's Adventures in Wonderland	Lewis	Carroll	8
Dark Tower, The (Series of 4)	Stephen	King	7
Wonderful Wizard of Oz	L. Frank	Baum	6
Through the Looking-Glass	Lewis	Carroll	5
Lord of the Flies	William	Golding	5
Chronicles of Narnia, The	C.S.	Lewis	5
Odyssey, The		Homer	5
Moon Pool, The	A.	Merritt	4
Watership Down	Richard	Adams	3
Heart of Darkness	Joseph	Conrad	3
Brief History of Time, A	Stephen	Hawking	3
Wrinkle in Time, A	Madeleine	L'Engle	3
Of Mice and Men	John	Steinbeck	3
Mysterious Island, The	Jules	Verne	3
Slaughterhouse-Five	Kurt	Vonnegut	3

I have provided above a list of sixteen works sorted according to the frequency of direct reference in the series. The reference frequency should not be considered accurate, and the list should not be taken as representative of the writers' thoughts regarding the comparative importance or value of any of the works referenced in LOST. This crude tabulation is merely my attempt to bring some structure to a discussion of the far-flung literary allusions that permeate the series.

While the list is certainly subject to debate, this is not my intention, either. I would never argue that the works of Lewis Carroll had greater influence on the writers than William Golding's "Lord of the Flies." I have no basis for any such claim. On the other hand, any of the books mentioned only once and not appearing on this short list, such as Joseph Heller's "Catch-22," probably can be assumed to have incidental or very modest impact on LOST's plot threads and characters.

ISLAND ALLEGORY

They survived the crash of their airplane on a deserted island. At first they believed they were alone, but they soon discovered they were sharing the island with a fearsome creature they called the Monster. Wild boar became a major source of food. Dreams and visions played a prominent role in the plot. Two leaders emerged, one of whom preferred to dress as a hunter, and they became bitter enemies. Eventually the other survivors were forced to choose sides, with half the camp following the hunter, and the other half following the more civilised leader. In a great rainstorm one of the survivors appeared to be a threat and was accidentally killed. Though the description may sound familiar, I am referring to a 1954 novel by William Golding, not the 2004 television series by Lindelof and Cuse.

"Lord of the Flies" bears striking resemblance to LOST. Lostpedia lists twenty-one specific themes shared between the two works, and these do not include the dozens of strong similarities between characters. If Jack Shephard moved the time wheel under the Orchid and found himself living on the island with these pre-teen British boys he would find many of the situations confronting him quite similar in nature to those he faced after the crash of Flight 815.

"Lord of the Flies" is allegory. It expresses in its pages one of the most profoundly unsettling and pessimistic views of human nature ever created in fiction. I will discuss allegory later in this book, and I will use "Lord of the Flies" as an example. For the concerns of this chapter, I wish to point out three important observations.

First of all, there are so many strong correlations between LOST and "Lord of the Flies" that I don't feel any of us can truly appreciate the series without having read Golding's novel. We would be foolish indeed if we tried to make sense of some of the more intricate plot points if we did not avail ourselves of the much simpler template provided by the atomic-era story of humankind's descent into savagery. Most readers, I suspect, have at least an acquaintance with the novel through studies in high school or university. But because of the formative influence of the work, I recommend anyone not conversant with plot details and characters review or reread the book. The novel is short, the prose is simple, and little time or effort is required to digest the straightforward themes.

Second, "Lord of the Flies" provides a terrific lesson in the complexity and uniqueness of LOST. Rereading Golding's masterpiece we may find ourselves tempted to draw more comparisons than warranted. We need to remind ourselves, as we plough through the literary works associated with LOST, that Darlton did not intend to rewrite "Lord of the Flies" or Shakespeare's "The Tempest" for the twenty-first century. Because this sixty-year-old novel supports more parallels with LOST than just about any other fictional work, it is a good place to start any compare-and-contrast exercise.

Finally, those who are familiar with both works will recognise that "Lord of the Flies" is significantly more pessimistic than LOST. In fact, LOST might be compared in some ways with "The Coral Island," an 1858 novel by Robert Ballantyne that would probably be considered overly cheerful by most readers, but does provide a valid counterpoint to Golding's vision of humanity. As we analyse LOST from several perspectives we will begin to isolate concrete instances of the series' more optimistic point of view. "Lord of the Flies" is a good touchstone for this gradual unraveling of thematic material. At the very least, we can contrast the two widely differing viewpoints of humankind's inner tendencies to arrive at some feeling for the plausibility of LOST's stand on human nature.

DOWN THE RABBIT HOLE

The works of Lewis Carroll were given prominent positions throughout the six year of LOST. The Looking Glass was an underwater Dharma station. Locke said of Jack's pursuit of his dead father that he was chasing "the white rabbit." In the sideways world, Jack told his son, David, that he often read him chapters from "Alice's Adventures in Wonderland." Many of the images each season provided visual allusion to themes or scenes from Carroll's novels. Since Alice's adventures were so frequently invoked, we will take time here to examine some of the themes a little more closely.

A STORY OF A GIRL, A RABBIT, AND GROWTH

"Oh dear! Oh dear! I shall be late!"

With the white rabbit's words, Lewis Carroll introduced the strange world of "Alice's Adventures in Wonderland." Alice followed the immaculately dressed white rabbit down the rabbit hole and there discovered a bizarre menagerie of caterpillars and pigs and frogs and a disappearing and reappearing cat, all ruled by the Queen of Hearts, whose only administrative acts seemed to be limited to the proclamation of writs of execution. "Off with his head! Execute him!" was her reply to anyone whose actions were not in accord with her caprice.

Hmmm...

Curiouser and

curiouser...

"Curiouser and Curiouser"
Peter Newell 1890 PD

This world made no sense at all to Alice. She often said, "How confusing this is," or "This is curious," or even "Curious and curiouser!" She ate cake or drank a beverage or chomped on a bit of mushroom and grew to nine feet tall or shrunk to three inches high. After nearly drowning in Alice's tears, the animals dried off by racing around in a circle until there was no winner. None of it made any sense to Alice, but she learned quickly. "Let me see," she said, "four times five is twelve, and four times six is thirteen, and four times seven is—oh dear! I shall never get to twenty at that rate!"

But this is not a nonsense world at all. "Alice's Adventures in Wonderland" is not a children's book of absurdities. It is satire, allegory about life in modern (1860s) Great Britain, biting commentary on the British Monarchy, the British Parliament, and current social norms. It is a book about the confusing, complicated world of adults and the simpler, more just, and entirely more proper world of children.

"Alice's Adventures in Wonderland" works at several levels. It is the story of a girl's triumph over confusion, it is a primer on growth from childhood through puberty and to adulthood, and it is Carroll's bill of particulars regarding a society he sees as depraved.

PHD MATHEMATICS IN A CHILDREN'S BOOK

Most of the book makes sense, though only after deliberate thought. Advanced degrees in mathematics, British history, and social anthropology may be required to fully appreciate Carroll's work. Let us consider as an example Alice's apparently nonsense multiplications:

$4 \times 5 = 12$

$4 \times 6 = 13$

$4 \times 7 = (14?)$

We don't know what the third product was going to be, since Alice didn't finish the thought, but it seems likely that the next number in the series 12, 13 would be 14. Recall that Lewis Carroll (given name Charles Lutwidge Dodgson) was a mathematician. All three of the multiplications above are correct, but the bases are different than the base ten system we are most familiar with.   Four   times   five   gives   this   many   items:

IIIII IIIII IIIII IIIII

In base eighteen, we must lump the first, second, and third piles of five and the first three sticks of the last pile into a single pile of ten with two left over:

IIIII IIIII IIIII III +   II   = 12

10 (base 18) +   2 (base 18) = 12 (base 18)

In the same manner, four times six in base twenty-one is equal to thirteen:

IIIII IIIII IIIII IIIII I + III   = 13

10 (base 21) +   3 (base 21) = 13 (base 21)

As for the final calculation, it seems likely that the next base in the series 18, 21 would be 24, and in base twenty-four, four times seven is indeed fourteen.

Even at this level, the imagery world of Alice's Adventures applies perfectly to LOST. Mysterious properties of numbers were a relentless theme throughout the show. Until only a few episodes from the end the numbers were as baffling as they had been from the crash of Flight 815. Yet, just as in Alice's experience in Wonderland, the numbers contained an inner consistency bearing significance to all the characters.

POLITICS AND PROGRESS

What about the other apparently nonsensical elements of the story? We will consider one more example before moving on. Anyone who has participated in a political caucus can appreciate Chapter Three of Alice's Adventures. The Dodo proposed that the animals dry off by participating in a caucus race, and off they went, chasing each other around and around. Discussions at political caucuses are the worst kind of endlessly circular arguments. No one is ever shy about supporting her particular faction. Everyone has a favourite position or candidate, and they're ready to tell you why, with excitement and conviction, even at two o'clock in the morning. Participants think themselves the party elite, the movers and shakers whose diligence and zeal will mold the platform into a document representing eternal truths equal in stature with the Magna Charta, more relevant than the Charter of Rights and Freedoms. That's what you think going in, anyway. What do you think after the ordeal is over? The political caucus is pretty much as Carroll described it: a bunch of zoo animals running around in endless circles.

We saw many examples in LOST of frenetic activity that seemed to have no purpose of any kind. Workers at the Pearl Station filled tens of thousands of notebooks with detailed commentary on events at the Swan, the Flame, and other Dharma stations, only to have their work carried by pneumatic tube to a dump in the middle of the Island. No one ever read any of the voluminous notes they had taken over so many years. Diligence and dedication to task were as useless as arguments at a caucus.

"Rabbit" by Airridi
2006 WMC PD

"Alice's Adventures in Wonderland" chronicles Alice's intellectual growth from childhood into adulthood. Most of what she experienced in Wonderland was not nonsense, but events that required a very adult, sometimes illogical but usually coherent, interpretation. Some of her experiences were indeed nonsense, and by the end of the novella she was able to separate meaning from truly random nonsense. She did not embark on the journey alone. She followed the lead of the white rabbit, who represented adult authority. The Queen of Hearts represented adult leadership gone awry, and the King represented forces of culture and propriety opposed to the Queen's selfishness.

For the purposes of LOST, it is important to remember that the White Rabbit of Alice in Wonderland was an experienced guide, an adult, and an authoritative leader. In LOST, Jack Shephard could be thought of as representing Alice, Christian Shephard as the White Rabbit, and the Smoke Monster as the Queen of Hearts.

In the Season One episode "White Rabbit," Jack has what he later interprets as hallucinations of his father. He sees his father in the waves just off the shore, standing without movement, dressed in a perfectly-tailored black suit. A few minutes later he sees his father again, motionless at the edge of the jungle. Jack abandons his discussion with Boone and runs toward the man in the black suit. Jack becomes obsessed, oblivious to his surroundings, and stumbles off a cliff, grabbing a bush to prevent his fall into the gorge below. Locke appears above Jack and pulls him up. The dialogue that ensues is the most quoted conversation of the twenty-first century.

THE FOUR DISCOVERIES

45.01 JACK: How are they, the others?
45.02 LOCKE: Thirsty. Hungry. Waiting to be rescued. And they need someone to tell them what to do.
45.03 JACK: Me? I can't.
45.04 LOCKE: Why can't you?

45.05 JACK: Because I'm not a leader.

45.06 LOCKE: And yet they all treat you like one.

45.07 JACK: I don't know how to help them. I'll fail. I don't have what it takes.

45.08 LOCKE: Why are you out here, Jack?

45.09 JACK: I think I'm going crazy.

45.10 LOCKE: No. You're not going crazy.

....

45.13 JACK: I'm chasing something—someone.

45.14 LOCKE: Ah. The white rabbit. Alice in Wonderland.

45.15 JACK: Yeah, wonderland, because who I'm chasing—he's not there.

45.16 LOCKE: But you see him?

45.17 JACK: Yes. But he's not there.

45.18 LOCKE:... then what would your explanation be, as a doctor?

45.19 JACK: I'd call it a hallucination....

45.20 LOCKE: All right, then. You're hallucinating. But what if you're not?

45.21 JACK: Then we're all in a lot of trouble.

45.22 LOCKE: I'm an ordinary man, Jack, meat and potatoes, I live in the real world. I'm not a big believer in magic. ***But this place is different. Special.*** The others don't want to talk about it because it scares them. But we all know it. We all feel it. Is your white rabbit a hallucination? Probably. But what if everything that happened here, happened for a reason? What if this person that you're chasing is really here?

45.23 JACK: That's impossible.

45.24 LOCKE: Even if it is, let's say it's not.

45.25 JACK: Then what happens when I catch him?

45.26 LOCKE: I don't know. But I've looked into the eye of this island. And what I saw was beautiful.

[Locke gets up to leave.]

45.27 JACK: Wait, wait, wait, where are you going?

45.28 LOCKE: To find some more water.

45.29 JACK: I'll come with you.

45.30 LOCKE: No. You need to finish what you've started.

45.31 JACK: Why?

45.32 LOCKE: Because a leader can't lead until he knows where he's going.

Water has already been a recurring theme in the first three acts of the episode; the survivors have nearly exhausted the Oceanic bottled water, and Claire may be suffering heat exhaustion. Just to be sure we understand the significance, Locke mentions water at the beginning of their conversation and also at the end. Coupled with the water motif is the theme of leadership. At 45.02, Locke tells Jack, "... they need someone to tell them what to do" and at 45.32, "... a leader can't lead until he knows where he's going." But these two themes are not the only ones repeated in the course of this brief discussion.

If you read the scene a few times some interesting patterns begin to appear. First they are discussing water and leadership, then the White Rabbit, then Locke steps out of the normal flow of conversation and makes an important statement that appears at first unrelated to the concrete issues of water, leadership, and Jack's fatigue-induced hallucination of his dead father. Then they resume their discussion about the "hallucinations," but the character of the discussion has changed, and finally they speak again of water and leadership. In the list below, "J" means Jack and "L" means Locke.

A	45.01	Water and Leadership. J: I'm no leader.
B	45.08a	L changes subject: Why are you here, J?
C	45.08b	J says he's crazy. L says Jack not crazy.
D	45.13a	J chases the White Rabbit.
E	45.13b	It's Wonderland—the chase has no reason,
F	45.17	The Rabbit is not real.
G	45.19	J says the Rabbit is an hallucination.
H	45.22a	The Island is not magic, it is real.
I	**45.22b**	**This Island is different. Special.**
H'	45.22c	The Island is not scary, but real (we all feel it).
G'	45.22d	L says Rabbit is probably hallucination.
F'	45.22e	What if the Rabbit is real?
E'	45.22e	It's the Island—the chase has a reason.
D'	45.22e	L says Jack's chasing the Rabbit.
C'	45.23	J says Rabbit not possible. L says it is.
B'	45.26	L changes the subject: The Island is beautiful.
A'	45.27	Water, Leadership. L says J not (yet) a leader.

This is a literary structure called a chiasm. Every statement in the passage is oriented around a chiastic centre at 45.22b. The entire scene is essentially an onion with nine layers. Statement A is the outside of the onion, the next layer is Statement B, and so on all the way to Statement I, which is the core of the onion. With Statement H' we move from the core to the next layer out, then to G', and so on all the way back to the outside of the onion at A'. The supporting statements flanking the centre mirror each other, so that Statement A mirrors Statement A', Statement B mirrors Statement B', and so on. Everything in the sequence points to the core statement, or thesis, and everything within the chiasm relates thematically to that core.

Because the structure is chiastic, we are able to draw certain conclusions, at least from a literary point of view. We are to understand, as we bore our way through the layers, that the topics invoked are intimately related to the core concept. Here the concept is the Island as a different, special place which is the ultimate arbiter of reason. The Island imbues all motifs in the chiasm with inherent rationale and deep purpose. Water is not the only thing that flows from (or actually because of) the very Source of the Island. The Island establishes leadership, reality, and beauty. Because the Island is, Christian Shephard is. Jack's vision is no hallucination.

Jack initiates the conversation at the beginning of the scene. It's clear to Locke that Jack is distraught, so he takes control of their dialogue by changing the subject, trying to get Jack to focus. But Jack is not ready to relinquish control, he's trying hard to centre the dialogue on the scientific rationale for his vision, and it's not working. He concentrates on his feeling of being crazy, of having experienced hallucinations. For the sake of Jack's argument, Locke is willing to grant that Jack is suffering hallucinations, but he doesn't believe it. Now that Locke understands the real issue, he drives home his response, and this time he wrests control of the conversation and never again surrenders to Jack.

Locke's point (thesis at 45.22b) is that the Island is special. The significance for Jack is simple: The Island has direct bearing on everything Jack seeks. When Jack continues to insist that the Rabbit cannot possibly be real, Locke again refocusses (45.26) on what he knows to be obvious: "I've looked into the eye of this island. And what I saw was beautiful." It is the beauty of the Island that will resolve all the water and leadership issues. It is the deep reality, harmony, and special nature of the Island that means all events transpiring there, even Jack's visions, are real. The White Rabbit is real, and it is directly related to the Island.

The above analysis was performed from a literary point of view, not from the standpoint of mythology. Although the analysis is valid, since it stands on well-accepted literary conventions, it cannot be understood as supporting any particular mythological interpretation. Mythologically we may say that Christian represented reconciliation (Jack's dead father), antagonism (the Monster), or an independent agenda (the Island), though any such mythological assignment could not be drawn uniquely from the literary analysis of Locke and Jack's discussion of the white rabbit.

THE FIRST DISCOVERY: JACK'S STATUS AS FOLLOWER

First he chased the White Rabbit, then he was beaten down twice in the same discussion by a man who had no understanding of science. In fact, Locke rejected every plausible scientific explanation Jack attempted. As if this weren't enough, Locke told Jack at the end of their conversation, "A leader can't lead until he knows where he's going." It was a double slap in the face: Jack didn't know where he was going, and he was no leader.

THE SECOND DISCOVERY: FAITH

In John Locke, Jack discovered an adversary who challenged Jack to his very core. Jack had squirreled away nothing in his personal or professional repertoire that allowed him to comprehend a faith-based approach to life. This conversation marked the introduction of the great struggle between science and faith. Locke gained the upper hand almost immediately. It would be nearly three years before Jack finally came to terms with Locke's wisdom. At this point in his journey, however, every word out of Locke's mouth seemed nonsense.

From Locke's standpoint, the most important truth for Jack was that his vision of the White Rabbit was real. Because it occurred on the Island, and because everything on the Island happened for a reason, the White Rabbit had to be real. It was more connected to Jack, more connected to the Island, and had greater purpose for Jack than anything he had previously experienced.

The concept of faith in LOST is not tied to traditional religion. By the end of the series LOST made entirely unique statements about faith, but in this first discussion only the mystery of the Island was invoked. In this early phase of Jack's journey and Christian's revelation of Island secrets, it was sufficient to say that Locke had faith in the power of the Island.

Symbolically, by having Locke pull Jack up from a certain fall and possible death, Jack was shown to be saved by faith, even if he rejected every aspect of Locke's faith-inspired vision of life and the Island.

THE THIRD DISCOVERY: WATER

LOST frequently invoked imagery from multiple, sometimes contradictory sources in a single scene. In the episode we are analysing, 1.05, Christian Shephard could be considered a representation of the White Rabbit, but another equally strong allusion could be posited. The name "Christian Shephard" evokes strong religious connections. The connections seemed particularly appropriate in light of the final scenes occurring subsequent to Jack and Locke's meeting.

Water was in short supply, and helping Jack find it was Christian Shephard's first order of business. Since it was at the top of Christian's agenda, it was the first thing Jack discovered after his talk with Locke. It was not until near the end of Season Six that we learned about the "special" aspects of Island water, but we knew there was some type of spiritual connection due to the nature of Christian Shephard.

Psalm 23
The Lord is my Shepherd; I shall not want.
He maketh me to lie down in green pastures:
He leadeth me beside the still waters.

Christian led Jack to waters, but they were not still. The agitated pool was a physical reflection of Jack's turbulent emotional state. His confusion only increased as the scene progressed.

Christian was Jack's guide, and he led his son directly to water. He was acting in his capacity as the Good Shepherd, who leads and cares for his flock. I don't believe LOST intends that we understand Christian Shephard to be the full embodiment of Jesus of Nazareth. In fact, I don't believe Christian is intended to represent a pastor in the traditional religious sense. I understand Christian to be a spiritual guide, and in fact, the supreme spiritual leader to everyone on the Island, but he represents no religious faction.

THE FOURTH DISCOVERY: THE EMPTY TOMB

Jack had no intellectual or emotional tools to deal with the airplane wreckage in front of his eyes, and still less to understand the significance of the wooden coffin so haphazardly placed amid the strewn wreckage. When he opened the casket and found it empty, the bewildering, frustrating, angst-ridden nonsense of the Island finally bested him. Jack busted that coffin into a hundred pieces. None of it made any sense, least of all the empty casket. Was this an hallucination, too, or did the empty tomb prove Locke correct?

During Season One I didn't know what to make of the empty coffin. I understood the strong religious symbolism of both the empty tomb and Christian's name, but with so many connections between characters, with no clear vision of where the story was going, I was hesitant to construct any frameworks involving Christian Shephard. Events beginning in Season Four gave me enough confidence to state early in Season Six that we would see the coffin again, and it would be empty.

I will have much more to say about Christian Shephard later in this book. It is my intention to deliver a mythology-based explanation of his activity on the Island, from Episode 1.04 through the final scene in the church pews. For now it is enough to say that Christian Shephard is probably the most enigmatic figure in LOST. He stands as an unparalleled exemplar of the idea that we will have to apply many types of analysis and invoke multiple literary allusions and forms to fully plumb the rich depths of this fascinating series.

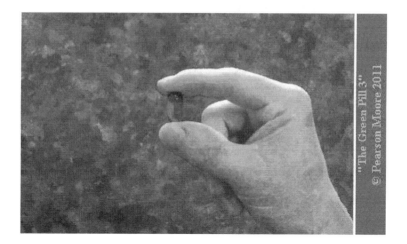

"The Green Pill 3"
© Pearson Moore 2011

We have no choices.

Morpheus offers us neither red pill nor blue pill. The range of human volition includes provision for neither deliberate amnesia nor grudging awareness. Enlightenment is not choice, but responsibility, and amnesia is not comfort in innocence, but oblivion in non-existence.

According to LOST, we have only the green pill.

We live and move and have our being in a world with firm foundation in rules known to all. LOST's premise is a monopole; the series is without choices, without dilemma, without unified conflict—even the antagonist has no name. Far from positing the vast, intricate, computer-generated, consciousness-bending false comic-book reality of the Matrix, LOST forces us to confront our world as a complexity beyond logic and cognition. Our daily reality is the chaos of the wreckage-strewn beach which we walk aimlessly, our muddled thoughts ruled by confusion, pain, and anxiety.

Lost is not drama, not science fiction, but a fresh genre, unique to fiction. LOST has a protagonist, Jack Shephard. But the antagonist is a nameless, formless black void that comes, fights, destroys, corrupts. Lost is not drama, but metadrama, for we are the story, and we know the antagonist, who bears seven billion names, who reads the words on this page in this instant. The antagonist is the Smoke Monster. We know this because we have met the Smoke Monster, and the Smoke Monster is us.

How deep does the rabbit hole go? There is no Matrix, no Wonderland. But the rabbit hole goes deep. The voyage is long, for the journey ends at the central core of our humanity, at the Source. There, bathed in brilliant light, stands Jack Shephard, bearing in his hand the single object of our contemplation: the green pill.

The plane crash was the enemy. In its aftermath three hundred passengers died and the survivors were dazed, confused, injured, and angry. However, we soon learned our initial judgment was flawed. As wounds healed and water became scarce, thirst for answers became the driving force. The survivors were not only hungry and without shelter, they were being watched, then hunted and killed. The plane crash was not the enemy. The Others were the enemy.

The Others moved in stealth, covered their tracks, lied, cheated, stole, and killed. Their leader, Benjamin Linus, was single-minded in thought and deed. His brilliant deceptions and manipulations seemed the embodiment of evil. But when the freighter arrived, we discovered the rationale for his madness and lies. Events showed us again we had been hasty in our judgment. The Others were not the enemy. Charles Widmore and Martin Keamy were the enemy.

Widmore, like Alvar Hanso's Dharma Initiative, wished to control the Island. Locke put his faith in that control, carved "In Marvin Candle We Trust" into the hilt of his Ka-bar and religiously pressed Execute every 108 minutes. But then at the Pearl he learned the Swan was a psychology experiment. Blind faith, Locke decided, was the enemy. He smashed the countdown computer and—all hell broke loose. Anger and pride clouded his thinking, caused him to confuse trust and control. Faith was not the enemy. Greed, selfishness, lust for power was the enemy.

Whoever was most greedy, we realised, would have to be the enemy. That person was identified at the end of Season Five.

JACOB: I take it you're here 'cause of the ship.
MAN IN BLACK: I am. How did they find the Island?
JACOB: You'll have to ask 'em when they get here.
MAN IN BLACK: [Grimacing] I don't have to ask. You brought them here.

Jacob. Jacob summoned the ships, the planes, the boats. Jacob enticed Magnus Hanso and Seth Norris, caused the deaths on the Black Rock, on Oceanic Flight 815, caused the dozens or hundreds of airliner crashes and shipwrecks over the millennia. Jacob, Protector of the Island, murderer of thousands. Jacob was the enemy.

But then we learned the Man in Black was Nemesis, opposed to Jacob, but no hero or even advocate for the Common Good; in fact, he hated humanity. He was the Smoke Monster. Not a guardian, not the Island's Cerberus-like "security system" as the Dharma Initiative believed. The Man in Black was, in Temple Master Dogen's words, "evil incarnate." The Man in Black was the enemy.

Jacob's brother, until he murdered the Protector, was a man of mundane self-interest, a creature of ordinary evils. But then Jacob beat him, kicked him, dragged him to the Island's great Basic Input/Output System. The BIOS will return only what it is given. If the Source is fed the raw precepts of civilisation (for example, the principles carved into the Cork Stone), it will intensify those tenets and return them as the Light of civility, social cohesion, and human kindness. If the Source is fed a man interested only in self, it will intensify those tendencies, spitting out an entity capable of pursuing only greeds and lusts, the formless black void of pure selfishness: the Smoke Monster.

WE COME. WE FIGHT. WE DESTROY. WE CORRUPT.

SAWYER: Tell me something, Jacob. Why do I gotta be punished for your mistake? What made you think you could mess with my life? I was doin' just fine 'til you dragged my ass to this damn rock.
JACOB: No, you weren't. None of you were. I didn't pluck any of you out of a happy existence. You were all flawed. I chose you because you were like me.

Indeed. All four of the final Candidates were just like Jacob. Flawed, damaged, hurt, capable of infinite selflessness, but capable also of unrelenting evil. In that respect not one of us reading is in any way different from the five gathered at the Candidates' final fire. We all have the potential, with Jacob, to wish on our brother an outcome worse than death. Which of us, if fed into the Island's BIOS, would come out as pure as Jack Shephard? Most of us—maybe all of us—would rush out of the deep cave as a shapeless dark void. Even a man who is pure of heart and says his prayers by night... all of us at one time or another, and most of us on a daily basis, place selfish caprice and desire over the basic needs of others. Every day we do our best to chip away at the foundations of civilisation. Every day we become the Smoke Monster. Every day we unleash on this world, in ways small and large, in thoughtlessness and cruelty, the full chaos of our unmeasured lusts.

Chaos is the antagonist, and we are the creators of its confusing and ill effects. Chaos has no linear etiology, no clear chronology, else we could approach the problem as an exercise in scientific empiricism. The pharmaceutical companies engaging me as consultant could simply send me to the laboratory to whip up an anti-chaos pill, and all the world's problems would disappear.

In proclaiming our shared identity as the Smoke Monster I bring nothing new to the discussion. The idea that individual evil characters can participate in a story that is allegory for human beings' inhumanity to human beings is not new to literature. In the introduction to this essay, however, I made a statement, as yet unsupported, that LOST constitutes an entirely new genre of fiction. This is a bold claim, certainly novel; even the unabridged Oxford Dictionary carries no entry for "metadrama."

Polar bears on a tropical island. A statue with four, not five, toes. Following a precise and undeviating northerly bearing leads a boat north, then west, and finally south. A ship doctor's dead corpse washes up on shore just as a group on the beach radios the ship, only to learn the good doctor is alive and well, and standing scant metres away from the ship's communications officer. A dark-haired man standing under the awning of a military tent in 1954 is not a day older when he is next seen in 2004. A rocket payload, traveling fifty kilometres per minute, shot from a boat fifty kilometres away, requires two hours to reach its target. A twenty-minute helicopter ride takes thirty-six hours. With the turn of a wooden wheel hundreds of metres below the jungle, John Locke instantly travels eighteen thousand kilometres and wakes up not in the jungle, but in the Tunisian desert, three years in the future, but not more than a blink of the eye later.

The situations and events followed neither rhyme nor reason. If there was logic to the laws governing the Island, it obeyed no syllogism that science or mathematics could divine.

The physical disorientations forced on the survivors of Flight 815, mind-bending and nose-bleed-inducing as they were, nevertheless paled in significance and impact when compared to the conceptual disorientations the newest inhabitants of Mittelos were forced to confront.

The weirdness of the Island, combined with the mindless violence of life on Mittelos, was too much for some. Rose and Bernard could not move past the ear-blasting disorientation of time travel through a purple sky. "Well, we built this place in '75... and then the sky lit up again. So God only knows when the hell we are now," Rose told Desmond. She didn't know which year a current calendar would proclaim, she didn't understand where the Island was, and she was in no position to predict anything that might occur in Jack's strange jungle world. But none of that mattered to her. Rose and Bernard, each handed a Number Two lead pencil and an official MIGSAT test (Mittelos Island Governance Scholastic Achievement Test), decided to skip the examination. They turned off, tuned out, and dropped out. Theirs was not a bad choice per se, but their action was tangential to the trajectory required of anyone seeking influence on Island events. The intention was not to provide a foundation for choice or a paradise for those too numbed by reality to continue an examined and thoughtful existence. Rather, the intention was to destroy the foundations of knowledge, understanding, belief—eventually thought itself—so as to render the would-be players in the drama susceptible and amenable to a new way of thinking.

LA VIE EN ROSE

Most of us engage superficially. Even if we are called upon to overcome adversity, requiring more than a typical level of collaboration, we nevertheless extend ourselves only to the degree that we are allowed to survive and make a minimal commitment. The life of singer Édith Piaf, portrayed by French actress Marion Cotillard, depicts one woman's struggle to make enough sense of her world to bring us a disciplined and compelling voice and songs expressive of the human heart. Out of her fractured and painful life came great music, great beauty, and an enduring contribution to the arts.

But Piaf was a helpless object of others' pity. She was blown about by chaotic circumstance and the whims of caring saviours and uncaring contemporaries, somehow managing in this purposeless milieu to train her natural talents into performances of hypnotic grace. But at the end of her life, the best she could say of herself was to repeat the refrain from her most famous song: Je ne regrette rien. I don't regret anything.

This is not enough for LOST. Overcoming adversity does not suffice. Indulging beauty, celebrating beauty, even creating beauty, is not enough. LOST finds no merit in Helen of Troy, as beautiful as she is.

Kate Austen certainly had beauty to launch a thousand ships, but she was not called to flaunt perfect smile, golden body, or attractive spirit. Her innate charm and grace were as useless to her as Jack's ability with a scalpel or Bernard's familiarity with a dental drill. The Island required not that Kate be something, but that she become something. She could be the Mona Lisa or Monica Callis or axe-wielding Lizzie Borden for all the Island cared. For the purposes of Mittelos, she had to move beyond her narrow understanding of life into a realm that would allow her to help the other survivors and bring enduring benefit to the Island. Kate Austen had to become not Helen of Troy, but Joan of Arc.

THE VISION OF JOAN OF ARC

"Jeanne d'Arc Au Sacre Du Roi Charles VII" Jean Auguste Dominique Ingres 1851 PD

Joan of Arc had to let go of childish notions of leading an ordinary life. Her destiny was to take charge of armies and lead a country to freedom. This was no small matter in the history of France, and it was no trifle to the young woman's turbulent and troubled soul. She faced doubts, distress, and demons every day, for long months and years. She defied generals and princes and kings. The psychological and spiritual confusion nearly killed her, and to any of her contemporaries she must have seemed given to madness, a hair's breadth removed from complete insanity. Such is the state of mind required of those who move mountains, who conquer nations, who save an Island.

Kate had to be broken down, her former self destroyed, before she could become the woman destined to save her jungle land. The pain and confusion she experienced off the Island was the necessary extension of the physical and mental disorientation begun on Mittelos. This was the expectation of all the Island's leaders. Jin had to move beyond jealousy and chauvinist expectations to the full appreciation of Sun's worth as a person and a wife. Sawyer had to grow from his self-centred "lookin' out for Number One" view of life to become the leader of his people during the Dharma Initiative's final pre-Incident years. Locke had to move beyond anger and frustration to acceptance of the Island's role for him, even to the point of accepting the painful inevitability of his own demise off-Island.

Jack Shephard's journey was the most perilous because it carried greatest importance to the Island. His story was chronicled more fully than that of any of the other survivors. I devoted a full 5700-word essay to Jack's story, but I have only begun to relate the significance of Jack's voyage from science to faith to Protector of the Island. He was one of the most fully-developed and multi-dimensional figures in fiction, and LOST is not understood without careful consideration of at least several of the deep facets of his well-mapped character.

Most important to LOST, and essential to this chapter on metadrama, is the reality of Jack's identity as fictional embodiment of Campbell's monomyth of the hero:

"A hero ventures forth from the world of common day into a region of supernatural wonder. Fabulous forces are there encountered and a decisive victory is won. The hero comes back from this mysterious adventure with the power to bestow boons on his fellow man." (Joseph Campbell, "The Hero With a Thousand Faces")

Kate, Locke, and Jack had to be destroyed and re-built. They had to come to the realisation that their knowledge and almost everything they believed they understood of life was incorrect, impractical, irrelevant to the Island. They were obliged, for the fulfillment of their destiny and for the welfare of Mittelos, to embark on the emotional and spiritual travails of a dangerous and soul-wrenching journey over continents and across decades. Their minds scrambled, their souls in despair, they would become the fertile and receptive vessels for a most precious vision: a vision of life as it was intended to be, a vision of the Light. Armed with a true understanding of life, carrying in their hearts a new-found vision of the Heart of the Island--the core of human civilisation--they would take charge of armies, defy a dark prince, and preserve the fragile heritage of our humanity.

THE REVERSALS OF LOST

In 2004 Jack was so faith-deficient he based his entire life on principles and logic that had no bearing on Island reality. After Locke threw the knife that killed Naomi Dorrit, Jack lost whatever calm façade he had been able to project to that point.

LOCKE: You're not gonna shoot me, Jack. Any more than I was gonna shoot—
[Jack pulls the trigger, but no bullet fires]
LOCKE: It's not loaded.
[Jack attacks Locke. Sawyer and Sayid pull him away]
SAWYER: Come on.
JACK: Let go of me! Do you know what he did?
SAYID: (Shouts) Yes, I know what he did!
[Locke gets up]
LOCKE: All I did, all I have ever done, has been in the best interest of all of us.
JACK: Are you insane?
LOCKE: I know I have a lot of explaining to do. But, I never did anything to hurt any of you. I even risked my life to tell you there was a traitor in your midst. (He points to Juliet).
JACK: She helped us, John. All you ever did was blow up every chance we had of getting off of this island. You killed Naomi.

Jack's life experiences, as broad and useful as they were in the outside world, did not equip him to understand the correctness of Locke's actions. To logical, law-abiding Jack Shephard, Locke's expert use of the throwing knife as deadly weapon was illegal, illogical, and insane. Three years later, every breath Jack pulled into his lungs, every step he took on jungle path, was informed by faith, trust, and hope. He not only understood the meaning and merit of all of Locke's actions, he knew them, felt them in his bones, consciously and unconsciously considered them worthy template for anything he might think, say, or do. Jack's reversal, from considering Locke a madman to revering him as mentor, was one of the major inversions in LOST. There were many such reversals. Possibly the saddest inversion was the one we experienced at the end of "The Life and Death of Jeremy Bentham." Locke, at the end of his life, had lost enough faith that he planned his own death. Jack became Locke. Locke became Jack.

But LOST depicted other, even more important reversals. One of the unique twists LOST brings to Joseph Campbell's template of the hero is the reversal of common and supernatural elements. Jack's destiny was not to bring Island knowledge or abilities to confront evils in the outside world. Rather, he experienced the greater part of the hero's journey of disorientation in the common, outside world, and carried back with himself to the supernatural Island a firm sense of purpose, a resolute dedication to serve the Island's needs. The corrective actions of the great hero were accomplished not at the hero's common place of origin, but in the realm of the supernatural itself—on the Island. One might consider that this fact did not constitute a reversal at all, though. When, after several years of searching, I abandoned the religious tradition of my youth and became a member of the faith to which I now subscribe, the pastor embraced me and whispered in my ear, "Welcome home." In like manner, we may well consider that Jack's upbringing in the outside world was a mistake of geography, that his true spiritual origin was on the Island. Campetin, Administrator at SL-Lost, made this statement with greater eloquence than my muddled thoughts can form into words ("Lost Season Five Official Trailer #1," available at YouTube).

REALITY ACCORDING TO LOST

Whether we understand Darlton to have accomplished a fresh and interesting examination of the hero monomyth, we are obliged to agree on this point: The Island is the focal point and most intensely real aspect of the series. With Locke, we understand Mittelos as "... different. Special." Perhaps we don't want to talk about it. Perhaps it is too scary. "But we all know it. We all feel it.... everything that happened here, happened for a reason."

The Island, source of phenomena beyond description or understanding, was more real than anything in the outside world. Jack's Island was metaphor and exemplar of our world--as it was and is (under Jacob), and as it could be (under Jack, then Hurley). The Heart of the Island is the repository of the most enduring and meaningful elements of our humanity, summarised in cuneiform script on the Cork Stone. These are the cultural elements of human society worth living for. They are the precepts of civilisation worth dying for. They are the only possible origin of our rebirth.

The Island is our home, for it is the Source. It is the place that most fully and faithfully expresses the widest range of who we are, that allows broadest latitude in culture and substance, that is the reliable and permanent foundation upon which we live and die and experience rebirth.

OUR REBIRTH

Every one of the thirty-five major characters across the six years had to experience life, death, and rebirth. Surgeon Jack died and was reborn as Protector Jack. Fugitive Kate died and was reborn as Dragonslayer Kate. Con-Man Sawyer died and was reborn as Responsible Leader James. They were ordinary, fractured, wounded souls whose essences were ground in a mortar, burned in agonising flame, and redistilled into lives of vital and unrelenting and committed engagement.

I feel a close kinship with the substantial and quite vocal minority of former LOST fans who now express contempt for this most compelling of television dramas. LOST did not end in a manner that anyone could have predicted. The series never engaged in linear, syllogistic, traditional storytelling. Darlton took frequent pains to expand not only the story, but the format in which the story was told. They were visibly and vocally proud of their flashbacks, flashforwards, and flashsideways. Darlton intentionally pushed the envelope in their storytelling. They never appealed to lowest denominators, never explained even the most irrelevant detail of this most complicated of stories. We were left entirely on our own to make sense of their creation. Even now, a year after the series ended, Darlton tell us the story speaks for itself. They are not going to explain it. We are alone, and we always will be left to our own interpretive devices with no help from those who gave birth to the series.

This is the true essence of the problem, I believe—the aspect of LOST that separates those of us who believe the story complete, and those who feel The End was a touchy-feely mess that left the greatest mysteries unresolved. For those who believe, "The New Man in Charge" is a pleasant but unnecessary epilogue. For those who lack faith, not even "The New Man in Charge" can begin to assuage their disgust. What we enjoy, those of us who consider the story complete, is full engagement with a very complicated piece of fiction. What we lack, those of us who consider the story incomplete, is a reference point common to ourselves and the story.

Darlton gave birth to LOST. We were never told, but we came to understand over six grueling years, that every one of us participating, the thirty million of us around the world, would be required to act as midwives to LOST's rebirth. In fact, little did we know, we ourselves would have to be reborn. With Kate and Jack and Sayid and Locke and Ben we would have to die to our former selves, embrace the truths of the Island, and understand events from the Island's point of view. With the characters, we would experience pain, confusion, loss, disorientation—whispering "Whiskey Tango Foxtrot" (or variants not appropriate to polite society) under our breath or even lobbing a symbolic tomato at the television—or at Darlton—every now and then.

Midwives we are, though, and ever will be. If we appreciate the story of LOST it is because we ourselves have been reborn. Our struggles and pains and eventual rebirth were not accidental, not unforeseen. They were planned, necessary and integral to the story itself; prerequisite, therefore, to any satisfactory understanding of the story as complete in its final 121-chapter form.

LOST is unencumbered with narrative structure. In fact, it barely has structure, and certainly lacks anything that could be recognised as traditional television storytelling. We, dear participants (and I do mean participants, and not "viewers"), supply the narrative structure. We are the ones who, with Leonard Simms' Connect Four, connect the disparate stories from flashback and the Sideways World and the Dharma Initiative of 1977 and the post-Dharma Island of 2004 into a cohesive whole that comports with our understanding of syllogistic cause and effect. Without this essential input from our overworked minds there is no story, and The End seems a cheat, a cop-out, a short sale that is really a cowardly foreclosure on something that should have had structure and permanence and closure. But thus will it forever be. For those who have faith, no proof is necessary; for those who lack faith, no proof is possible.

To say we believe is simply to acknowledge that we are no longer beholden to logic as final arbiter of significance and value and causal priority. We have perceived something of enduring grace and beauty and wholeness and magnificence. Through our struggles, we have risen to the mountaintop. Our eyes truly have seen the Glory—it matters not whether we are black men or white men, Muslim or Jew, Protestant or Catholic, for we see now the fog-shrouded green expanse before us, the Island that is Source, the destiny that is freedom, the Light that enshrines the content of our shared culture and depth of our character.

EXPOSITION VERSUS DEMONSTRATION

Expository drama is descriptive, matter-of-fact, "spoon-fed" fare. The detective says he's going to speak with the victim's daughter, we witness the interrogation, the detective's partner and her boss look on through the two-way mirror. "I don't believe her," the partner says, pointing to the daughter. "Her story's a little too tight, isn't it?" the boss says. We know what the partner and the boss are thinking, because they tell us. The story is spoon fed to us. We don't need to think about what is transpiring. All we need is an ear to hear, sometimes an eye to see. The descriptive cues are usually audible, and more often than not, verbal. There were very few instances of expository drama in LOST. One memorable occurrence was Michael's appearance to Hurley near the end of Season Six.

[Michael steps out of the jungle.]
HURLEY: You're stuck on the Island aren't you?
MICHAEL: [nodding] 'Cause of what I did.
HURLEY: And...there're others out here like you, aren't there? That's what the whispers are?
MICHAEL: Yeah. We're the ones who can't move on.

We do not have to think about Michael's words or their significance. He told us the significance; the entire short dialogue is expository. As is the case for much of expository work in film, we can close our eyes through the whole scene and miss none of the information; everything we need to know is contained in the dialogue.

The writing style I am employing in this section is expository. I am relaying in a matter-of-fact way a description of a couple of ideas useful to the better understanding of metadrama. Exposition need not be dry writing, but it is often perceived in this way. This is fine, though, since the objective is not necessarily entertainment, but the cold, accurate communication of factual information.

The tenor of this section is quite different from the flavour of previous sections in this chapter. Most of the time I style my prose in the manner of an essay, and you have the vague but accurate sense that I write not from a position of authority, but from the point of view of opinion. I use metaphorical language or I write in symbolic terms. For instance, I have invoked the symbol of the green pill as a stand-in for the notion of metadrama. But in this section, I am staying clear of metaphor and relying on description alone. Just the facts.

Demonstrative drama is not descriptive. The writer or director shows you what is transpiring; it is up to you to decide the significance of the event, what it means to the characters, how they feel about it, and so on. Locke is moving through the nighttime jungle, torch before him, but his face is downcast, his brow wrinkled in a frown, his legs moving sluggishly, as if pulling a great weight. He stops for a moment, lifts his eyes to the starry sky, and we see his red eyelids, the tears pooling in his eyes. His eyes move about, as if searching for something. A voice calls out from far away. Locke's eyes open wide and he pivots on his foot, scanning the jungle near and far, making a fast, broad sweep with the torch.

In this scene there is not even a word of dialogue. No one within the scene is telling you what to believe about what you have seen. From previous events, immediate context, and whatever you know of the character's motivations, behaviours, beliefs, and disposition you need to decide for yourself what is going on. The scene is entirely visual, as is the case for many types of demonstrative drama.

Demonstrative writing is the style preferred by most popular fiction authors, and it was the style used almost exclusively in LOST. Even when there was dialogue in a scene it was not the only element containing information. Emotion, voice inflection, the stance of the characters, the background elements of the scene, the context, and many other considerations had to be brought to bear in determining the significance of the interaction. The words themselves were often secondary to the other elements of the scene, and even when the words were important, we had to be on guard at all times to evaluate the trustworthiness of the speaker.

If most popular fiction is about seventy-five percent demonstrative, LOST relies almost exclusively on demonstration in its scenes. Perhaps ninety-five percent of LOST is show, not tell (demonstration, not exposition). This means that LOST requires much more of its viewers than just about any other television drama ever created. In fact, I believe we should consider that LOST constitutes an entirely new type of fiction—something I call metadrama.

Metadrama is not a frequently employed word, though it enjoys occasional use among academics and literati. The word is defined by neither the Canadian Oxford Dictionary (my authority of first resort) nor Webster's Unabridged Dictionary. The English Oxford may well provide a definition, but I am decidedly North American in syntax and orthography and have not consulted this across-the-pond authority.

From the few academic authorities I have become familiar with, I have learned that metadrama can be thought of as describing a play within a play. A frequently invoked example of this type of metadrama is "A Midsummer Night's Dream" by William Shakespeare. But this is not metadrama as I understand the concept to be applied to LOST.

"A Midsummer Night's Dream Act IV Scene I" Henry Fusell 1796 WMC PD

Metadrama as I define it is virtually unique to LOST. No other story or theatrical production of my acquaintance (several hundred classics, modern general fiction, historical fiction, and several hundred more works within the genre of science fiction; scores of plays attended over my lifetime) places such an immense burden on audience or reader. In fact, for most of fiction, those on the receiving end of an author's creative work can be referred to quite accurately as audience or reader or viewer. This designation is not appropriate for those participating in the artistic creation called LOST. If we merely break out the beer and pretzels, plop down on the sofa, and "watch" LOST, we will never make sense of the work. LOST demands our sustained and active engagement. We, the viewing participants, supply the narrative structure.

Without our input, LOST lacks dramatic wholeness. With our active involvement, the piece comes into its own, shining as few other works of fiction ever have. This is my understanding of the new fiction format created by LOST:

Metadrama is that form of nonlinear, theatrical fiction whose narrative or causal structure is evident through neither chronology nor clear etiology, and must be supplied by engaged audience-participants.

In metadrama, the effect of events in Act Three may play out in the first scene of Act One, a flashback in Act Two may contain the full background required to make sense of the first words of the play, and the penultimate scene may have no apparent connection to the final scene, but may be the precursor to events in Act Two. "Rosebud" in Citizen Kane is a weak example of nonlinearity of this type, though Citizen Kane is a story told in mostly linear fashion, and it certainly requires not anything close to the audience engagement demanded by LOST. The events and character arcs and plot are engineered by the audience, who may require several sessions to bring coherence and internal consistency to the structure.

Metadrama does not consist in a single event or significance held until the end of a work to provide the dénouement. It is more akin to a literary treasure hunt. A dying man utters a clue to finding a map, which leads to an idea, the articulation of which uncovers a key, which opens a door to a room containing a symbolic painting that contains several meanings simultaneously, on multiple levels. The Dungeons-and-Dragons-style quest continues, but it finds keys and maps and secret passages behind each of the painting's symbols, all of which are inter-related and whose significances change as we progress through the multi-dimensional maze. We keep our wits about us by supplying the narrative structure that unites the strange, disconnected mess into a cohesive story. We weave histories, motivations, biases, cultures, symbols, religions, myths, literary allusion, and storytelling devices into a vast drama that defies satisfying analysis from any single angle. We adequately describe its significance only by approaching from multiple conceptual levels.

IMMERSION VERSUS PARTICIPATION

Some of you are puzzled by the assertion that LOST's demand that we immerse ourselves in the story indicates a new form of drama. You have read novels or seen movies in which you have felt yourself immersed in the story. You're thinking to yourself that there can be nothing unusual in even a continual sense of attachment to the plotline or characters or the entire world created by the work. I agree. In fact, my primary objective, when I construct a scene, short story, or novel, is to bring the reader into my story. I want her to experience such a level of anxiety about the fate of the characters that she feels compelled to stay with the story until the very last page, preferably without even taking a break between reading sessions.

But the desire to become immersed and the need to become a part of the story are two different states entirely. One can read good fiction without feeling any particular attachment to characters or plot and still come away understanding the story. If this were not true there could be very few passing grades in literature courses. Metadrama, by definition, requires more than immersion; it requires participation. Active involvement is not optional.

Consider for a moment the reactions of bloggers and reviewers after the LOST finale. Reviews were mostly positive, but fifteen or twenty-five percent of reviews were negative, sometimes even bitterly so. The chief complaint seemed to be that the finale did not tie up loose ends. The show introduced plotlines, events, concepts, and situations that demanded resolution, but no explanations were provided. The producers responded that LOST had always been about characters, not about mythology. I find myself in disagreement with the position they took. When I look at LOST as a whole I see few unresolved questions, even among the most esoteric of problems posed by the show. I have spent the last year writing essays addressing the hundreds of questions that have been posed over the years. These essays are not difficult to write; the corpus of LOST resolves almost every question that I have read or heard.

Neither am I unique in believing that LOST fully explained just about every question that has been raised. A quick search for "Lost Questions" on Google will reveal hundreds of bloggers and commentators, well-known and obscure, who have taken on any LOST-related question and found its answer within the 121 broadcast episodes and thirteen mobisodes of the series. My first assignment as a regular weekly contributor at Dark UFO was to address the seven top "unresolved questions" of LOST.

I submit this idea for your consideration: Those who do not believe that all remaining questions posed by LOST were resolved in the finale were not immersed in the series. They approached LOST as they would any other offering on network television. Rather than understanding the commitment and effort required of them, they considered that the level of involvement they found satisfactory for other television series would be adequate to the full comprehension of LOST's final scenes.

There are a handful of questions that resist facile response. Who was the Guardian ("Mother") and how did she affect Jacob and the Man in Black? Who was the Man in Black, and how did he affect the other characters? What was the significance of the Christian Shephard apparitions? We will see that responses to these questions require the kind of close participation I discussed in this chapter. Especially in the case of the nature of the Smoke Monster, important parts of the final answer were sprinkled throughout the six-year run of the series.

THE GREEN PILL

We can choose to engage with the story, or not—accept the green pill, or reject it. If we accept the pill, we provide the narrative structure, we make the connections between disparate events within the six-year series. The only possible causality filter for the events is the one we provide through our own observation and understanding.

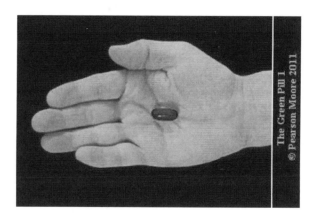

LOST is metadrama not only because it requires disorientation and establishment of a new conceptual order. It is metadrama not only because it requires active audience participation. It is metadrama because it requires both of these commitments simultaneously. LOST provides the minimal structure—the green pill, with its associated Island rules. We provide the remainder, through our focus, willingness to submit to disorientation, and commitment to ferreting out the wonders of its conceptual richness.

THE AUDACITY OF TRUST

Darlton entrusted us with the narrative and the plot. They had their own idea of the way in which the 726 pieces (acts) of this 121-chapter, six-volume masterpiece were to be understood. But we will never be granted the privilege of reading or hearing their own interpretation. These two writers trusted us to create the narrative. Never has a collaboration of this type endured the test of six long years. Never have artists thought so highly, or expected so much, of the participating recipients of their most prized creation. I am humbled, grateful, and very happy indeed, to have been a most active participant in this drama beyond dramas.

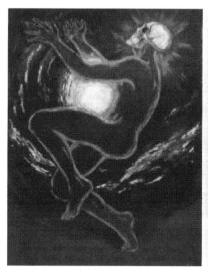

"Chaos" by Hlamo 2005 PD
"One must have chaos inside oneself to give birth to a dancing star."

He always seemed to have a weapon at his side. He wrestled with so many deep, personal issues that his girlfriend abandoned him. He didn't get along well with his father. His group of survivors recognised him as their leader, though in private they expressed uncertainty about his suitability. He had expert technical training and professed a desire to help people, though his efforts seemed primarily oriented toward his own benefit.

If you identified this man as John Locke, you are correct. If, on the other hand, you identified him as Jack Shephard, you are likewise correct.

Personality traits were not the only attributes John Locke and Jack Shephard held in common. They shared a destiny. They seemed to cover the same ground and to pass through the same challenges to their development and understanding. But this was not a matter of accidental similarity of character. They fell into the clutches of a chaotic, unpredictable force that led to the same patterns of thought and behaviour. We commonly refer to this force as "fate" or "destiny," but such a designation is nebulous and incomplete, and does not express the idea I will develop here.

John Locke and Jack Shephard were not only drawn to the Island—they affected each other to the very centre of their beings. In scientific terms we refer to the force determining their future as a Lorenz attractor, or a strange attractor. It is the idea of a multi-faceted attractor that provides the basis for the analysis in this chapter. In considering nine pairs of strange attractors, focussing on the most mythically-charged of LOST's characters, we will come to understand the story of LOST as never before, permitting a fully-reconciled knowledge of characters and plotlines that until now have resisted even the most dedicated of analysts.

RANDOMNESS AND PATTERNS

The spontaneous explosion of dynamite is one of the most random events we've seen in LOST, but we've witnessed it twice. On both occasions the explosion killed only the person handling the dynamite, even though several individuals stood in close proximity to the blast. The victim was an expert, with significant training in explosives. Arzt and Ilana each had been leading a group of survivors toward a particular objective. In both instances the victims seemed to exude only a slight air of cockiness, though one could have interpreted their words and expressions as indications of expertise, not as any sign of arrogance.

The events of course were not random. All of the above similarities between the two situations were necessary, used to achieve a number of storytelling objectives. From an author's point of view, the events had great utility in increasing the danger to the survivors. From the perspective of viewing participants (we—the audience) the explosions served to increase the survivors' reliance on each other, and they also became a sign of the unseen presence of some unifying effect.

The events were recurring. Even though we accept the wisdom of the notion that occurrences such as these should be considered random, we have the feeling that the events were not random at all, but exhibited dependence on recurring conditions. In scientific terms, we would say the occurrences were periodic. Considering the state of dynamite in Jack's pouch or Locke's or Ilana's at any given moment, we predict that the state will not change in Jack's or Locke's backpack, but it has a good chance of changing in Ilana's sack. In fact, we predict that any non-Candidate carrying dynamite and also acting in some role critical to a faction on the Island has a high probability of death by explosive chain reaction.

The events are not random at all. In the midst of unpredictable outcomes, we begin to see patterns emerge. The connection between Arzt and Ilana is feeble. In many cases, though, we are aware of strong connections between major players. Jack and Locke, Jacob and the Man in Black, Hurley and Ben, all seem to be connected in ways that indicate symmetry and similarity, but also opposition and contrast. "They are polar opposites," we say, but we are uncomfortably aware of strong characteristics which these black-and-white pairings share in common. All of these are indicative of a phenomenon known in science as strange attraction. The concept sounds anything but scientific. I suppose the idea may appear to be something out of a kinky erotic romance novel, but I assure you, the thought is entirely scientific. Strange attractors have become the basis for deconvolution (explanation) of all manner of chaotic activity: the growth of leaves and crystals, the development of weather patterns, the changing gravitational forces in the solar system, even sociological forces at play in an angry crowd. We are going to use the concept to explore nine critical mythic pairings in LOST.

PERIODICITY

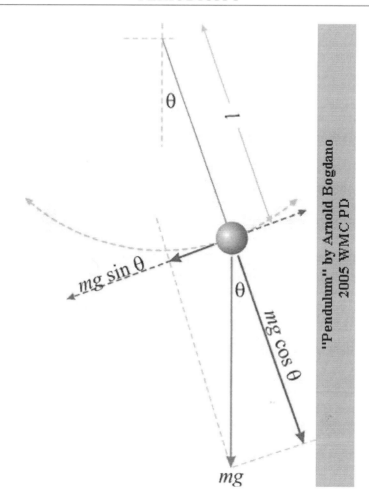

There's nothing new under the sun. The more things change, the more they stay the same. Those who do not study history will invariably repeat the mistakes of the past.

The periodicity of existence can be difficult to understand. When we were children, our parents told us not to touch the hot burner on the stove or we would get burned. We went ahead and did it anyway, and we suffered the inevitable consequences. In the same way, if a mother's child is violently taken from her on a mysterious island, she's going to behave in a certain extreme but imminently predictable manner. But other examples of periodicity may resist cursory analysis. In the course of this article we will discover a number of superficially unrelated or random events that are in fact tied to each other. A study of periodicity and strange-attractor chaos will allow us to make these connections.

Periodicity is the idea that there are certain rhythms in nature, and that outcomes tied to these rhythms are both repeating and predictable. Dmitri Mendeleev's periodic table of the chemical elements is probably the most widely-known example of natural periodicity, but the idea is much easier to understand, and applies even to simple motions, such as the repeating movement of a clock pendulum.

In the context of LOST we might refer to periodicity in literary terms: recurring motif, common theme, and so on. However, these ideas are broader than that of periodicity, they focus on the principle of a unifying event, and they do not take into account the recurrence of conditions or events alongside the unifying element. It is the strong connection between periodic elements of an episode and the recurring conditions present at the time of the event that we will examine in this section. To make the most of this discussion we are going to begin with a short, non-technical examination of some of the concepts.

THE PENDULUM

A periodic event does not occur in random fashion. The event recurs because it experiences an outside force. In the case of a pendulum clock, the periodic motion is initiated by pulling the pendulum up and away from its equilibrium position and then releasing. Gravity acts on the weight at the lower end of the stick or string, pulling the weight back toward the ground. Since the other end of the stick is free to move in a sideways direction, the pendulum continues traveling up and away from the ground until the force of gravity overcomes the diminishing forward momentum, and the pendulum falls back over the same path it cut moving forward. The back-and-forth motion repeats endlessly, or until friction stops the pendulum.

Periodic Motion in a Pendulum

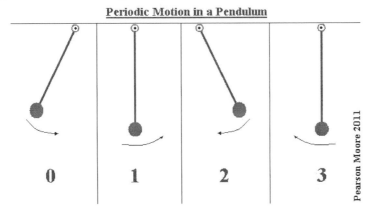

Pearson Moore 2011

The motion of the pendulum can be represented in any way that suits the observer. Imagine the speed of the pendulum as it proceeds through its flight path. When I set the pendulum in motion it is moving slowly. But as it approaches the lowest point in its trajectory it speeds up. Moving past the low point and toward the high point it slows down. When it finally reaches the high point of its path, gravity cancels the effect of momentum and forward movement stops. However, gravity continues to act on the pendulum, and now it reverses course, first slowly and progressively more quickly toward the low point, where it again achieves maximum speed. If we plot a graph of pendulum speed versus time, this is what we get:

You may wonder how this simple motion is relevant to the very complex interactions on the Island. This is a valid concern, and I believe I can demonstrate the connection by adding a simple complication to the pendulum system.

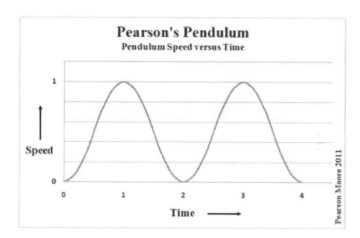

Let us imagine we have set up an experiment using two pendula. The first pendulum is started at Time Zero and the second pendulum is started at Time One. If we again draw a graph of speed versus time, this is the chart we obtain:

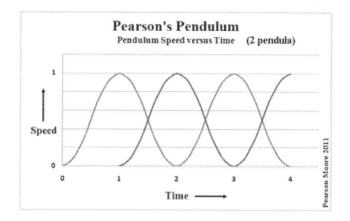

We're doing this work for our boss, but she's a busy woman and doesn't have time to figure out every detail of the graph. She instructs us to deliver a graph showing a single line: combined pendulum speed versus time. For every

195

time point in the graph we have to add the speed of Pendulum One to the speed of Pendulum Two.

For the first time interval, from Time Zero to Time One, only one pendulum is in play, so our graph of combined speed looks exactly the same as the one above, at least until we arrive at the first time point. At Time One the first pendulum has reached the maximum speed of one, but the second pendulum is at speed zero: $1 + 0 = 1$. At Time 1.5 the first pendulum has a speed of one half, and oddly enough, the second pendulum also has a speed of one half, so we get $0.5 + 0.5 = 1$. At Time Two the first pendulum is not moving (speed zero), while the second pendulum has reached maximum speed, so we get $0 + 1 = 1$. In fact, if we plot combined speed at any point after time one, we always obtain a speed of one. Here's what the graph looks like:

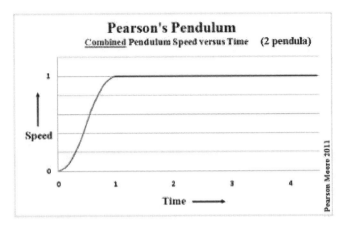

The above graph looks simple, and we might normally consider this to be a good thing. But as we will see, simplicity is going to lead to some severe complications that have direct bearing on the chaotic conditions we find on the Island. To give you a better idea of what I mean, consider a new experiment, this time with three pendula, each given different starting times, and each having a different maximum speed. If we plot the individual speeds of these three pendula we obtain this graph:

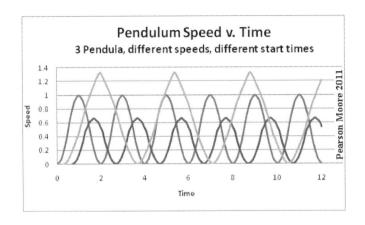

196

Even though the three lines have different amplitudes, all three repeat any given speed at regular intervals. The graph is a little complicated, but by following the speed graph of any one of the three pendula we see a regular repeating pattern—periodicity. Now let's look at the graph of the combined speeds:

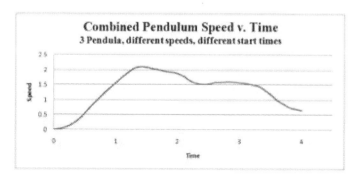

Even though only three speeds are represented we discern no pattern at all. Sometimes the combined speed is low, sometimes it is high. Perhaps if we follow the pendula for a longer time period we may see a trend emerge:

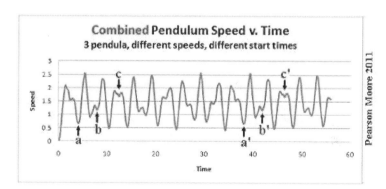

We begin to see periodicity (repetition) at Point a', occurring at Time 37.8. The speed reaches a minimum at Point a', and this speed is exactly the same as at Point a (Time 3.8). Comparing Point b to Point b', and c to c', we note correspondence between the first segment (Time 3.8 to 37.8), and the second segment (Time 37.8 going forward).

This plot of combined pendulum speeds is simpler than the graph of three pendula in that a single line is represented, but in at least one respect it is considerably more complicated. When the pendulum speeds are deconvoluted (separated from each other) we immediately discern a repeating pattern in each one of the speed graphs. When we combine the speeds, much time and effort is required to discern a pattern. Deconvolution of real-world events may require weeks or even months of time on a supercomputer.

We do not have the luxury of deconvoluted graphs when we analyse human behaviour. What we see in a person's expressions or activities is the combined result of any number of variables that together determine a person's thoughts, words, or actions. But underneath there is often a set of periodicities or symmetries that will provide us with much deeper understanding.

Imagine that you have a printout of Danielle Rousseau's jungle movement for the month of May, 1994. She regularly travelled between Points A and B across an open field.

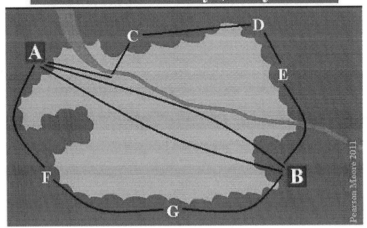

The log of her movements is accurate to the second, but the activity is complex and at first glance has no rhyme or reason. Sometimes Dr. Rousseau crossed the field directly, but on other occasions she moved from Point A to Points C, D, and E within the jungle, and then to B. Even without a glance at the map we can use mathematics to deconvolute the activity. We note trips directly across the open field occurred during early to mid-morning or very late afternoon, while she opted for the more circuitous path through the jungle from late morning to late afternoon. Thanks to accurate timing of her jaunts we are able to determine that she preferred shade during the hottest part of the day. Notice we have two "pendula" in our analysis of Rousseau's movements: The need to move from A to B, and the desire to stay out of the sun.

We notice curious exceptions to the correlation with daily weather patterns (periodicities). On two occasions she took the long route through the trees, even though the sun was not yet up. We find three instances of her movement directly across the field during the hot early afternoon hours.

Date	Departure Times				Arrival	Travel Time (minutes)
	A	C	D	E	B	
3	7:19	7:33	8:59	9:17	9:34	135
12	12:21	---	---	---	1:02	41
15	7:12	7:22	7:41	10:04	10:31	199
22	12:19	---	---	---	12:26	(7)
29	12:15	---	---	---	12:48	33

Rousseau's Peculiar Movements

May, 1994

Note: Short travel time

The strongest deviation from her routine occurred on May 22, when she ran from A to B at midday, bounding across the field in seven minutes. On May 12 and May 29 she again made the direct traverse in early afternoon, but she covered the distance in her typical thirty to forty minutes. Perhaps the seven-minute sprint indicated she was training for a long journey, but more likely she was fleeing imminent danger at Point A, or some emergency drove her to Point B.

Notice that we have gleaned substantial information from nothing more than a time table. But assignment of rationale for the exceptions to diurnal travel patterns will probably require a third "pendulum" (behaviour template). We locate weather records for the period and find there was light rain throughout the afternoon on the 12th and the 29th. We surmise that Rousseau favoured open spaces during rain showers. The long trips through the trees on the third and the 15th are attributed to the setting of new traps at locations C and D. But the mad dash across the field on the 22nd remains unresolved. The weather that day was warm and sunny. We have insufficient information to account for her alarm.

We plough through the New Otherton vital records of the period. Goodwin Stanhope's fifteen-year-old son, Burt, went missing on May 21. His body was recovered near Point B on May 23, together with a Polaroid of the grizzly remains of his body and a simple note: "Give me my daughter!" We conclude that Danielle spied movement in her trap at Point B on May 22 and ran across the field to kill her quarry before he could escape.

DYNAMIC INTERACTIONS

The deconvolution of pendulum data and the analysis of individual movement patterns require nothing more than sound detective work and common sense. While these phenomena involve movement, the behaviours are static. The more difficult—and interesting—interactions in LOST involve dynamic, evolving conflicts between opposed yet connected major characters.

Time and temperature data will not help us divine the powerful forces guiding and reshaping these characters' lives. A mechanical pendulum will not enhance our understanding of the chaotic forces at play between complex individuals.

I invoked the simple example of a pendulum to introduce ideas of deconvolution and behavioural templates. Chaotic phenomena are orders of magnitude more complicated than harmonic movement and periodicities of night and day, yet the deconvolution of chaotic data can yield surprising, even shocking symmetries that offer profound understanding of complex events. Through exposure to the elementary ideas of periodic movement we will achieve a more satisfying appreciation of the underlying rationale for chaotic behaviour.

CHAOS

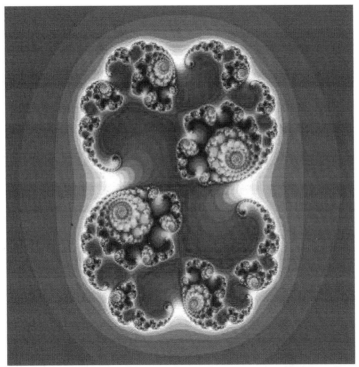

A scale-independent chaotic fractal structure (Wikimedia Commons, Public Domain)

A chaotic system seems random but contains hidden, non-linear symmetries. A chaotic system is not random at all, and can be distilled into simple equations. Chaos differs from linear systems in three important ways. First, the system is nonlinear, meaning it does not obey linear mathematics' behaviours around scale, dimension, or time. Second, chaotic systems do not repeat themselves—as we would say now, these systems are aperiodic. Finally, the outcome of a chaotic interaction depends to an extraordinary extent on the arrangement of the starting conditions. In some chaos experiments a change in position of only one millimetre can result in outcomes 200 metres apart along a flight path as short as 500 metres. A tiny change has an effect far out of proportion to its size.

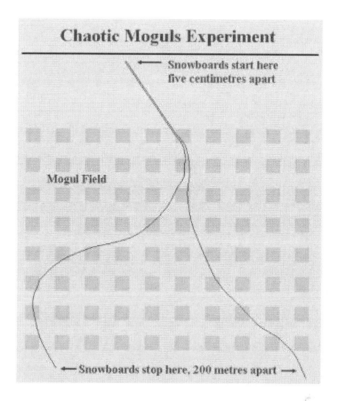

Chaotic systems are not limited in scope to esoteric laboratory experiments or hyper-intensive computer modeling programmes. Nonlinear events are more common than those obeying linear mathematics. Consider, for instance, a pinball game, or a skier on a mogul hill. Not every chaotician (scientist who studies chaos) would classify these as chaotic, but they certainly serve as excellent examples of phenomena exhibiting high dependence on initial conditions.

In the above experiment we have created a perfect mogul hill. The slope at all points on the hill is the same and the snow is completely smooth except for the moguls, which are identical in every respect. We have enclosed the entire hill inside a climate-controlled building. Two narrow snowboards, each carrying five kilograms of lead but no passengers, are placed at the starting position five centimetres (two inches) away from each other. As they proceed through the field they hit the first mogul at just slightly different positions. The mogul causes a perturbation in the flight path, but because the mogul is rounded, the effect is slightly different from one location to another. The result is that the snowboards' flight paths are further apart than before they hit the first mogul. When they hit the next mogul, the flight paths deviate even more, and the effect is exacerbated as they proceed through the field.

CASE STUDY: JACOB AND THE MAN IN BLACK

In Jacob and the Man in Black we are no longer considering the harmonics of a pendulum. There is no perfect repetition, but a very chaotic trajectory. The most appropriate metaphor was the game of Senet. It was a deadly game, played out over two thousand years. For years or even centuries it may have appeared that neither side made a move, but then a sudden cascade of events would reveal that both sides had been preparing and calculating and moving critical pieces into position during periods of apparent calm.

Those who have played Senet know of several metaphorical connections to LOST. One such connection concerns the rules of the game.

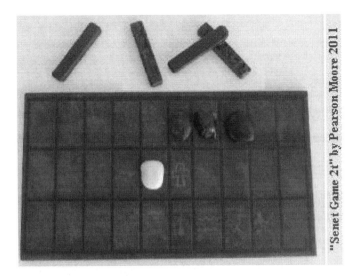

"Senet Game 2r" by Pearson Moore 2011

In the game in progress above, four pieces (called "dancers") remain on the board: three dark dancers at the top and one light dancer at the centre. Because the dark dancers are arranged in adjacent squares they are protected; the opposing player cannot remove them from the board. The light dancer, on the other hand, is vulnerable. If Dark throws the right combination of sticks, she can remove the single light dancer from the board and win the game. We know the interpretation Jack Shephard would apply to these positions: Live together (occupy adjacent squares) or die alone (occupy a lone square, without protection from other dancers).

Jacob and the Man in Black whirled about in their chaotic dance for centuries. The important aspect of the dance is that it was governed by rules. There were four crucial elements to the game. Two elements are obvious: "Two players, two sides. One is light, one is dark." The third element is the game itself; the players are obliged to obey the rules of the game.

The fourth element is essential to our discussion, because it relates to a crucial aspect of the chaos analogy we will construct. The players interacted with each other and with the game. The rules of the game were set, but different rules came into effect depending on location of dancers on the board and the disposition of dancers relative to each other. That the opposing players interacted with each other and with the game is central to our discussion in this chapter.

The chaotic system most applicable to our discussion of Jacob and the Man in Black is called a Lorenz Attractor, or a strange attractor. The Lorenz Attractor starts with three equations. It is not important that you understand them. I produce the equations here only so that I might point out one feature bearing on our discussion.

The Lorenz Equations

$$\frac{dX}{dt} = \sigma(y - x)$$

$$\frac{dY}{dt} = X(\rho - Z) - y$$

$$\frac{dZ}{dt} = yx - \beta z$$

The Lorenz attractor comprises three equations with three variables x, y, and z. The other terms (σ, ρ, β) are constant. The equations are dependent on each other. The x equation depends on y, the y equation depends on x and z, and the z equation depends on x and y.

Pearson Moore 2011

All three equations depend on each other. If x changes, y will also change, because x is multiplied by other factors to give the value of y. In the same way, if y changes, x will also have to change, because y is multiplied by other factors to give the value of x. This is true for all three variables in the equations.

Applying the equations to Jacob and the Man in Black, we can say that if Jacob makes a move or changes his behaviour the Man in Black will be obliged to make a move or change behaviour in response, and his move will depend on Jacob's move. Also, because the two men have reoriented themselves relative to each other, different rules of the game come into effect, or the rules affect the two players in slightly different ways than they did before the two of them made their moves. The two players and the game itself are affecting each other in an endless, chaotic cascade of moves and counter-moves and changing strategies and tactics as all three variables (players and game) evolve due to their interactions with the other players.

Now here is a crucial observation about both the Lorenz equations and the deadly game between the two brothers: We cannot assign priority or causality. That is, we cannot determine from the equations, nor can we determine from the two brothers' moves, who caused whom to do what. We cannot decide whom to blame for any particular event. We can't blame the game, either, since alone it could do nothing to bring about a particular result. All three variables had to come together to realise any particular outcome.

Whom do we blame for Jacob's death? Jacob, the Man in Black, or the game that was initiated when the Guardian killed their mother, Claudia? In the story of Romeo and Juliet, do we blame the House of Montague, the House of Capulet, or do we accuse the good people of fair Verona? In tragedy everyone is guilty, and everyone is a victim. The feud can be taken to its inevitable conclusion, or the Hatfields and the McCoys can agree to stop playing the game.

Many more crucial observations can be made using the Lorenz attractor as the basis for discussion. Several points could be made about various types of symmetry in Lorenz scenarios. In the case of Jacob and the Man in Black, we are aware of both mirror image (opposing) symmetries and symmetries of similarity or exact duplication. These are not accidental, and in fact they point to an even more important truth about the brothers.   Let's take a closer look at the Lorenz attractor so that we can reveal these critical aspects of the brothers' relationship with each other.

NONLINEAR SYMMETRY

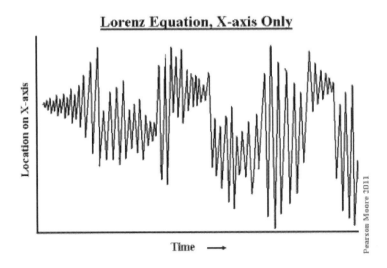

The graph above depicts a particle moving along the X-axis according to the constraints of a Lorenz attractor. The movement seems entirely random, but it is not. If we were to extend this graph outward indefinitely, though, we would not see even one perfect repetition of any part of the pattern. Also, the particle never reverses direction in the same place twice (and therefore is not periodic in its movement). However, its location along the X-axis is framed by upper and lower boundaries that do not move. These boundaries are inherent to the equations.

We see the beginnings of symmetry in some parts of the graph. The particle tends to reverse course about an apparent axis of symmetry, but then the symmetry is suddenly broken and a new, unstable axis of symmetry seems to develop. The new axis appears to be in effect for a while, only to be suddenly destroyed again when the particle veers into new territory.

Recall, however, that the Lorenz attractor consists of three variables. If we wish to faithfully represent the position of the particle, we will have to do so using a depiction in two or three dimensions. This is where we see the spectacular nature of the nonlinear symmetry of the Lorenz attractor.

Lorenz Attractor, 2 Dimensions

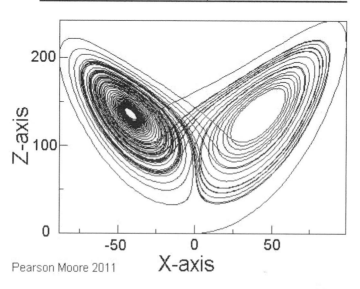

Pearson Moore 2011

This is the so-called butterfly pattern, made famous in Dr. Edward Lorenz's 1972 paper on weather prediction, when he asked, "Does the Flap of a Butterfly's Wings in Brazil set off a Tornado in Texas?" The Butterfly Effect is an idea fascinating to chaoticians because it suggests there is a rich domain of investigation at the interface between chaos and randomness, that even the most complicated behaviours, such as weather, may yet be assimilated into relatively simple algorithms such as strange attractors. If we look at weather patterns in only two or three dimensions we see utter randomness. But recall that when we examine the Lorenz attractor in just one dimension we likewise see only randomness. When we expand to two or three dimensions we see a beautiful, almost perfect symmetry. Perhaps by expanding weather patterns to five or six dimensions we would discover symmetries that allow accurate long-range forecasting.

Jacob and the Man in Black did not sit down as young men and spontaneously decide to play a game in which one or both of them could die. One might reasonably argue that the two of them were never obliged to hate each other, and that they could have decided at any time to end their feud. However, their enmity was not merely a matter of chance or choice. Attitudes and priorities formed in their youth, based on events of highest importance to them, shaped their lives forever.

Their mutual antagonism had its genesis in events outside their control, beginning with the Guardian's murder of their mother, Claudia. The Guardian's studied decision not to bestow the Man in Black with a name was the second important decision. This would affect the Man in Black in ways I will discuss later in this book.

The origin of their deadly game can be traced to four sets of conditions imposed by the Guardian. First, the Guardian granted the boys immortality and created a rule that the boys could never hurt each other, which the boys understood to mean they could not kill each other. The rule was the natural outcome of their status as Candidates.

Next, the Guardian groomed the Man in Black to become Protector, while she moved to make Jacob into a kind of human check on the Man in Black's power over the Island. Deceit was an attribute the Guardian felt necessary to preservation of the Heart of the Island, and she never found fault with any of the Boy in Black's fibs, large or small. On the other hand, she expected Jacob to convey the truth, even in small matters, since he would have to serve as counter-weight to the Man in Black's tendency toward deception. She must have considered this the best scenario for preservation of the Heart of the Island.

The critical event occurred here:

GUARDIAN: What were you and your brother doing down at the beach?
JACOB: We were just... walking.
GUARDIAN: Do you love me, Jacob?
JACOB: Yes.
GUARDIAN: Then tell me what happened.

This constituted the third relationship-changing condition imposed by the Guardian. She made Jacob's honesty a requirement of her love. She reinforced his love of her—an action she never took with the Boy in Black. This simple act of polarisation (Darlton's term) ensured that Jacob would forever feel strong attachment to the Guardian, while the more aloof Boy in Black would have good reason to turn on the woman who raised him.

The final condition was the Lie. She lied about the Island, about the existence of people across the sea, and about the boys' origin with those people. Most importantly, though, she lied about her identity as mother, and she also neglected to tell the brothers she murdered the woman who bore them. Since the Boy in Black had no strong attachment to the Guardian, the revelation of her deception was sufficient cause for him to leave her. Though Jacob loved his brother, he loved much more the woman who had raised him, and he could not follow the Boy in Black to his exile.

The polarisation of the two brothers was complete. Living across the Island from each other, they inhabited entirely different spiritual and emotional spaces. Jacob lived to serve the Guardian, while the Man in Black lived only to leave the Island and return to his people.

They shared genes, language, and the woman who raised them. In almost every other respect they became opposites of each other. The analogy of a mirror reflection is most appropriate, as they were originally cast from the same mold.

They each bore an equal weight of pain due to bounties the other had been given. Jacob received most of the Guardian's love, while the Boy in Black received most of the Guardian's favour. Something that should have been Jacob's (the Guardian's favour) fell into the Man in Black's possession, while an essential aspect of character rightfully belonging to the Man in Black (the Guardian's love) was wrenched from his soul and given to Jacob. Thus, they were not only mirror reflections of each other. In spiritual terms, they started life not as fraternal twins, but as spiritually identical twins. Due to the Guardian's intervention, they each carried something important belonging to the other. They were connected, as if by unbreakable cable—perfect images of the Lorenz Attractor.

The analogy to Lorenz is strong. The men could no more quit the game than surrender their wounded and incomplete identities. Equations determined not only the game they would eventually play, but every aspect of their attitudes toward each other. The game was chaotic because they would never cover the same ground twice. They would learn from the efficacy of their actions, from the Island, from each other, plotting new tactics every time a move failed to give the results they sought.

BROTHERS OF THE LIE

Ben was the master of deceit, second in abilities of manipulation and deception only to the Man in Black. Hurley, on the other hand, seemed incapable of telling a lie. But their dance around the bright flame of truth involved more complicated issues than the opposing periodicities of honesty and deception. Their dance was chaotic, and it was ruled by the Island and its needs.

Episode Two of Season Five was titled "The Lie." Just before the Oceanic Six left the Island, Locke told Jack, "You're going to have to lie." If they did not lie, more of Widmore's mercenaries would arrive by freighter. Everyone left behind would be placed in jeopardy. Jack realised the deadly nature of the stakes, and he worked for the next six days at sea to convince five of the six (he probably didn't spend much effort on Aaron...) that they would have to agree to lie about what had happened to them. The only person who did not readily agree to the Lie was Hurley.

Jack continued to work on Hurley, and he reluctantly supported the deception. His inability to tell a lie forced his return to the Santa Rosa Mental Health Institute. Hugo had not yet learned that the world is willing to hear only certain varieties of honesty, that in most situations a lie is expected, even socially required. Upon escaping the facility he was sought for murder, and it was in this curious situation that the true nature of Hugo's abiding relationship with truth was revealed.

When Ben approached Hurley to return to the Island, Hurley realised the predicament he was in—having to hide from the police—was due to the extraordinary agglomeration of fibs, fabrications, and falsehoods that he and his friends had been obliged to create. All of these deceptions, Hurley was convinced, originated with one man: Benjamin Linus. In that instant something spectacular occurred. In order to rid himself of Ben, he concocted the most fantastic lie imaginable: "I did it!" he screamed, running outside to the squad car. "I killed them, all four of them!" There had been only three murders, but it didn't matter. The important thing, in Hugo's mind, was distancing himself from Ben.

Hurley was no longer opposed to falsehood per se. He was opposed to the person he considered the personification of deceit, Benjamin Linus. In fact, he was willing to fabricate falsehoods to bring himself into opposition with Ben. In personifying deceit, rather than living according to the dictates of honesty, Hurley was foregoing the possibility of referencing an independent set of objective laws. He was leaving the linear world of springs and pulleys and laws of nature and man and entering the chaotic world of the Lorenz Attractor, tethering himself forever to the supreme object of his soul's concern, Benjamin Linus.

Ben had his own epiphany around the logic of deceit. Manipulation of others' perceptions had served him well all his life, until the young woman he truly loved—his adoptive daughter—was dragged before him by Widmore's goons. He cared more about Alex than anyone else, even more than the Island. He had to preserve the Island at all costs, but he thought he might be able to save Alex with a simple lie. "She's not my daughter. She means nothing to me. So if you wanna kill her, go ahead and—"

Ben learned in the most horrifying manner imaginable that one does not lie to a hired thug. People whose profession is murder have no allegiance to virtue, no temperament for others' feelings or needs. The young woman's death devastated Ben. In virtually every scene following Alex's murder, Ben's face was a picture of anguish, of sadness that would not be assuaged.

Toward the final days Jack was no longer issuing commands or dispensing ideas. He felt he had to learn to listen and follow. People began to turn to Hurley for counsel, but there was danger in being a leader on the Island.

Michael appeared at Libby's grave, warning Hurley that people would die if he allowed Richard and the others to destroy the airplane. Never comfortable with leadership, he was being forced into the role. When Richard made clear his intention to destroy the plane, Hurley took action. He lied to the entire group, leading them to believe he supported Richard's plan. Meanwhile, he arranged to arrive at the Black Rock ahead of everyone else so he could destroy the dynamite that Richard needed to wreck the plane. Even this extreme action did not stop Richard, who knew of a store of explosives at the barracks. Desperate, knowing he must save the plane but having no idea how to stop Richard, he told an even bigger lie. "Jacob says we have to talk to Locke [the Man in Black]."

Perhaps it was a fib born entirely of frustration and fear. Or possibly Hurley carried some innate awareness of Jack's need to confront the Man in Black directly. Regardless of any other factors contributing to Hurley's decision to utter this monumental lie, Ben's presence in the group was unquestionably a factor, as Hurley's decision ensured their close collaboration through the remainder of the story.

Ben and Hurley were the second Odd Couple at the Source. The rope they held as they lowered Jack was symbolic in so many ways: Tied to the Island, tied to Jack, tied to each other. Hurley had long ago thrown in his lot with Ben, and now Ben was reciprocating, perhaps sensing that through the most honest man on the Island he might gain redemption. The rope they lowered in tandem, the rope that bound them in a common goal, was the symbol of their necessary and inevitable connection. Neither character could discern the complicated dynamics of truth in a single dimension. But by merging their knowledge of honesty, by recognising their connection to each other, they would begin to discern the higher symmetries of truth in multiple dimensions.

UPWARD DECONVOLUTION

To visualise the symmetries of competing pendula we resolve a multi-dimensional graph into its single-dimensional components. This is the most elementary kind of analysis, applied in the laboratory, at crime scenes, in meeting agendas, and so on. We deconvolute, or resolve apparent complexity into lower-dimensional, less complicated elements.

But when we consider attractor phenomena the only way to appreciate the chaotic symmetries of the system is to unite individual elements into a multi-dimensional scheme. We do not analyse, resolve, or pull apart. Rather, we combine elements into a finished composition. We seek understanding of a synthesis in progress. When our feeble analyses uncover common threads, we bring to bear all of the details of the plot or character dimensions to reveal the meta-symmetry that exists as a dynamic system guiding both characters and the plot. We deconvolute into higher dimensions because this is the only way we can understand the symmetries of a constantly changing story.

We do not understand Jack without reference to Locke, and vice versa. In fact, without Jack there is no Locke, and absent Locke there can be no Jack.

The original Odd Couple of LOST began with the same questions. Jack and Locke were told repeatedly they didn't have what it takes, that they couldn't do it. In both cases, their response was to say, "Don't tell me what I can't do!" Locke conveyed his response verbally; Jack responded with his actions, in a lifetime devoted to fixing people to prove that he did have what it takes. Both men began their lives confronting the two-sided coin stamped SCIENCE on one side and FAITH on the other. Jack turned toward science even though his primary teacher—his father—discouraged him from taking that route. Locke turned toward faith even though his primary teacher—in high school— encouraged him to pursue science.

Attractor systems evolve. They operate in three dimensions: the two interacting characters and the rules by which the characters dance or play their game. We cannot ask Locke the tenets of his faith and expect that these will guide both Locke and Jack in some linear progression toward common epiphany. The characters are tethered in push-me-pull-you fashion to the object of their common fascination and reciprocal deficit. Ben lacks honesty, Hurley lacks fraudulence; both characters consider they seek different things, but in fact they seek the same objective. The crucial aspect of their character is not a static relationship with truth or falsehood, but Ben and Hurley's dynamic relationship with each other.

BONDS OF IDENTITY

In the same way, we should not posit an unmoved connection between Jack and Locke and Science/Faith. Jack did not worship at the altar of rational scepticism, and Locke did not work in the laboratory of belief and destiny. The most durable connections are not with concepts, but with identities. The question "Who am I?" is just a short, concise way of asking "What are the most relevant connections between the essence of my being and the elements of life that are most important to me?" In this sense Jack is no more a scientist than he is a janitor or a soldier. He is first of all the person who seeks to resolve the question of his identity. Jack does this by asserting that his identity includes the ability to fix things, despite contrarian claims of learned counsel that he lacks any such ability.

Jack lacks faith, Locke has it. Locke lacks scepticism and logic, Jack has them. These deficiencies are not objective aspects of reality, but darknesses of the soul—they are deficiencies of identity. They are not monolithic; logic and faith are different ways of stating a preference for an investigation of the universe. They are not static. The only constants in the tethered struggle are the presence of the two characters and the rules that bind them. They choose to refer to their debate as a dialogue regarding logic and belief, but these are almost accidentals to the greater reality of their dynamic struggle together toward the fulfillment of their identities and the discovery of a unifying truth. This unifying truth, of course, is not something linear or conceptual or objective, but something subjective and spiritual that satisfies the need to establish identity.

IDENTITY AND PERSONALITY

Kate is not connected to Claire through some abstract concept of motherhood. The ties that bind are human spirit and soul. They connect two people at the deepest level of personality and identity. In Kate and Claire we cannot even appeal to an objective concept as touchstone or metaphor. For these two women the ties that bind are a baby boy and the unending responsibilities and joys emanating from their mutual commitment to his care.

Kate is no less Aaron's mother than is Claire, and out of her love for Aaron, she is willing to risk her own life—but not Aaron's—to reunite blood mother and beloved child. We cannot possibly understand Kate without reference to Aaron and Claire. So strong is her love for Aaron that she leaves her Constant, Jack, to face death on the Island, alone. Kate is tied to Claire in a way that is proof to adversity. Kate can leave her beloved, Jack, because the overwhelming reality of their relationship is that they are always together in a spiritual sense. Kate's relationship to Aaron and Claire, on the other hand, requires physical presence and action. Nothing can keep them apart, not even a supernatural force that defies normal means of destruction, because Kate is not a complete person without Claire. Together, they will care for the only person who could cause Kate to stop running: Aaron.

ILLE QUI NOS OMNES HABET

Daughter to Widmore, wife and lover to Desmond, Penny is the tie that binds these two men together, but she does not create the rules. The Island holds all characters in its sphere. Mittelos is the object of Widmore's fancy, the bane of Desmond's odyssey, and the firm reality that will yield to neither of them.

"None of this matters," Desmond told Jack just before he and the Man in Black lowered the intrepid Scotsman into the Source. Desmond always had a neurotic, almost psychotic relationship with the Island, saying first the Swan Station accomplished nothing, but almost in the same breath warning that entering the numbers amounted to nothing less than saving the world. But as Jack told Desmond, all of it matters. The Island pulled both Widmore and Desmond into its grip, regardless of their feelings about the reality of its decision to impose its rules on their lives. The Island is a constant force in every strange attractor in the series, determining the constraints on every one of the dynamic systems dancing within the Island's sphere.

SINGULARITY

The Island is home to dozens of strange attractor pairs. Aaron and Ethan have strong and complementary ties to the Island. Stuart Radzinsky and Daniel Faraday were scientists with very different concepts regarding the proper place of science in the world. Their mutual misunderstanding of science led to the great catastrophe we know as the Incident. We can march through the list of characters major and minor and create strange attractor pairings that satisfy every reasonable expectation regarding plot points and character arcs.

But two characters resist our most determined efforts at pairing. We are stymied in our attempts at deeper understanding, even to the point that we cannot perform a logical, linear analysis of the characters' greater meaning to the series.

The woman who raised Jacob and the Man in Black, the Guardian, was in relationship with just two other people. She imparted priorities and attitudes about humanity and life on the Island to both of them. Is it possible to say she had a stronger relationship with one or the other? Are we obliged to conclude that the Guardian established strange attractor connections with both Jacob and the Man in Black? Or must we instead believe that she was a singularity, without strong connection to anyone?

The most intractable analytical problem is posed by the character who has consumed the largest fraction of my time and energy over the last two years. His connection to other characters ought to be a very simple assignment, but none of the dozens of essays I have read about him satisfactorily explains the vast reach and deep significance of his place in the story.

Christian Shephard was Jack's father. He was primary exemplar of the "daddy issues" that were a recurring motif during the entire six years of LOST. On this basis we ought to be able to sum up his significance over the course of a few short paragraphs. But no such cursory determination will stand up to detailed scrutiny.

The crux of the problem is that an apparition—a disembodied vision—was the instigator of some of the greatest events of the series. He called for the Island to be moved. He led John Locke to the Light and brought his own son beside Island waters. But he also stole Claire's baby away from her and on at least one occasion served as the spokesperson for the Smoke Monster. Christian's name and actions were imbued with religious symbolism. He told those in his presence to follow him, indicating the promise of one who would serve as shepherd and saviour. But he also acted as representative of the Island's darkest form of evil, pledged to commit murder and destruction.

This book will examine both the Guardian and Christian Shephard in detail. I will demonstrate that the account of their significance most consonant with their true effect and most pleasing to our sense of balance will be achieved through higher levels of chaotic symmetry than those examined here. Our journey has only just begun.

CHAPTER 14 ADVANCED TOPIC I:
THE SOURCE

"Stromboli Eruption" © Wolfgang Beyer 1980 GNU FDL 1.2

You believe.

I cannot know every particular of your thoughts on LOST, but I do know you consider that the series had relevance to you personally. I know this because of your emotional condition the first time you saw the finale in 2010. You at least had a lump in your throat—and if your troubled state approximated the extreme condition of millions around the world, you succumbed to warm tears after the first or second revelation—in hospital with Sun and Jin, or at the concert with Kate and Aaron and Claire and Charlie. I was among the stoics who fought tears through the finale. I lost my battle at the candy machine with Juliet and James.

You believe. Faith commands the centre of our shared appreciation of LOST, and it provides the essential foundation of any real understanding of the series. Our ranks used to include millions more. With warehouse worker Hector, they screamed, "We deserve answers!" If only they understood what we know: LOST gave us faith, and faith provides the answers. This chapter is about the provider of faith, trust, and hope, the giver of Light: The Heart of the Island. The Source is the basis for everything that occurred since September 22, 2004. Let us take a closer look at this foundation of our common fascination.

Some months ago I undertook a scientific explanation for the mysteries of LOST. Two facts surprised me. First, I found a technical basis for almost every one of the major properties of the Island, down to the green glow of the water at the Source and the destruction of the Taweret statue. Even the extreme compass needle deflections which caused Sayid so much consternation (Lost 1.13) have been explained by scientists (in Hawaii, no less. Read the complete technical article in this geology journal: http://www.agu.org/journals/ABS/1995/95JB00148.shtml). Second, the one phenomenon I was sure I would be able to explain—the red glow emanating from below the pool around the Cork Stone—has resisted every attempt at reconciliation with current geological theory. I consulted with volcanologists at the University of Alaska Fairbanks Volcanology Group and at the University of Hawaii. I spoke with geologists and paleomagetologists in California and British Columbia. Given the features of the light cave and the extreme electromagnetism of the Island, not a single scientist was able to construct a model consistent with the observation of a red glow originating beneath the floor of the pool.

One might argue that the red glow would be ascribed to lava or magma by those of us—including myself—who are not experts in volcanology. Surely Darlton could not have been expected to delve so deeply into the geological underpinnings of their fictional creation. Even those who demand answers to every question posed during the six years of the series would be willing to grant Darlton licence to fabricate a minor geophysical impossibility to advance the story. I would be willing to grant this, too, if I believed a scientific or quasi-scientific explanation was the writers' intention. But this was not the intention.

BASIS IN FAITH

There is a point at which we are obliged to bring an end to our quest for objective truth.

CLAUDIA: Where are the rest of your people?
GUARDIAN: There's only me.
CLAUDIA: How did you get here?
GUARDIAN: The same way you got here. By accident.
CLAUDIA: How long have you—
GUARDIAN: Every question I answer will simply lead to another question. You should rest. Just be grateful you're alive.

"Across The Sea" was not the writers' attempt at a scientific or historical or social explanation for the Island. Every frame of the 43-minute episode stated emphatically that the explanation was mythological in character. The mythos of LOST had its origin in conditions and events that unfolded naturally from the Guardian's time as Protector through Jacob's reign and

Hurley's ascension to the See of Light. We are permitted to speculate about events and conditions prior to the images and words of Episode 6.15, but we cannot expect objective, non-mythological explanations.

The Source is literally and figuratively the defining boundary of LOST mythology. It is the starting point for every condition and event, every plotline and character arc. It is not subject to explanation or understanding. Rather, it is the common reference point for everything in the series. The Source explains; it is not in itself an object of our understanding.

Darlton did not intend to fashion a story predicated on known truths of science or history. LOST is not a procedural show like NCIS or House; there are no ruthlessly logical connections between characters and events, and there is no proof for any of the great mysteries, nor even for some of the small questions.

For instance, we know Jin-Soo Kwon, not Sun, was the sixth Candidate. We do not rely on advanced knowledge of Korean language and culture in making this assessment (according to Korean practice, Sun's name would have been PAIK Sun, not Sun Kwon), but rather on the consistency of LOST mythology. Candidacy was conferred not by Jacob's touch alone, but by Jacob's intention combined with tactile contact. The scene at Sun and Jin's wedding confirmed only the touch. We didn't learn Sun was not a Candidate until the flight of Ajira 316. All of the Candidates traveled through time; since Sun, Frank, and Ben did not travel through time, they were not Candidates. Jin, unconscious on the floating remains of the Kahana, did travel through time, and therefore he was a Candidate. We have no proof to back this interpolation, but we require no such proof. Reliance on mythology is sufficient.

In like manner, we rely on the integrity of LOST mythology and apply judicious interpolation to arrive at solid answers for any of the questions posed during the series. Since the Source is the starting point for LOST, it must contain within itself an unambiguous answer to the foundational question of the show. Yet, other than the Guardian's quite obviously biased statements about the Heart of the Island, we have very little information about the Source itself.

We rely on faith to understand LOST. I need to point out that this firm reliance is not the result of an incomplete story. The story is complete. In fact, even without "The New Man in Charge" epilogue, the story is complete. Everything that occurred in the little eleven-minute film could have been extrapolated from the 121 one-hour episodes; in fact, some of us correctly predicted events as portrayed in the epilogue several weeks before it was leaked to the Internet. We rely on faith because the writers intended precisely this type of understanding. Faith allows us to arrive at quite unambiguous conclusions regarding the nature of the Source.

THE HISTORY OF THE CORK STONE

The dearth of logical, objectively true information about the Source must have been a stumbling block to those who sought a mechanistic understanding of the show. We have no reliable, non-mythological information about the Light, the Source, or the Cork Stone. No single character was given definitive insight into the nature of these elementary objects. From a sterile, logical point of view, LOST must seem to have been an extraordinary waste of time and effort.

We know nothing of the history of the Source. However, we do possess some information on the history of the Cork Stone, provided by Darlton during the audio commentary accompanying "Across The Sea."

Damon Lindelof: If I were to have a theory that that apparatus we see in the finale with the stone sticking in the middle of the pool that's sort of blocking the light, maybe that apparatus wasn't created until after this event [the creation of the Smoke Monster].
Carlton Cuse: I think that's an incredibly likely deduction, Damon.
Damon Lindelof: It's possible people went down there and basically...
Carlton Cuse: They built something.
Damon Lindelof: Some people think the light went out in that shot [when the Smoke Monster rose out of the cave for the first time] but it was just the smoke monster obstructing the light. The light has not been diminished in any significant way but is probably largely responsible for what just happened.

This is useful information, especially since it superficially contradicts the written record contained on the Cork Stone. According to Lost Encyclopedia (not Lostpedia), the Cork Stone is etched with two lines of Egyptian hieroglyphs and two lines of Sumerian cuneiform script. These are the four lines of ancient text, translated into English:

Line 1: "Embrace that which the Balance hath weighed, let a path be made for the Osiris in the Great Valley, and let the Osiris have light to guide him on his way."

Line 2: "He hath reconciled the Two Fighters (Horus and Set), the guardians of life."

Line 3: "Break the immovable yoke that we may sleep."

Line 4: "That silence may reign and we may sleep."

The superficial contradiction is found in the languages chosen for the inscriptions. Egyptian hieroglyphs were current during the Classical Roman period depicted in "Across The Sea"; Sumerian cuneiform script, on the other hand, was an ancient and unknown form of writing by the time Jacob and his brother were born. The cuneiform symbols were not placed in error, though. We need to dig deep into the mythological significance to make sense of the Cork Stone.

THE MYTHOLOGY OF THE CORK STONE

"Horus" by Pearson Moore 2011

The painting above should seem somehow familiar. The figure is that of an idealised falcon, rendered in the Egyptian fashion with wide body, wide head, and small wings held close on either side. The figure is idealised because it depicts an Egyptian god, in this case Horus, the god of daylight. The strange feature of traditional representations of Horus is the nature of the eyes. One eye is entirely white, with no pupil. The other eye is painted dark. This depiction of light and dark eyes is done to conform to the Egyptian myth of Horus and Set.

Horus and Set battled each other after Set, the god of darkness, killed Osiris, Horus' father. Set plucked out one of Horus' eyes, and the fight raged on. With no prospect of a victor, the other gods assembled to decide their colleagues' fate. Initially the gods sided with Set, but Osiris, from the land of the dead, sent a message to the gods, instructing them to choose Horus. The gods obeyed Osiris, Horus was declared winner of the contest, and Set was cast into the darkness, though not killed. After his victory, the gods located Horus' missing eye and restored it. Horus was originally the god of Lower Egypt, while Set was the god of Upper Egypt. The myth of the struggle between Horus and Set, with Horus installed as victor, is understood as a parable for later unification of Egypt under the single god, Horus. The Pharoahs, after they died, were considered to personify Osiris.

The light and dark eyes are understood as the unification of night and day under the control of Horus. The light eye sees as the sun, while the dark eye sees as the moon, symbolically indicating Horus' position as supreme ruler of both night and day. Horus is often depicted with a single eye, and sometimes, as in Jacob's tapestry, only the eye itself—the Eye of Horus—is used to symbolise divine power from on high.

We didn't see Jacob's tapestry until the end of Season Five. But we had an important glimpse of Horus long before that. In fact, we saw a novel and quite memorable depiction of the Egyptian god in Episode 1.10, "Raised By Another."

Claire's dream showed Locke with one dark eye and one light eye in the configuration typically used to represent the post-battle, victorious Horus who reconciled night and day and Upper and Lower Egypt. I will not analyse Claire's dream here. I mention the Season One dream because it supports the claim that the Source determined the survivors' fate, and even their thoughts and dreams, from the earliest days.

The importance of Darlton's statement that the Cork Stone was installed only after the Man in Black became the Smoke Monster is understood through the inscription. Since the Cork was installed on Jacob's watch as Protector, he would have placed the Cork himself or he would have directed its installation. Having won the battle over "Set" (the Man in Black) he could justifiably consider himself the personification of wise Horus. That he commissioned the second line of the inscription ("He hath reconciled the Two Fighters [Horus and Set], the guardians of life.") can be taken as an expression of magnanimity, declaring both himself and the Man in Black as equal "guardians of life."

The cuneiform script is more difficult to explain. We may well imagine dozens or even hundreds of interpretations of their significance supported by the events leading up to Desmond's descent into the cave. Due to the antiquity of the writing we know the script did not originate with Jacob. The symbols and their significance would have been handed down from the Guardian, who would have known them herself or received them from the Protector before her. These two lines were the most precious words the Guardian knew. Jacob ensured their eternal propagation through history by inscribing them on the single object he knew would survive any change over the millennia.

The two ancient phrases inscribed on the Cork Stone hold the key to understanding every event in LOST. But before we can propose their meaning, we need to return to a deeper consideration of the Source.

THE GROUND OF ALL BEING

I AM.

Not a single person living or dead can make such a bold statement. Even if anyone could summon the audacity to utter these two impossible words, we would immediately seek clarification through qualification: "You are *what*, pray tell?" I am my father's son, my daughter's father, my wife's husband. I am a chemist, a writer, a linguist. I am, but only in relation to something or someone else. I cannot say simply I AM, because to do so would be tantamount to claiming non-dependent, necessary existence. There is in this world only one entity that can legitimately claim necessary existence, and She is not human.

"God Appears to Moses in the Burning Bush"
Eugene Pluchart 1848 PD

Perhaps you considered my earlier claim, that "The Source explains; it is not in itself an object of our understanding," was an innocent but unremarkable statement. It was not unremarkable at all. And it certainly was not innocent. In fact, in certain circles the claim would be considered tantamount to blasphemy.

Only the Creator can utter the unqualified statement "I AM." The Creator is the only necessary (non-dependent) entity. No one created the Creator. The Creator exists before all else that is or ever will be, and is contingent on nothing.

The exploration of the Creator's character is complicated in ways we need to delineate in order to make sense of the Source. I am going to consciously refrain from appealing to the revelation of any particular religious tradition, not because I wish to remain neutral, but because such discussions would unnecessarily complicate an already difficult philosophical concept. I do not dispute any aspect of revelation, and nothing stated in this essay should be considered a denial of the veracity, efficacy, or necessity of any religious doctrine or revelation. For the purposes of our discussion I am going to make statements that may be at odds with your understanding. In fact, some of what I write in this chapter will not comport with my own understanding of the reality outside LOST. I am consciously framing the discussion to illuminate the core ideas of the series.

The Creator is not a being. Beings are those objects that are brought into existence by the Creator. In fact, the great twentieth century theologian, Paul

Tillich, referred to the Creator not as a being, but as The Ground of All Being. The Creator is the necessary source (ground) of all created things, and as such is no being at all, but something above being. Tillich sometimes referenced the Creator as "God above God," meaning the true, unknowable Creator above the divine entity we understand through revelation.

PROFESSOR PAUL TILLICH

This understanding of the completely Other—the Creator—is essential to a productive approach toward the Source. The few characteristics we might reasonably ascribe to the Creator I believe are best understood, for the purposes of coming to know the Source, as being founded on this radical concept of the Divine.

The Creator creates. Therefore the Creator has power. The Creator creates everything, and can create anything. Therefore the Creator has infinite power, contingent on nothing, answerable to no one. The Creator can create anywhere, at any time, simultaneously or sequentially, and is therefore omnipresent and not subject to the constraints of calendar or clock. The Creator adds to and subtracts from creation at will and uses the same infinite faculties to create and destroy, to unify and tear apart.

The Creator does not answer to us, does not necessarily conform Her will to ours, is not obliged to bring any particular aspect of creation into a form we understand. Because the Divinity is not a being, not a part of creation, not an entity we can understand or interact with in any way (again, not including or referencing mechanisms of interaction that may be available as proclaimed through revelation), the Creator's presence is not going to be understood or appreciated as such. Fear and trembling are the most likely responses to an encounter with the Divine, for the Creator is completely Other, completely beyond anything we have ever experienced, completely beyond our faculties of comprehension.

The Source behaved in a manner consonant with an entity beyond any human understanding. It was powerful—perhaps infinitely powerful. Its power appeared in a form that virtually demanded of us a sense of fear and awe.

I do not claim that the Source is the Creator, or even that the writers intended that we devise or imagine any mental associations between Source and Creator. What I claim is that conceptualising the Source as something beyond human understanding is the most effective route toward a deeper appreciation of the series. You may choose to believe that nothing even remotely similar to the Creator as understood in established religious tradition was invoked by the writers. However, I hope you will at least consider the possibility that something akin to Tillich's Ground of All Being has direct bearing and proximity to the behaviours of the Source.

I believe the Source was not Creator but rather the connection between the world we understand and the world knowable only to the Creator. The Source—the Island—is the umbilical connecting us to the Divine.

The writers were quite deliberate in their decision to leave the Source unexplained. We know only the colours it imparted to the cave above it and something of its behaviour. When the water flowed and the Cork Stone was in place, a bright, greenish-yellow glow emanated from the pool. When the Cork Stone was removed the water stopped flowing and drained into the Source. When no water remained, a dull, reddish to reddish-brown glow emanated from below the empty pool.

But we can assign phenomenological effects as well. The true character of the Source is beyond comprehension, the behaviours are inscrutable, but the results of the Source's activity are well catalogued. Some of the results of the presence or actions of the Source were entirely beyond systematic understanding. Locke's ability to walk was instantly restored. Rose's cancer was cured. Wounds that should have required weeks or months to heal were instead mended in short days. Whispers engulfed anyone who walked the abode of the dead.

Some phenomena unfolded in a manner we believed consistent with the rudimentary theory of emerging, cutting-edge science. Places deep underground in close proximity to the Light were found capable of sending objects—or even the Island itself—instantaneously across the globe and forward or backward in time. We attributed these phenomena to the presence of exotic matter, manipulated in such a way that a Casimir Effect was propagated through the local environment, creating a displacement of material through a temporal vortex.

Other outcomes were of a type we believed partially or completely understood by long-established science. Pregnancies that should have been routine became instead death sentences for both mothers and babies. Metal behaved in strange and sometimes unpredictable ways. Forces at play on the Island were capable of loosing mercury amalgam fillings and instantly sending them through tissue and bone, carving a path through the brain and killing the hapless victim. Planes flying thousands of metres above the Source were subject to its strange effects, all of which were explained as an extreme form of electromagnetism seen nowhere else on Earth.

We should take care to avoid confusion regarding the true extent of our understanding. The observation of events unfolding in a manner consistent with theory does not indicate any triumph of our scientific knowledge. The dolphin inhabits salt water and possesses a sleek body similar in form to the shark. A large book could be filled, cataloguing the long list of similarities between dolphin and shark. We might be tempted to conclude the two animals are virtually identical, but they're not.

In the same way, we might believe ourselves ready to conclude that because several Island behaviours conform to the well-worn conventions of electromagnetism we are therefore entitled to proclaim our perfect understanding of the events. We must keep in mind that any understanding of the true cause of Island phenomena is beyond our limited capacities. We have no knowledge of the true range and nature of the Source's abilities.

THE PERSONALITY OF THE SOURCE

From the earliest episodes of LOST we were witness to the strange affinity of John Locke for the Island. During his first heart-to-heart conversation with Jack (Episode 1.05) he revealed that the Island was "different... special." He was beginning to formulate the idea that their presence on the Island was no coincidence. By the end of Season One, the night air illuminated by bright torches, he conveyed to Jack his understanding of their purpose.

JACK: Who brought us here, John?
LOCKE: The Island. The Island brought us here. This is no ordinary place, you've seen that, I know you have. But the Island chose you, too, Jack. It's destiny.

These few pronouncements could have been understood as a peculiar manner of speech, an unintended personification of a rock he knew to be inanimate. But Locke made many such statements, conveying the clear idea that the Island had not only a purpose, but an awareness, a consciousness.

LOCKE [To Boone]: The island will send us a sign.

LOCKE [To Charlie]: What I know is that this island might just give you what you're looking for, but you have to give the island something.

LOCKE [To Boone]: The island will tell us what to do.

LOCKE [To Eko]: Boone made it fall. Then he died. A sacrifice that the Island demanded.

If Locke had been the only person attributing conscious awareness to a piece of ocean real estate we might have been able to dismiss his rantings. But he was not alone. Almost everyone who had inhabited the Island for an extended period spoke casually of the Island's intentions, desires, and caprices.

BEN [To Locke]: I'm not going in there with you. The island wanted me to get sick and it wanted you to get well. My time is over, John. It's yours now.

ELOISE: I'm sorry to have to tell you this, Desmond, but the Island isn't done with you yet.

WIDMORE: The Island needs you, John. It has for a long time.

LOCKE: What makes you think I'm so special?
WIDMORE: Because you are.

JACK: You know, when we were here before, I spent all of my time trying to fix things. But...did you ever think that maybe the island just wants to fix things itself? And maybe I was just...getting in the way?

Several statements assuming an Island consciousness were made in such a way that we knew the parties to the conversation had a shared understanding of the Island's personality.

RICHARD [To Widmore]: Jacob wanted it [saving Ben's life] done. The Island chooses who the Island chooses. You know that.

BEN: You're the one who wanted her dead, Charles, not the Island.
WIDMORE: I hope you're right, Benjamin, because if you aren't, and it is the Island that wants her dead, she'll be dead.

INDEPENDENCE IN THOUGHT AND ACTION

Knowing the cause of a particular event can be crucial to our broader understanding of Island phenomena. Although it is tempting to build complex theories around the actions of a particular character, we must challenge ourselves to avoid interpreting a situation in a way beneficial to a favourite participant in the Island drama. We must never become comfortable with convenient theories that do not take into account the details of a scene.

Many commentators, I think, lost sight of the complexity of interaction on the Island, especially in the final season, and particularly with regard to interactions between Jacob, the Man in Black, and the Guardian ("Mother"). These three were not the only characters in "Across the Sea" whose actions had the potential to drastically affect others' lives.

We have seen broad consensus among the major characters that the Island not only had an awareness of self, but it was conscious of the characters roaming about its jungle and beaches. But the Island was no mere observer of events.

Ilana was one of the leaders in the last season of the saga. It was her job to protect Jacob and the Candidates. Though she arrived too late to do anything for Jacob, she did have the training and knowledge necessary to help the Candidates achieve the goal of wresting control of the Island from the Man in Black. She had been tutored one-on-one by the Protector himself, who treated her as a daughter. Jacob deemed her crucial to the responsibility of protecting the Island. With her unique and essential knowledge of Mittelos, we do not overstate her significance by claiming that she was the most important figure on the Island after Jacob. With Jacob's death she became the most critical player in the 2000-year-old game.

But long before she could assist in the selection of a new Protector she stopped on her hike with the Candidates, wiped her brow, and removed the dynamite bag from her shoulder. It was her last act on the Island.

BEN: Ilana. There she was - handpicked by Jacob, trained to come and protect you candidates, no sooner does she tell you who you are, then she blows up. The Island was done with her. Makes me wonder what's gonna happen when it's done with us.

It's hard to know why the Island decided to remove Ilana from the game. Perhaps she would have become an impediment to Jack or Kate. Perhaps the single task she needed to perform had been accomplished. But we can be sure of at least one thing: Ilana's death was not in keeping with Jacob's plan. Jacob had groomed her for years for a task she had not yet completed at the time of her death. Neither was she executed by the Smoke Monster. Rather, she died because the Island needed her to die. The Island had an agenda different from that of Jacob.

We have off-Island confirmation of the Island's conscious independence. Recall that Jacob could not see dead people, and that Isabella (Richard's wife) died on the Canary Islands, and then consider this interaction from Episode 6.09 (Ab Aeterno):

HURLEY: [Isabella] kinda said one more thing. Something you have to do.
RICHARD: What?
HURLEY: She said you have to stop the Man in Black. You have to stop him from leaving the island. 'Cause if you don't... todos nos vamos al infierno.

Isabella consulted neither with Jacob nor with the Man in Black to arrive at this understanding. In her apparition to Hurley she was acting as messenger, delivering crucial instruction to Richard through Hurley. She was not in the employ of Miles, the only other person known to harbour the ability to communicate with dead people. If she was neither Jacob's nor the Man in Black's agent, some other figure of authority entrusted Isabella with the courier mission. The only other authority figure capable of communication with dead people was the Island.

The Island could detonate explosives to remove people no longer needed, such as Michael, Ilana, and Arzt. It could manipulate conditions to prevent cancer in Rose but stimulate cancerous growth in Ben's back. It influenced or directly intervened in dozens or even hundreds of events over the last two thousand years. And it accomplished all of these things without consulting Jacob, the Man in Black, Locke, or Jack. Those who survived this terrifying and wondrous place were the individuals who took to heart this truth: The Island has a mind of its own.

"The Ark Passes Over the Jordan" James J. J. Tissot ca. 1900 WMC PD

Coming into the presence of an entity possessing complete power over life and death and rebirth must be the most frightening task anyone can imagine performing. Two thousand years ago, someone took on this fearsome burden, placing an inscribed stone into the hole at the centre of the pool. The task had never been performed before because the Monster had never been created in the way Jacob had, by physically throwing his brother into the cave. He knew he had offended the Island, and in fact all of creation. He had unleashed a terrible evil on the world. In fitting the stone into its place in the pool, Jacob ensured that the Man in Black could never leave the Island, and he made amends with the powerful entity he had offended.

Careful preparation would have preceded the installation of the Cork Stone. Perhaps the pool itself and the aqueduct to the temple had to be constructed. But the most important consideration was the stone itself. It would serve as the physical impediment to the Man in Black's departure from the Island. More than that, though, it would also serve as a promise—a covenant—between the Protector and the Source. Jacob fashioned a stone containing four important covenant statements, two in Egyptian, two in the ancient language of Sumer.

THAT WHICH THE BALANCE HATH WEIGHED

The first covenant statement would have to acknowledge the Source's power over life, death, and rebirth. This was perfectly accomplished with a tribute to Osiris, the continually reincarnated Egyptian god of death and life, in a quotation from the Egyptian Book of the Dead:

"Embrace that which the Balance hath weighed, let a path be made for the Osiris in the Great Valley, and let the Osiris have light to guide him on his way."

Osiris was the pharaoh of old, killed by his brother, Set, and consigned in death to the underworld. But he held power over life and death, and so he was reincarnated as the next pharaoh, the pharaoh after him, and then the next one, and so on, in perpetuity. Osiris was master of the underworld, and was the final judge to all who died, weighing souls in his balance pan to determine whether they deserved life with him in a perpetual state of bliss or gruesome death in the jaws of the god Amenti, who would consume the soul. The Great Valley was the valley of the dead, but because it would also be the starting point for Osiris' next journey among the living as reigning pharaoh, the Great Valley would be looked upon as the nexus of life and reincarnation as well as death. In the mythology of LOST, the Heart of the Island corresponds to the Great Valley, since it is the place in which the power of life, death, and rebirth dwells.

THE GUARDIANS OF LIFE

"Set and Horus Adoring Rameses" ca. 1200 BC Abu Simbel, Egypt

The second statement addressed Jacob's error in violently forcing his brother to enter the holiest place on the Island and lose his identity as a human being. In setting himself above his brother as the Man in Black's judge, Jacob had violated the rules established by the Guardian. Jacob made amends by drawing another statement from Egyptian mythology:

"He hath reconciled the Two Fighters (Horus and Set), the guardians of life."

This reference to Horus and Set was meant to symbolise Jacob's relationship with his brother. Rather than declaring himself the Man in Black's superior, the quote is meant to restore to the Man in Black the dignity he lost at the Source, and declares that both Horus (Jacob) and Set (the Man in Black) are equal guardians of life.

It was not Jacob (Horus) who reconciled the two fighters, but rather the Source itself, with the Cork Stone correctly in place to prevent either of the brothers from gaining ascendency over the other. As long as the Cork Stone remained in place, the brothers would maintain a balance that would serve the Island's need for stability and protection. Thus again Jacob deferred to the power of the Source rather than assuming power or the appearance of power to his person. The quote made Jacob and the Man in Black equals, both subservient to the Source, both guardians or servants of life.

JUSTICE

The Code of Hammurabi
Upper Stele
ca. 1700 BC PD

Jacob believed in progress. From the Guardian he learned a saying that stuck with him all his life: "Break the immovable yoke that we may sleep."

The quote is from Tablet One of the Enûma Eliš, the Babylonian story of creation. At this early point in the story the gods were in strife with each other. Some of the gods were creating such unbearable noise that no one in the care of Tia-mat, who gave birth to the gods, could sleep during the night. Instead they found themselves sleepy during the day from their lack of repose in darkness. The situation was intolerable, and a delegation of the gods appealed to Tia-mat, imploring her to intercede among the troublesome gods on their behalf, saying to her, "Break the immovable yoke that we may sleep."

There was no literal yoke, of course, but only the dreadful, unrelenting noise that created unnecessary strife and imposed an uncivilised disorder on the gods in Tia-mat's care. The situation was not just, and it was not civilised. The call to "break the immovable yoke that we may sleep" was an urgent appeal to divine justice and human civility.

Jacob incorporated this pivotal covenant statement into the Cork Stone as his own pledge of justice and civility, and in recognition of the fact that justice and civility could reign over the world only when humanity yielded to higher authority. By inscribing this ancient appeal to justice on the stone that was at the very heart of this world's contact with the forces of life and death and rebirth, Jacob was establishing justice and civility as supreme among the virtues. By placing them at the heart of the holiest place on Earth, he established these virtues as those to which all human beings and civilisations must defer.

No civilisation can be opposed to justice and civility. This ought to be evident. The statement requires no syllogism; it is, in fact, a raw statement of identity standing on its own. But Jacob knew, and we see evidence every day, that those in power over others take delight and comfort in placing yokes on others' necks, enslaving them, compelling them to conform to their unjust and uncivilised rules. The third statement is a pledge to bring an end to our tendency to wish to enslave each other. It is a hope for our future—for the progress Jacob knew we were capable of demonstrating.

HARMONY

The final covenant statement was also drawn from the first tablet of the Enûma Eliš. It is a desperate appeal to end the strife in the world. "That silence may reign, and we may sleep."

When there is justice in the world, when women and men are civil with each other, with their neighbours, with those whom they serve and with those who serve them, when everyone can live together, none of us will ever have to fear that we will die alone. Silence will reign. That is, the world will know neither strife nor discord. The gods and humans and the rulers of women and men will live in harmony with each other. This was Jacob's hope, his promise, his covenant carved in stone.

If we can't live together, we're going to die alone. If silence does not reign, we will never know peace, we will never possess justice, we will never enjoy any of the fruits of civlisation.

The message of LOST is that we can live together. We need not die alone. We know that we can do this because there are women and men like Jacob, Jack, John Locke, Sayid Jarrah, and Charlie Pace who consider these precepts, these foundations of our civilisation, more meaningful than even their own lives. In their sacrifice, we understand the essentiality of our shared humanity. It is something to savour, to appreciate, to share with our neighbours and especially our enemies, to teach to our children, to carry in our hearts.

"Eve." The Dormition Church on Mt. Zion, Jerusalem Radbod Commandeur ca. 1950 CC SA 3.0

Hebrew Scripture begins its story with an account of the origins of human civilisation in an ancient paradise as told through the exploits and foibles of the very first couple, Adam and Eve. The progenitors of humanity did not wish to leave the Garden of Eden, but they ate of the forbidden fruit of the tree of the Knowledge of Good and Evil, and the Creator drove them out of paradise.

Our Island story similarly began in a mystical paradise as old as the stars. The fish of the sea and the fruit of the trees were likewise sufficient to support all life on the Island, and there was also a single tree of which the fruits were forbidden. The sole occupant of paradise called this forbidden tree the Source—the Heart of the Island. She wished to leave the Island, but her destiny was to guard the centre of life, death, and rebirth with her eternal life, and the Source prevented her from leaving paradise.

We might take exception with a story that posits a murderous, conniving, bitter old woman as the first and most important example of commitment to a cause greater than oneself, acting essentially as the exemplar for all of humanity. After all, she hated us, to the point that she instilled that hatred in the two boys in her care, whose mother she murdered on the day of their birth. But the story accepted as foundational by the three great monotheistic religions of the world maintains that the single facet of human character warranting a Rule of Life, the most important part of our humanity, was destroyed when Adam and Eve ate of the forbidden fruit. In what way were Adam and Eve any better than this bitter old woman? After all, she was not driven out of paradise for disobedience—she faithfully protected the only Rule of Life on the Island. Seen in this light, our nurturing by this bitter old woman was more in keeping with the full breadth of our humanity than the intimately flawed example set by Eve and her helpmate, Adam.

The Guardian ("Mother") was the starting point, the catalyst that ignited the passion and imagination of boys who became masters of the Island, defenders of life, purveyors of death. She was evil harnessed for the protection of the Source, goodness for which there was no outlet, love for which there was no object. She was a jumble of contradictions, a loving mother who despised people, a woman with no beginnings who plotted her own end. Most of all, she was scared. Fear filled her eyes, changed the tone of her voice, for she knew her time had come, but no Protector appeared.

She protected the Source, the Light which all people seek. To fulfill her mandate she would commit any act, fabricate any falsehood, suffer any wound. The Source was well protected from the elements, fed by clean water, and not subject to natural paths of degradation. Animals had no interest in the Heart of the Island. Her sole duty, the one she feared and loved, was the protection of the living, breathing Island from the only predators that could harm the Source. Like the Man in Black, she had no name. She was adoptive mother to boys, Protector of the Source, but transcending both roles, she was custodian of the greatest myths and mysteries of the Island. We will call her the Guardian.

GUARDIAN OF FOREVER

The Guardian of Forever [from the original series (TOS) of Star Trek] had no beginning, no history, no interests or ambitions other than the single task of guarding the history of the universe. This strange entity from the Star Trek TOS episode "City on the Edge of Forever" marks an appropriate starting place for our analysis of the Guardian of Mittelos.

Both Guardians were gatekeepers. The Guardian of Forever guarded the history of every time and place; the Guardian of Mittelos watched over the treasure she believed the most important on Earth. She knew the Source, she saw the Light. More than likely she lived for thousands of years, since before the first pharaohs. With Claudia, we feel the urge to pose questions.

We think our questions worthy of the story, of her character, of finding a place for her in Island lore. In fact, some of us may consider her well-informed answers to our questions vital to our understanding. After all, we know who she really is. She is the gatekeeper for the kernels of mythology and axioms of human character that are the foundations for the story we watched unfold for six years. But the questions are problematic and any answers the Guardian provided would be pointless, since they would reveal no truths useful to our limited understanding.

The Guardian told Claudia, "Every question I answer will simply lead to another question." We see the exasperation in the Guardian's face, we hear the lack of patience in her voice. Perhaps she was simply tired of providing answers. We also know that she intentionally hid information and even prevented her two young teenage Candidates from gathering the knowledge they would require if they were chosen to become the Protector of the Island. Possibly, then, her secretive nature determined her unwillingness to provide answers. We can imagine other possibilities. Perhaps the writers were lazy, we think. Or perhaps they simply didn't give themselves enough time. Maybe if they had had just one more episode they could have laid out every truth and intricate bit of knowledge about the Island.

If we think about that possibility long enough, though, it becomes clear that one cannot pose questions and provide answers ad infinitum. At some point we have to accept axioms as they are, even if we don't like them or understand them. One cannot explain an axiom; it just is. Perhaps some are disappointed in this approach to LOST. Others of you may have decided that this is the only reasonable attitude we can cultivate, and that the significant and rich mythology we have been given is more than sufficient to the task of understanding this cinematic masterpiece.

I find myself disagreeing with both camps. I believe some elements of the story are beyond understanding, but not because of the inherent impossibility of completing an infinite progression. More importantly, though, I believe LOST provided more stuff with which to construct durable and meaningful answers than adherents of either of these two positions have been able to grasp.

The problem with the unlimited question and answer period is not a function of diminishing returns or infinite progressions or unrequited human lust for knowledge or any other challenge due to infinities. The problem is a result of the limited capabilities of our minds. Read the words the Guardian of Forever spoke in response to Captain Kirk's questions.

Kirk: What are you?
Guardian: I am the Guardian of Forever.
Kirk: Are you machine or being?
Guardian: I am both and neither. I am my own beginning, my own ending.
Spock: I see no reason for answers to be couched in riddles.
Guardian: I answer as simply as your level of understanding makes possible.

Some may understand this as an unnecessary affront. But if we consider the type of question we might wish to pose, we begin to understand the nature of the problem. We might, for instance, ask the woman about the duration of her stay on the Island. She could tell us, but the answer would provide no additional insight. Whether she had been on the Island for ten months or ten millennia is irrelevant because we know the Protector lives forever, provided she is not killed in certain ways. The questions that might have relevance are the ones we could not understand. What is the nature of the Source? As I have explained in other parts of this book, the Source is not subject to our probings. The Source is the mythological floor of the grand six-year parable. No interrogative we ever pose is going to elucidate any bit of information beyond the knowledge we have been given. If you are of like mind in analysis, a second difficulty arises. I consider that the Source is nothing less than humanity's connection to the Divine. If so, there can be no way to explain the Source in linguistic terms. Stated simply, there are no words. The Source is at the very interface of a world that exceeds human capacities for understanding.

EDITH KEELER

There is an important sense in which LOST provides more answers than even the most insistent fan of the show has requested (or demanded!). LOST provides a fertile ground for both questions and answers. If we look at the problem of a mythical being from this point of view, there is no distinction between question and answer; they are two sides of the same fascinating little coin.

Edith Keeler was framed by Harlan Ellison as a statement: Edith Keeler must die. Mention Edith Keeler to any Trekkie and you will receive in return a thoughtful nod and verbal acknowledgement of the grandeur of the name. Keeler's name bears greater significance than any character other than James T. Kirk or Mr. Spock. It is as meaningful as the phrase "Kobayashi Maru" (http://en.wikipedia.org/wiki/Kobayashi_Maru) has become to more casual moviegoers.

I will not divulge Edith Keeler's significance here. Hers is a story best experienced as originally performed, in Star Trek TOS 1.28, "The City on the Edge of Forever." The fifty minutes required to take in the episode are time well spent. Many believe "The City on the Edge of Forever" is the best hour of science fiction ever to appear on television.

The significance to us is that the problem of Edith Keeler could be posed as a question with no change regarding the philosophical power of the problem: Must Edith Keeler die?

Whether we render the philosophical conundrum as question or answer matters not. Even though the original 1967 teleplay stated that Keeler had to die, the debate rages on, among Trekkies, science fiction enthusiasts, and philosophers. Damon and Carlton weighed in on the question; Eloise Hawking was used as the spokesperson for their position on the matter. Their conclusion was simple: No, Edith Keeler did not have to die. As Eloise Hawking told us, the universe tends to course-correct. That is to say, there is nothing inherent or inevitable about any particular action. If the universe is tending toward a certain course of events, nothing we do will succeed in forcing the universe to follow some other route more to our liking.

In the same way, Darlton could have couched their questions as answers. It wouldn't matter in the end, because we would consider every answer to be a question subject to our consideration and debate.

Was the Guardian's bifurcation ("polarisation" was the word Darlton used) into Good Jacob and Bad Boy in Black inevitable? Must good always be accompanied by evil? Was the Boy in Black evil at all? Upon becoming the

Smoke Monster was the Man in Black evil, or was he merely carrying out the evil that Jacob had commissioned by throwing him into the Source? Was Jacob as evil as the Man in Black? Does evil come only in deep black, or is it flavoured in gradations of grey and even white? Was the Guardian fully human? Did she commit evil acts (lying, killing) only to preserve the Source, or did she have other motivations?

These are some of the questions arising naturally out of 6.15 "Across the Sea." They could be rendered as answers: For instance, "the Guardian imparted only good character elements to Jacob and only bad character elements to the Boy in Black." Or, "good is always accompanied by evil because good and evil are relative terms without objective value or meaning."

Rendered as statements, we immediately turn the ideas into questions anyway, and we go about the business of supporting an alternative answer. We know Jacob could not possibly have received only good character elements because he answered his "mother's" death with something worse than death for his brother; since he sought greater punishment than warranted by the crime, Jacob was evil. Therefore the Guardian imparted both good and evil elements to Jacob. Another person might chime in with the position that anything the Guardian did in this matter was irrelevant; either by genetic pre-disposition or by character, Jacob was the person he was. Yet a third participant in the discussion may opine that the whole question of good and evil was never raised by LOST and that the debate is therefore irrelevant.

At the foundational level of the Source and the Guardian, LOST examined the core values of our humanity. There can be no objective, universally embraced set of answers at this level. All we can hope for is what we received: Ideas about the human condition that stimulate thoughtful exploration, response, and debate.

THE RULES OF THE GAME

Senet Game 1 © Pearson Moore 2011

The Guardian was subject to the same rules binding any other Protector. Her only mandate was protection of the Island. Although we can think of this mandate as a "rule," we would probably do well to envision it more along the lines of the Island's firm preference. If we think of it as a "rule" we will be obliged to consider an infinite variety of corollaries to the prime directive encompassing every possible threat to the Island. While this way of looking at the Protector's responsibilities may appear to be quite reasonable, it carries potential to cause a misunderstanding of cause and effect.

For example, Keamy's team has violated the Island perimeter. If we have seen in the past a corollary to the prime directive indicating that the Protector must take immediate and direct action against the invaders, we may be surprised when we see the Protector take no action whatever. This inactivity on the part of the Protector may seem to violate the corollary rule, and the deviation may cause us to question the applicability of any other such rules. However, inactivity does not necessarily violate mandate; the Protector may employ any number of tactics against an invader, after all, as long as she is successful in the end.

We might consider the other "rules" as incidentally derivative of the prime directive. For instance, the Protector and the Candidates could not take their own lives. We may choose to see this as a distinct rule, but if we instead think of it as a natural outcome of the prime directive, we may be better served in our thinking. The acquisition of new Candidates was a most difficult undertaking. The Island was almost impossible to find, and we might consider this fact as also being derivative of the prime directive. The defence of an easy-to-locate Island would be virtually impossible.

The identification of Candidates was time consuming. Oceanic Flight 815, with over 300 passengers and crew, brought not more than a few dozen Candidates to the Island. Of these, only six were "finalists" for the position of Protector, and one (Kate) was Jacob's secret seventh weapon. There must have been very few suitable Candidates over the centuries, and all of them were eventually killed or found deficient in some critical way. The Protector had to endure long enough to find suitable replacement, and this would require extreme longevity. We can think of the unusual electromagnetism of the Island as conferring the requisite immortality through a slowing of the processes of apoptosis, but this entirely scientific way of looking at the Island imposes a logical artificiality that is perhaps not useful to our deepest appreciation of Island phenomena. Better, perhaps, to see immortality as the natural result of the Island's need for protection.

Seen in terms of the prime expression of the Island's will, the other "rules" can be understood as natural corollaries. Suicide was out of the question because the Island required protection by a knowledgeable Protector. The Island controlled life, death, and rebirth. We might consider the Island's ability to prevent suicide as being derivative of the greater ability to control vital functions. We might also consider that the prime directive is not the Island's protection, but life, death, and rebirth themselves. If there must be life, death, and rebirth, and order must be imposed over these, the maintenance of the necessary process would become the prime directive.

Thus, we might even consider that life, death, and rebirth was a single process that naturally dictated the set of conditions that we understand as "rules." Life, death, and rebirth, we might say, are the very stuff of the universe. Everything in our existence that we understand as some independent and arbitrary rule is actually a natural and necessary corollary to the unending expression of these three requisite functions of the universe.

PREGNANCY

She would not have waited long—no more than a few centuries, I imagine—before a shipwreck appeared, with survivors. The survivors were of no direct use to her. People were greedy, manipulative, untrustworthy, and selfish. But she needed a replacement. Ideally it would be someone bright, able and willing to do anything to protect the Source, and completely malleable to her will and her understanding of the world.

Probably she would have helped the sailor rebuild his vessel. When they were finished, she would have given him a heavy sack full of jingling yellow metal coins. "That's twelve minas of gold," she might have said. "Go out and get me a woman in her last month with child. I'll give you twelve more."

Perhaps she relied entirely on the caprices of wind and wave to bring her the perfect, untainted bundle of human flesh she required to teach and bend to her will. I doubt it. Claudia showed up on the beach because of human greed—and because the Guardian had been plotting Claudia's arrival for centuries. This is certainly conjecture, but it is not an unsupported guess. It is valid and plausible hypothesis, supported by every bit of Island history. More important, it is supported by the prime directive. The Protector was charged with finding a replacement. As we saw in the case of Jacob, identifying the replacement required centuries, even with professional navies plying the waves and commercial aircraft crossing the skies. In the Guardian's time, without the benefit of air travel, the identification of a suitable replacement would have required even more time. It therefore seems likely that she helped ships find the Island.

H. F. HARLOW'S ISLAND

Sixty years ago H.F. Harlow conducted studies in motherhood and childhood development. He was interested in determining the aspects of childhood conducive to normal development. The prevailing theory in the 1950s was that parents' most important contribution was material support: food, clothing, shelter. Dr. Harlow was sceptical. He separated rhesus monkeys from their mothers and gave them either terry cloth or wire "mothers." The terry cloth mothers had no food to offer, while the wire mothers were fitted with milk bottles. When the monkeys were dropped into strange environments with terry cloth mothers, they clung close to the soft figurines. When they were put into new environments with the wire mothers, they sat in the middle of the room, crying, or ran frantically around the room, looking for "mother."

Dr. Harlow established in several sets of experiments that psychological comfort was more important to the infant monkeys than even the best milk. The monkeys forced to grow up without real mothers were easily frightened, incapable of interacting with other monkeys, and generally disturbed and unhappy for the rest of their lives. When asked which condition of childhood provided for the best development of well-rounded children, Dr. Harlow gave a simple, one-word response: Love.

Jacob and his brother grew up without their mother. The woman who adopted them—or, more accurately, took on the job of raising them in the proper hatred of human beings—was not a soft and cuddly terry cloth adoptive guardian. She was more like the wire monkey, giving food, clothing, and shelter. Is it any wonder that, when left alone, Jacob and his brother more often than not ended up beating each other to a pulp? They had no concept of love, no remembrance of love, no certainty of worth and belonging that comes of a mother's embrace. No one showed them affection, and they were not loved. They belonged to neither mother nor father, and not once did they feel even a parent's touch. They belonged to no one, not even to the woman who stole them. They did belong, but to an entity they both wished to reject: the Island.

The Island was more important than the boys, at least in the Guardian's mind. They had to be blindfolded as the woman led them to the heart of Mittelos because the Island had greater value than their sense of wonder, their autonomy, even their very lives. Most of all, the woman could not allow them to figure out where the Light originated, because she could not trust them.

She taught Jacob her version of "love." When the boy returned to the cave without his brother, the woman asked where the Boy in Black was. Jacob didn't know. "Do you love me, Jacob?" she asked. When he responded "yes," she said, "Then tell me what happened." Love, to the Island-Protector, didn't mean giving Jacob a hug. It meant quizzing him, shaming him into ratting out his brother.

What most disturbed her was the tendency of her chosen Boy in Black, the one who would someday replace her as Protector of the Island, to stare out at the ocean, to think on it, to wonder what might be found across the sea. This was most dangerous, because the boy was otherwise precisely what she had longed for. He used deception and cunning and loved to stalk prey—the very qualities the Guardian held most dear. The boy who preferred dark tunics was "special" in every way that she was special.

They had no personal freedom. Volition was not among the aspects of human life cultivated by the woman, and she rigorously sought out any sign of dangerous independent thought in either of them.

The Guardian was no mother. "Mother" has become the almost universally used name for this character. But because she murdered the boys'

236

real mother, because she treated the boys in a manner unbefitting even the most callous and unfeeling of any mother I have ever seen in literature, because she was anything but a mother to these boys, I have never referred to her as "Mother."

DUTY BEFORE DEVOTION

Duty to the Heart of the Island outweighed every consideration, even devotion toward the Man in Black, whom she had favoured to inherit her responsibility. Her feelings for the man she had raised as her son were evident. But he and the Roman shipwreck survivors were meddling with the underground water and the Light that suffused it above and below.

"Morning Colours, Canada Day"
Brett Morton, USN, 2010 PD
USN ID 100701-N-8539M-013

MAN IN BLACK: I began to think--what if the light underneath the island-- what if I could get to it from someplace else? Figuring out how to reach it took a very long time.
MOTHER: The people with you, they saw this, too?
MAN IN BLACK: Yes, they have some very interesting ideas about what to do with it.
MOTHER: Do with it? You don't have any idea wh—
MAN IN BLACK: I have no idea because you wouldn't tell me, Mother.

Her adoptive son was attempting to use the Source. It was precisely the type of danger to the Source that she had sworn to prevent. One does not "use" something apart, something entirely beyond human understanding. The problem was not that the Man in Black wished to leave the Island. The problem was that he conceived of the Source as something that could yield to his will, be used to serve his ends. This thought was anathema to the Guardian, its utterance was darkest blasphemy, and its physical manifestations were abominations. If there was one truth on the Island, it was this: One does not interfere with the Source.

The Guardian's destruction of the Roman village and the murder of its inhabitants again invites mythological questions. Was the Guardian also a Smoke Monster? If so, did she become a Smoke Monster in the same way as the Man in Black? These again are pre-Source or sub-foundational questions that have no relevance to the story. We will never be able to make a determination regarding the status of the Island prior to the arrival of Claudia.

MOTHER NATURE

We might envision the Guardian as having relinquished those parts of her character that separated her from the Island. There was no separation for her. That she had no happiness on the Island was more than clear. But at some point the dreams of leaving the Island must have ceased. The dreams didn't end because she lost hope. Rather, her fantasies and deepest desires and every aspect of her imagination must have been oriented toward the single goal of protecting the Heart of the Island. Just as the flowing water of the Island and the Light from the Source were the lifeblood that ensured Jacob's immortality, the Heart of the Island must have been the Guardian's only connection with anything outside herself. She became more than herself, more than human, more than Eve. She was most akin to the entity we envision as Mother Nature.

That she was Mother Nature, that she was myth and immortality and primal force, does not nullify the fact that she was human. As a human being, she had the same need for companionship that we all share, and she found this companion in the Island. But if she was human, according to LOST she would also have to be linked with another entity to form a strange-attractor pair. The mythical part of her found this strange attractor in the love/hate relationship with the object of her pain and the origin of her desire: the Source. In fact, she was the only human (or partially human) character in the six-year series to be paired in a strange attractor with an entity other than a human being. Since she was more myth than human, this pairing was obvious and logically sound. But logic does not get the final word.

If you are not convinced of the authenticity of these words, think to the Guardian's pronouncements regarding humanity. We come, we fight, we destroy, we corrupt, and it always ends the same. We're greedy, manipulative, untrustworthy, and selfish. In what way are these statements any different from those of any of the major organised religions? Ah, you say, but my religion tells me that in spite of all our faults, the Creator loves us. The Guardian, on the other hand, hated us. Yes, the Creator loves us as She loved Jacob. That phrase sounds familiar to your ears, I know. The original citation is from the book of the prophet Malachi (Mal. 1:3) and repeated in the Christian Scriptures (Rom. 9:13), but this is not the origin in our mythology. The original quote is from the Room 23 brainwash video. "God loves you as He loved Jacob" was one of ten statements in the video, and one of four sayings given prominence during Karl's brainwashing in Episode 3.07 ("Not in Portland"). The Creator loves us. The Guardian hated us. These statements indicate the same reality. It is the Green Pill again, this time masquerading as a distinction between love and hate. For the Island loved both the Guardian and Jacob, and the Guardian loved both the Island and Jacob. The Guardian is the Island's strange attractor twin.

One might find one's Constant in something other than a human being, but a human/non-human Strange Attractor coupling could not last. According to Daniel Faraday the Constant need not even be a living thing—it could be inanimate. But to become involved in a strange attractor pair with something other than a human being requires that one constantly exchange essences of self that have no grounding in emotion and no bearing on deepest identity. The strange attractor goes deeper into our nature than even the Constant. If the nature of the strange attractor is to act as the expression of one's deepest self, this expression cannot be sustained if there is no deep exchange. One of the twins would have to leave the couple, spinning out of control away from the strange attractor. This, of course, is exactly what happened to the Guardian, who was at least partially human.

The Guardian was only partly myth. The more important part of her character was conveyed through her humanity. I am not entirely convinced that she was human in ways we might understand from science or history. But even such a distant deviation would not prove problematic to the story. Mr. Spock is only half human, but we see generous evidences of his humanity in every episode of Star Trek. Even if Damon and Carlton someday confess that the Guardian was a space alien, it nevertheless remains true that she felt happiness and dread and sadness and anger and every other human emotion. She was compassionate to a degree—at least to the extent that she genuinely regretted having to inflict pain on other human beings. In the ways that truly matter, she evinced every characteristic of human beings.

The hypothesis I find most attractive is simple: The Guardian, like the Man in Black, lost her humanity in the millennia preceding the boys' arrival. Whether she became a Smoke Monster we can never know. Certainly she receive power equal in magnitude to that of the Smoke Monster. Perhaps it was in the acquisition of this power that she also surrendered any claim to the completeness of her humanity.

The Guardian, for Darlton, is the introduction of the non-mechanistic, non-mythological human element into the story. In her interactions over the years with Jacob and the boy she never named, she was confronted with choices. Her daily decision to put the Source first, above even the most essential needs of the boys, had consequences antithetical to her primary objective. Her lies and manipulations served as immediate but short-lived protection for the Source because those same deceits were a constant affront to the dignity and humanity of the boys she had raised as her own. The Boy in Black left her, never to return. Even the disturbed mama's boy, Jacob, agreed to stay with her, but only "for a while."

Her deceptions served to convince both men of the need for independent thought, and forced them to rely on their own resources for the acquisition of information. Deceit, fueled by her lack of trust, removed any basis for the sharing of common priorities, and therefore undermined every other aspect of their relationship. It is in these conflicts over trust, faith, devotion, love, desire, assertion of control, and lust for power that we see LOST shine most brightly.

DEATH

She burned the Roman village to the ground, filled in the deep well, and killed every one of the inhabitants. Descendants of the survivors of the shipwreck, they had survived peacefully on the Island for forty years until the Guardian recognised the opportune moment to kill them and use their deaths to further her nefarious plans.

Her intention, thought out for centuries, was to so enrage Jacob's brother that he would release her from the millennia of captivity she had endured on the Island. Perhaps in her youth—maybe before she lost her own humanity—she had dreamed of returning to her people. Maybe she had nurtured this dream even after she became something less than human. But after so many millennia, she too must have been praying at the statue of Tawaret, begging her or any deity who would listen, to send a child she could teach in the ways of the Island and then leave—by boat or by death—so she could end her unhappy existence and hateful responsibility to protect the Light.

Hers was not the first death reckoned a release. Kelvin Inman sought precisely the same escape from his lonely responsibilities at the Swan Station. His hatch mate, Stuart Radzinsky, found the situation underground so depressing that he believed his only choice was suicide. Richard Alpert, after serving Jacob for at least two lifetimes, wished only to escape the immortality he had gained.

These instances of unhappiness constitute a common thread with multiple shared elements. All of these characters were performing repetitive, sometimes boring tasks over long periods of time. All of them were to some degree immune from the vagaries of life in the greater world, insulated from dangers and accidents.

We might draw from our own experience to fashion a hypothesis uniting these deaths and suicides under the cause of boredom. But boredom is not one of the themes of LOST. I doubt, too, that the tasks were so odious or so boring as to have become the cause of a wish as profound as murder or death. Rather, I believe the Guardian's planned death, Radzinsky's suicide, and Inman's wish to leave the Island were directly related to Jack's proclamation in Episode 1.05: "If we can't live together, we're going to die alone."

By isolating themselves from human civilisation, the Guardian, Inman, Radzinsky, and Richard (isolated in that he did not share in human mortality) were alone. Though not physically dead, they were dead to the rest of humanity. "If we can't live together, we're going to die alone." The significance is not that by violating some tenet of civility we will be doomed to die without our loved ones surrounding us. The meaning is much simpler: If we do not cultivate friendships, we will die. Jack's words, in light of the Guardian's lonely existence and her outright refusal of companionship and disdain for anything human, meant simply that human life is impossible without friendship. Friendship, in the form of the idea of the Constant, was a major theme in LOST. Without each other, we are dead. Without each other, we are Lost.

In her loneliness and in her perverse and sad preference for an unhappy solitude, in her contempt for human society, the Guardian was the instigator of a two-thousand-year legacy of distrust, murder, deception, loneliness, and death.

"Let me help," Captain Kirk said to Edith Keeler as they strolled the shops on Main Street. "A hundred years or so from now, I believe, a famous novelist will write a classic using that theme. He'll recommend those three words even over 'I love you.'"

Jack Shephard, if he were still alive, would be nodding, noting his firm agreement with Captain Kirk. Let me help, because by helping I come to share in your troubles and challenges, I come to share in your life. By sharing in your life, I find my own life. And by sharing all things together, we find ourselves, and each other, and we are no longer Lost.

"Light and Dark" © Pearson Moore 2011

He had no name, no family, no history, no future. His people lived far away, across the sea. The one who professed love for him took away his job and gave it to his brother--and then she killed every one of his friends.

At forty-three he was trapped on an Island with the woman who killed his mother and the infantile mama's boy who doted on her. He shared nothing with his brother, not priorities or desires or diversions--not even hair colour. His thoughts lacked any point of reference other than his home, across the sea.

His situation was infinitely worse than this, however. We have heard his story before. We know him from the holy text of every ancient religion. Mary Shelley wrote about him, and Edward Everett Hale fifty years after her. We have heard his story before, but every aspect of him is new. He is the Man in Black, Cerberus, the Smoke Monster, but he is so much more. He's not so different from you and me. In fact, we understand him best by looking at ourselves.

Good and evil are abundant inside each one of us, as they were inside the Man in Black. Perhaps we believe we understand the nature of goodness. But the origins and expressions of evil we may consider beyond our grasp. Let us take a close look at the one character in LOST who exhibited every defining characteristic of evil. Through this study we will come to understand good and evil in an entirely new light.

THAT WHICH WE CALL A ROSE

"I only picked one name."

Claudia was exhausted after delivering the first boy, Jacob. Delivering the second she was too tired to think of a name. The Protector scrambled to find a rock suitable for cracking a skull, not because she wished to deprive the woman of any contact with her babies, but because it was imperative that the second-born have no name.

From this early moment in the Protector's plan, she had already chosen the Boy in Black (BIB) as her successor. He was the second-born, the runt of the litter, the one normally disfavoured by society. She would raise him to be comfortable in taking control of any situation or person. No one would exercise control over the BIB; no one would even try to displace him from the exalted position of Protector. This was the Law of the Island.

He could have no name. The Protector herself had no name, and the Protector she replaced so many millennia before likewise carried no moniker. Her adopted second-born son, heir to the most powerful position in the world, could never be subject to anyone's call. If he had a name, people could invoke him, petition him to do their bidding. Such was his responsibility that any petition was out of the question. He would have a single function, expressed in his title: Protector. He would answer to no one.

Friends or even casual acquaintances may address us by our first names. But in a formal situation we are addressed by title and surname. "Pearson" becomes "Dr. Moore." The way in which we address someone is determined by relationship and context. For the Protector, there can be only one context, determined by the absolute requirement to protect the Light. For the Light is everything: "Life, death, rebirth. It's the source, the heart of the island." Likewise, there is only one relationship: We are all subordinate to the Protector.

But the prohibition against naming the Protector goes far beyond the normal constraints of relationship and context. To name something is to control it.

The ancient belief in the power conferred by the naming of things is featured in the opening pages of the Hebrew Bible. The first chapter of Genesis says, "God said to them, 'Be fruitful and multiply, and fill the earth and subdue it; and have dominion over... every living thing that moves upon the earth.'" (Gen 1:28, NRSV) Dominion was achieved in the second chapter, with the naming of the animals: "So out of the ground the Lord God formed every animal of the field... and brought them to the man to see what he would call them; and whatever the man called each living creature, that was its name." (Gen. 2:20, NRSV) The Creator controls humankind, and therefore gave us names: woman and man. However, human beings control all the animals, and therefore we, not the Creator, named them.

In many aboriginal cultures one does not address a person by name. To do so is more than disrespectful; addressing a person by name indicates an attempt to gain spiritual power over the person. Even today in some major religions one does not presume to affix a name to the Creator of the world. For instance, the Tetragrammaton—the four-letter (thus "tetra"-"gram") name of the Creator in the Hebrew Bible—is never intoned, at least in most Jewish tradition.

"Tetragrammaton" 1868
Grace Episcopal Church, Decorah, Iowa

Recent proclamations by Roman Catholic and mainline Protestant leaders have restricted or eliminated the now-declining tradition of transliterating the Tetragrammaton and providing an English pronunciation. Speaking the revealed name of the Creator from the Christian pulpit was a common weekly event not too long ago, but is becoming all but unthinkable in modern liturgical practice.

The custom of addressing certain high-ranking persons by title rather than by name is maintained even today. One does not address the President of the United States as "Mr. Obama" or even "President Obama." The correct form of address is "Mr. President." Likewise, one does not address Cardinal Marc Ouellet of Québec as "Cardinal Ouellet." The correct form of address is "Your Eminence" (or, in his native language, "Votre Éminence").

No power spiritual or temporal, physical or mystical, would gain ascendency over the Boy in Black. Such were the rules, rigorously enforced by the Protector. The Boy in Black (BIB) would never, ever have a name.

BY ANY OTHER NAME WOULD SMELL AS SWEET

A person's name is the sweetest word that person can hear. Psychologists and human resource managers and professional interviewers know the best way to gain a person's confidence is to address her by name and to refer to her name in a complimentary manner. "Pleased to meet you, Susan. My brother named his daughter 'Susan.' It's a beautiful name." Susan has just made a friend for life, and the person addressing her in this way knows it.

If we do not hear our name intoned in friendship and respect, some other acknowledgment of who we are must take the place of verbal address. In this respect the BIB was more than fortunate. The person who raised him, the woman he knew as Mother, made him the centre of her life. His brother, Jacob, had second place in her heart, and everyone knew it, most of all the BIB. While Jacob performed chores around the cave, the BIB was out exploring, investigating, trying to make sense of the world. Whenever he had questions, Mother was there to answer them. She favoured him with time, affection, and every resource available to her. His domination of the world around him was confirmed in every action he took, even in the game of senet he played with his brother.

BOY IN BLACK: You can't do that, Jacob.
JACOB: Why not?
BOY IN BLACK: Because it's against the rules.
JACOB: You made the rules.
BOY IN BLACK: I found it.

One day the BIB would make all the rules, and they would bind Jacob no less than anyone else. Everything was proceeding according to the Protector's plan, and everything was happening according to the BIB's pleasure.

HONOUR THY MOTHER AND FATHER

I am my daughter's father. I am my wife's husband. I am my father's son.

We establish our identity in any number of ways: Our name, the work we do, the place we inhabit. But probably the most important means by which we establish identity is through relationship. If I am not my son's father, my wife's husband, or my mother's son, who am I? If these relationships are taken away I have no means of orienting myself in this world. The mandate to "honour thy father and mother" is one of the greatest of the commandments because it is a directive aimed at establishing identity. This single commandment gives purpose, priority, and place to three living human beings: The daughter or son, the mother, and the father. To disrespect mother or father is to disrespect oneself, and to disrespect—even remove—one's place and priority in this world.

The BIB had abilities not shared with his brother. He saw dead people, something his brother would never be able to do. But more important to the story, he could converse with them. The woman in red was not only beautiful, she had the closest relationship with the BIB that one person can have with another: she was his mother.

Claudia's revelation destroyed the BIB's world. The woman he had loved as mother turned out to be a thoughtless, vile pretender, a murderer, a destroyer of anything of value or worth. By killing his mother, the BIB's Guardian was saying the mother had no worth, and therefore the BIB himself had no value.

The BIB had neither name nor relationship of any kind. He had no identity, and therefore he was nothing. He would have to find some other means of asserting his identity.

In the Roman village on the other side of the Island he found his identity. He was Roman, like them, a shipwreck survivor, like them. They were his people. He regained his identity. He belonged. For thirty years he enjoyed the reassurance of shared humanity. The people were "greedy, manipulative, untrustworthy, and selfish," but they were his people. Best of all, they were working together toward a great and worthy objective: Finding a way across the sea.

THINGS UNDER THE EARTH

"Socrates is an evil-doer, and a curious person, who searches into things under the earth and in heaven, and he makes the worse appear the better cause; and he teaches the aforesaid doctrines to others."

This was the accusation leveled against the Sophist, Socrates, in 399 B.C. He was peering into matters not suited to philosophical exploration. The abode of "things under the earth and in heaven" was not to become the subject of human examination or feeble attempts at understanding. This was the abode of the gods, and of beings beyond our comprehension. Human beings did not belong in such places, for we had no right to meddle in the affairs of the gods. For his disobedience of this fundamental principle of Athenian law, Socrates was executed.

The mixture of water and Light under the earth was the Island's abode of supreme power. The Light was more powerful and more dangerous than even the Protector herself. The power and danger were so great that the Protector would allow not even the Man in Black to know its location. When they were yet boys she blindfolded them so they would not be able to figure out its place on the Island.

When the Protector found the Man in Black underground, with access to the Light, she was shocked. The Man in Black had no business underground, and certainly not anywhere near the Light. While she was still trying to make sense of this revelation, the Man in Black told her the unthinkable: He and his Roman friends were figuring out how to manipulate the Light to do their bidding—to allow them passage across the sea. The Protector was beyond shocked and moved into the realm of pure anger. This meddling in the affairs of life and death and rebirth would have to end, immediately.

She said nothing to her adopted son, for there was no benefit in alerting him to her extreme displeasure. She pulled him in, as if to embrace him, and then pushed him into the stone wall, knocking him out.

THE MAN WITHOUT A VILLAGE

The Protector killed every one of the Romans, destroyed their village, and filled in every mine they had dug. In less than a single afternoon she spent her fury and destroyed everything that had ever had meaning to the Man in Black.

A man whose friends were all murdered has suffered bewildering loss. The deaths are disorienting because the individuals to whom he was connected established his place in the world. Many people, suffering such awful depths of loss never recover. Having lost their essential connections to the world, they become only fractions of the people they once were.

Most people who experience loss of even the closest relationships will eventually recover. They count on their other connections to reality to provide the foundation upon which they can rebuild their lives. They belong to a synagogue or church, have membership in professional organisations, take night classes, or do volunteer work. The key concept in all of these connections is belonging. We find our place in this world, we establish our identity, by belonging.

With the burning of the village and the murder of every one of his friends, the Man in Black had no relationships, no friends, no social connections, nothing to which he might claim to belong.

THE MAN WITHOUT A COUNTRY

In the classic novel by Edward Everett Hale, Philip Nolan is a young U.S. Army lieutenant on trial for conspiring to treason with Aaron Burr (circa 1807). During the course of the trial he shouts, " Damn the United States! I wish I may never hear of the United States again!" The judges, all Revolutionary War veterans, decide to grant the man his wish. Rather than executing him, they sentence him to spend the remainder of his life aboard U.S. naval vessels, never again to set foot in the United States, the crews sworn to silence regarding any aspect of history or current events in their country.

Nolan spends the remainder of his life at sea and through a masterful narrative we experience the development of the saddest, most pitiful character in fiction. The man loves his country, of course. The conclusion of the novel depicts Nolan, hours from death in 1863. Displayed in his tiny room are a flag, a partial map of the United States, and other tidbits he acquired over the decades. The navy lieutenant who has been fighting for his release disobeys orders, enters Nolan's cabin, and spends the next several hours relating American history of the last sixty years. The only fact the officer leaves out is that the country Nolan so deeply loves is now at war with itself. The Civil War has literally torn apart the land he loves, and the officer cannot bear to tell the dying man anything about the destruction in his country.

I doubt most readers can finish this novel without shedding tears. Every one of us needs to belong. We understand the man's sadness but also his nobility in never giving up hope of seeing the land he loves.

The sadness of the Man in Black runs deeper than even Philip Nolan's. Nolan at least had memories of his country. The MIB knew only that his country was out there—across the sea; he had never seen his land. The long-promised inheritance of the Protector position had been given to Jacob. The Guardian destroyed every single contact he had. Even this was not enough for her, though. She took steps to ensure he would never leave the Island, would never once know his roots in Rome, far across the sea. She removed from him every shred of belonging.

The Man in Black was a man without a name, without mother or father or brother, without friends, without a history, without connection of any kind. He had no identity. He did not belong to anyone or anything.

RETRIBUTION

Only a truly evil woman could commit the deeds the Guardian had performed. She had robbed the Man in Black of even the smallest morsel of identity, torn from him any sense of belonging.

The implement of retribution was the pugio the MIB carried. He and Jacob thought it had to be a pugio, but they learned soon enough—two thousand years later—that any knife whose metal was subject to electromagnetism would work. The knife had to be subject to a power greater than the Protector's. He struck from behind, before she could utter a word. If she had gotten a word out, she would have rendered the dagger useless—she would have named her attacker, and in the naming, she'd have controlled him.

Seconds before she died, the MIB posed the only question that had ever been on his mind.

MAN IN BLACK: Why wouldn't you let me leave, mother?
GUARDIAN: Because I...I love you.

She had a warped concept of love, but it was in keeping with the extreme negative bias she had toward people in general. Her legacy found expression in many ways. Her philosophy of contempt for humanity was propagated directly in the thoughts and actions of the MIB. Her lack of compassion and warped values continued in Jacob, who spent most of his time conniving to bring hundreds of innocent people to the Island, only to have them die. As people died in horrible ways they certainly never would have chosen for themselves, Jacob was yet able to comfort himself with the thought that in forcing them to the Island he was somehow allowing them full expression of personal autonomy. Jacob's warped sense of things was similar to the Guardian's.

The Guardian's last two words expressed gratitude for the MIB's act. "Thank you," she said. He had released her from a life that had become a burden. With Jacob in control of the Source, she knew she could finally leave the Island by the only means available to her.

A FATE WORSE THAN DEATH

Jacob knew his brother could never die. But he knew of a punishment far worse than death.

GUARDIAN: Just promise me. no matter what you do, you won't ever go down there.
JACOB: Would I die?
GUARDIAN: It'd be worse than dying, Jacob...much worse.

The type of interaction we have with the Source depends on our state of being. "For everyone who has will be given more, and he will have an abundance. Whoever does not have, even what he has will be taken from him." LOST teaches that we have value only to the extent that we cultivate relationships. In fact, the only way to "move on" from the sideways purgatory is with a Constant at one's side on entering the Church of the Holy Lamp Post.

The MIB had been stripped of almost everything: name, family, relationship, village, country. We might believe that he had in fact lost everything. Two things yet remained: His human body, and his status as a human being. When Jacob threw him into the cave at the centre of the Island, he lost those two remaining shreds of identity.

RICHARD: But if you are the black smoke...
MAN IN BLACK: You aren't the only one who's lost something, my friend.
The Devil betrayed me. He took my body. My humanity.

The Source operates much like the basic input/output (BIOS) system in a computer. Whatever goes in comes out, but intensified. Jack went into the cave with faith, and came out with assurance of his faith. The MIB went into the cave with selfish intentions, and came out as an entity of pure selfishness, not connected to anything or anyone. It is not the existence he chose.

PATHOS

He was almost nothing. He had no identity of any kind. He was not even a man anymore. All that remained was desire. Above all else, he desired to belong. His single goal over two thousand years was to find his home across the sea where he would finally have a place in the world. His is almost certainly the saddest story in the six years of LOST.

SAWYER: What are you?

MIB: What I am is trapped. And I've been trapped for so long that I don't even remember what it feels like to be free. Maybe you can understand that. But before I was trapped, I was a man, James. Just like you.

SAWYER: I'm havin' a hard time believin' that...

MIB: You can believe whatever you want, that's the truth. I know what it's like to feel joy... to feel pain, anger, fear... to experience betrayal. I know what it's like to lose someone you love.

His words to Sawyer were not only true, but they were from a place that was once his heart. It was not the last time he would confess his feelings to those he sought to destroy.

MIB: I know what you're going through.

KATE: And how do you know that?

MIB: Because... my mother was crazy. Long time ago, before I... looked like this... I had a mother, just like everyone. She was a very disturbed woman. And, as a result of that, I had some growing pains. Problems that I'm still trying to work my way through. Problems that could have been avoided had things been different.

STRANGE ATTRACTOR

We need to belong because we need to be able to say "I am." These two words are necessary to our existence because they express our identity. But our identity must be connected to something or someone. We are allowed these two powerful words only if we know at the deepest part of ourselves that we are connected to something outside ourselves. We cannot simply say, "I am"; we must say, "I am X," or, "I am Y." For example, I am my father's son, or I am a bicyclist. The only entity with necessary, non-contingent identity is the Creator. If I cannot identify a single connection with reality outside my fragile existence, I have no connection, therefore no identity, therefore no existence.

The strange attractor is the fundamental expression of our identity. It constitutes the baseline statement of who we are. Jacob, like Cain, decided he was not his brother's strange attractor twin. Or, as Cain asked, "Am I my brother's keeper?" Jacob's response and Cain's response to the question were identical. The outcomes were the same. Cain was physically marked as a sign of his identity as killer of the first-born son of Eve. Jacob was spiritually marked: He was flawed, all alone in this world (Episode 6.16, Act 5.2) because he rejected even his strange attractor brother.

The Man in Black appeared before the Source as an entity devoid of connection to anything in this world. But there never has been and never can be a single entity without fundamental connection to something outside itself. Created things are created, they do not pop into existence on their own, and therefore they obey the rules of existence that state that existence is a condition of connectedness to other created things.

We cannot know the exact nature of the transformation the Man in Black underwent inside the Cave of Light. We might speculate that his fundamental orientation was toward evil, or that his murder of the Guardian was the act that weighed most heavily in Osiris' balance pan—that the Source judged him according to his deeds and found him lacking the humanity to survive in human form. This seems a perfectly logical possibility. However, I would like to present an alternative that I believe has merit.

I do not believe it is necessary to envision the appearance of the Man in Black before the Source as requiring judgment. That he enjoyed not a single connection to the world was partly his own choice, but mostly the natural result of the Guardian's evil and Jacob's violent reaction to the Guardian's murder. Perhaps the only aspect of reality with any bearing on his strange appearance at the Heart of the Island was the fact of his spiritual nakedness, that he was the barest shell of a being. If connection to something outside self is necessary to existence, perhaps the most benign or positive action the Source could take was to provide a connection for the Man in Black. He came out of the cave connected not to any one person, but to all of humanity.

He was good, because he wanted good things, because he desired connection above all things, because he only wished to return to Rome, across the sea. He was good because he was connected to all of us, and even the worst among us carries some of the Light and dreams of things fair and beautiful and just.

He was evil, because he cared for no one, was connected to no one in particular, because he disconnected himself from the only woman who cared for him, from the man who had wished for his happiness. He was evil because he came, he fought, he destroyed, he corrupted.

But these assignments of character miss the important fact of his innocence. He had no evil intent prior to stabbing the Guardian. The murder itself was nothing more than retribution for her murder of everyone in the village. The Man in Black was content to find a peaceful way off the Island. No one, not even the Guardian, had ever told him that meddling with the Light and its waters was forbidden. In all his travails over the thirty years before the destruction of the village he never once contemplated or carried out murder or even the slightest crime. He was a man without a country who merely wished to go home.

There is no good, no evil, no judgment. There is only existence, identity, attraction, connection, and a happy Constant to ensure one's ability to "move on." In the Man in Black we see pure desire devoid of belonging. Even if he had somehow completed his great voyage to Rome, he would have found there no one willing or able to make him into a complete, connected human being. He would have been eternally alone, eternally drinking from a cup that could never quench his thirst. We did not see him in the church, or anywhere in the sideways world. There is some satisfaction in this realisation, but no joy—and much sadness.

ANTITHESIS

The MIB was LOST's antithesis. He was the worst-case opposite of everything required of us as humans. Stripped of every particle of humanity, he was pure desire, willing to sacrifice any number of people to satisfy his whim. Selfishness is a necessary constituent of our existence, but it is not properly an element of our humanity. We all must die, but we do not hold death to be one of the abiding principles or great expressions of our essential selves. When death becomes our focus, we become something less than human. In the same way, when selfish desire becomes the guiding principle in our lives, we can no longer claim to be fully human.

According to LOST, we express our humanity only to the extent that we cultivate and uphold the value of human interaction, friendship, trust, faith, and love. Connections are essential to our identity as human beings. In valuing trust, faith, and love above all else, we learn to give up our selfish desires and see in others the full culmination of everything we wish to be. "You can't take it with you", but to move on past the sideways afterlife, we must have lived life in such a way that we cultivated enduring friendships and gave up selfish desires to serve the needs of others.

These are the teachings of LOST. Our identity is grounded in belonging. If we can't live together—that is, if we can't give up our morbid concentration on self—we're going to die alone. Jack (the personification of LOST's thesis) articulated this truth back in Season One. Everything we witnessed over the next six years was proof of Jack's prophetic wisdom.

The story of the MIB is sad. But even in his wretched, lonely journey, there was hope. At any moment he could have made a decision like Sawyer's or Ben's. Ben was not far from the MIB in the degree to which selfishness ruled his life. Yet under Ilana and then under Hurley he worked for the common good, and he was offered redemption after death.

The sight of the Man in Black's broken body was sad, but we did not mourn for him. He received his due. Halfway across the Island a noble soul, a man pure of heart also died, and the moment was sad. But we did not mourn for him, either. For we knew that Jack Shephard had a billion strong connections in this world and the next--the connections for which Jack willingly sacrificed his life. He also received his due. He belonged.

CHAPTER 17 ADVANCED TOPIC IV:
THE VALENZETTI EQUATION

Freedom is responsibility.

Science is faith.

Adversity is opportunity.

As Kris Kristofferson wrote, "Freedom's just an another word for nothin' left to lose." The great battle of science versus faith that consumed John Locke and nearly took Jack Shephard's life was a war over complementary means of knowing. Elements of reality that appear to work against each other from a linear point of view are seen to work in harmony from a multi-dimensional standpoint. Those who understand the true nature of the world know that "impossibility" is another way of stating "infinite potential."

The Valenzetti Equation predicted the end of the world. "It predicts the exact number of years and months until humanity extinguishes itself. Whether through nuclear fire, chemical and biological warfare, conventional warfare, pandemic, over-population... the results are chilling"(Sri Lanka Video). The Dharma Initiative maintained a single objective: find a way to avoid the Valenzetti outcome. But science, in its logical, linear approach to the problem, would never find an open-ended solution to the equation. Humankind was doomed.

We know LOST constituted an optimistic statement of humankind's ability to overcome obstacles to Jacob's Progress. Jack saved the Island, kept the light shining in the Heart of the Island so that it could always burn in the hearts of women and men. He found the open-ended solution to prevent the extinction of humanity. But how did he accomplish this feat?

FAILURE IS NOT AN OPTION

Gene Kranz, NASA Flight Director during the manned Gemini and Apollo Space Programs, is revered in the engineering and scientific world for prevailing against no-win conditions. He and his ground-based team faced essentially impossible odds on April 13, 1970, when the Number Two oxygen tank in the Apollo 13 service module exploded three hundred thousand kilometres from earth. The explosion led to the immediate failure of the Number One oxygen tank, and within minutes all three fuel cells were dead. The command module's vital supplies—electricity, light, oxygen, water—were gone. From the point of view of a reasonable observer the three astronauts on board were doomed to rapid death through hypothermia or asphyxiation.

"Gene Kranz" NASA ca. 2005 PD

Four days later, all three astronauts were back on Earth aboard the USS Iwo Jima, fifteen kilograms lighter, but otherwise in good physical health.

A triumph of science and engineering? Certainly Kranz's White Team (called the "Tiger Team" by the press) represented his country's best minds in engineering know-how. In the space of three days they accomplished mechanical and electrical feats that are considered miraculous to this day. But Kranz did not attribute mission success to scientific prowess. Something much more important was in play. It is this characteristic of Kranz's team, applied forty years later on the Island, that turned the tide against the Smoke Monster, and guaranteed that the doom-and-gloom predictions of the Valenzetti Equation would never again darken our thoughts.

THE EQUATION

The Valenzetti Equation is canonical to LOST. Verbal reference to the equation was never made, but the idea was prominently displayed in one of the most cherished iconic images of the series. Around Day 60 (Episode 2.17, "Lockdown"), Locke discovered a map of the Island inscribed on the blast door in the Swan Station. The lower left corner of the map contained this cryptic remark, written in bold letters:

--LOW PRIORITY ZONE FOR
 EXPLORATION--
POSSIBLE SITE FOR ABOVE-

GROUND STUDY OF FLORA
LOW RELEVANCE TO
VALENZETTI-RELATED
RESEARCH ACTIVITY.

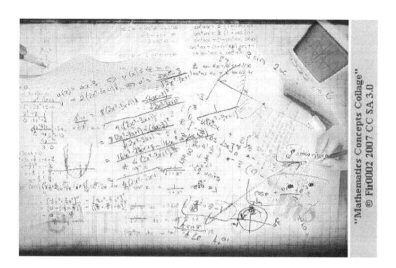

The semi-canonical Sri Lanka video explained the significance of the Valenzetti Equation. The Cuban Missile Crisis of 1962 spurred the United Nations to investigate the mathematical basis for the preservation of humanity. Enzo Valenzetti reduced all global activity and conditions to six core environmental and human factors and fitted them into a single equation returning the number of years and months remaining before the disappearance of the human species from the planet. The coefficients representing the six core factors were 4, 8, 15, 16, 23, and 42. Regardless of the assumptions and changes made to the model, no solution to the equation allowed for the survival of humankind.

According to film narrator Alvar Hanso, the Dharma Initiative was created specifically to address the problem of human extinction as predicted by the Valenzetti model. Hanso said he and his executives "have assembled the greatest minds in the world and given them unlimited funds and access." His passion and energy were focussed on finding a way to prevent our demise, and he would commit his personal fortune to fund the initiative in perpetuity. "Only by manipulating the environment, by finding scientific solutions to our problems we will be able to change those core factors, and give humanity a chance to survive."

Jacob assigned numerical values to each of the Candidates. By the time the Man in Black brought Sawyer to the cave under the cliffs, only six names had not yet been crossed out:

04 Locke
08 Reyes

15 Ford
16 Jarrah
23 Shephard
42 Kwon

While Sawyer looked on, the Man in Black crossed out 04 Locke, who had died days before. Only five remained.

That the number assignments of the final Candidates corresponded to the coefficients of the Valenzetti Equation could not have been coincidental. Jacob would have known the significance of the Valenzetti Coefficients since Richard reported on Dharma activities. It seems unlikely, however, that he would have assigned the numbers in response to knowledge of the equation. First of all, at least one of the Candidates, John Locke, was born before the development of the equation. But most importantly, Jacob had his own mind about things. He did not believe as his adoptive mother had said, that people were greedy, manipulative, and untrustworthy. He preferred to base his actions on a perception that humanity was on a trajectory toward improvement. More likely, it seems to me, the six coefficients represented something inherent to the structure of the universe; the numerical assignments were inevitable because they expressed immutable, structural necessity.

Jacob must have mused on the significance of the Candidates' numbers while he worked on his tapestry. Perhaps he had "insider" knowledge of the larger significance; indeed, this may have been the origin of the mystical lighthouse, where he observed the daily activities of the Candidates over the last decades before their arrival on the Island.

Despite his longevity and laudable drive to make provision for a successor, I don't see Jacob as a super-intelligent mastermind. He did not have "special" abilities, such as his brother's ability to speak with dead people. He didn't want the job of Protector, after all. I understand Jacob not as unusually bright, but as unusually gifted with optimism and determination. He may or may not have understood the underlying significance of the Six, but he did spend decades studying the limitations and abilities of his chosen ones. If we are to understand the ability of six individuals to overcome the inevitability of human self-destruction, we must understand the factors critical to their success. Let's begin by taking a closer look at Candidate #8, Hugo Reyes.

MULTI-DIMENSIONAL CANDIDATES

The characters of LOST were not attracted to abstract ideals. Hurley is a perfect representative of this truth, since he was the character most closely associated with a resilient moral code. He had an innate sense of right and wrong and he was loath to violate his principles. Of the five adult members of the Oceanic Six, Hurley was the last one to buy into the need to lie about their activities on the Island, and he agreed to the great deception only grudgingly.

It was on Penny's boat that Hurley realised he was being asked to subsume the principle of honesty to a greater moral value. He resisted this re-prioritisation of virtues for many reasons, not the least of which was scepticism regarding the ability of deception to ensure the islanders' safety. In the end, he was able to convince himself that this grand falsehood would serve the common good. Agreeing to the lie was significant, though, because it was a fully-examined decision, studied over the course of a week. It demonstrated that even a morality as firmly entrenched as Hurley's was susceptible to change.

Hurley was shaken out of his comfortable world of abstractions when Benjamin Linus showed up at his house, using his slippery tongue in an attempt to convince Hurley to return to the Island. Ben presented him with an ultimatum he must have believed unopposable. Hurley didn't have a choice in Ben's mind. The police were waiting outside the house, ready to take Hurley into custody when he appeared. He could follow Ben, or go to jail for murder. When Hurley ran outside and claimed responsibility for murders he did not commit he was lying in the most spectacular manner we ever witnessed on the show. Hurley surpassed even Ben in the audacity of the fib. The lie was not inconsequential but rather a bold, conscious act that would turn justice on its head, leading to the perpetual incarceration of an innocent man. With this grand falsehood, Hurley loosed himself from any attachment to the concepts of honesty, justice, temperance, and virtue of any kind.

Relational Map for 08 Hugo Reyes

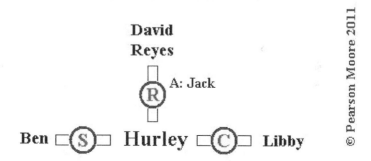

This action was not an abandonment of his moral bearings. Throughout the scene he retained complete allegiance to a morality that determined the words he spoke and the path he trod. Hurley's bizarre outburst revealed one of the strange truths of LOST: The values that motivate us are not abstract but personal; we are connected not to ideas, but to people. At the deepest level of our individual selves we are connected to others. Without these connections, we have no identity, as I explained in detail in Chapter 13, "Strange Attractors." Hurley had a constant, Libby. We might use LOST's symbolic shorthand, like so:

(Hurley) C (Libby)

That is, Hurley and Libby were Constants. Though there is no rule that each member of a Constant pair must act as the other's Constant, this seems to have been the case in most close relationships we witnessed, as evidenced by the final meeting in the church pews at the end of the series.

The other deep relationship was the Strange Attractor, or struggle-relationship with Benjamin Linus, represented by the symbol "S":

(Hurley) S (Ben)

That is, Hurley and Ben were a Strange Attractor pair. Put another way, Hurley struggled with Ben. Ben goaded Hurley into taking leadership actions that required compromising the truth, while Hurley exhorted Ben to abandon deception in favour of honesty. If we had any question that these two men were involved in a spiritually intimate odd-couple relationship, any such question became moot when we saw Hurley and Ben working together to lower Jack into the Cave of Light, and later, when Ben became Hurley's second in command. They needed each other because the dynamics of honesty and deception were at the very core of their beings.

In the world of LOST, anything bearing personal value is expressed in relationship. The value of relationships is so great that they cannot be broken. When they are broken, agents are dispatched and the universe course-corrects to ensure complete repair. Using the symbolism of LOST, we use "R" to represent "reconciliation" and "A" to represent "agent." In Hurley's case, we have this expression:

(Hurley) R (David Reyes) A (Jack)

Hurley reconciles with David through Agent Jack. That is, Jack was the agent dispatched to repair the broken relationship between Hurley and his father, David. When David left his son and his wife he took away Hugo's ability to believe in himself. He ruptured the fundamental connection in Hugo's life. Jack accomplished the repair by telling Hurley the words that had been lacking in Hurley's relationship with his father: "I believe in you." (Episode 6.18, Act 12, Scene 2)

It may not be entirely obvious, but no agents were required for the Constant and Struggle (Strange Attractor) relationships. Each twin in the pair acted as agent of the other's progress.

JACK TO THE FOURTH DIMENSION

Jack's Constant, of course, was Kate.

(Jack) C (Kate)

Jack needed to reconcile with his father, Christian. Toward this end, the people of the sideways world created for Jack a son, David, who was the agent of reconciliation with Christian. David provided Jack with a father-son relationship to nurture. Jack's success with David brought an end to the Shephard family legacy of broken paternal relationships.

Relational Map for 23 Jack Shephard

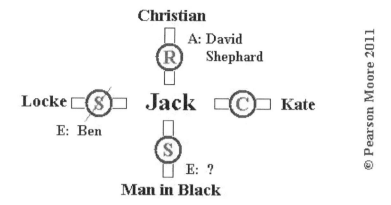

Christian
A: David
Shephard

Locke — Jack — Kate
E: Ben

E: ?

Man in Black

© Pearson Moore 2011

(Jack) R (Christian) A (David Shephard)

For most of the series John Locke was Jack's Strange Attractor twin, but Ben Linus killed Locke. Using the symbolic notation of LOST:

(Jack) NS (Locke) E (Ben)

That is, Jack does not struggle with Locke, due to Executioner Ben. Jack achieved much in his three-year struggle with Locke. He found faith, courage, and knowledge of his final destiny. But in the world of LOST we are not static beings. We do not achieve some plateau of excellence and coast along through the rest of life. We must continually improve ourselves ("It only ends once. Anything that happens before that is just progress."). The core of who we are must continually express itself in relationship with others. For this reason, Jack would require a Strange Attractor twin to replace Locke and complete a pair. He found this twin in the Man in Black. The Man in Black was available for this deep-level bond because he had successfully coerced Ben into killing his Strange Attractor twin, Jacob.

As with the Hurley/Ben odd couple, the scene at the waterfall inside the cave was used as proof of the Jack/Man in Black Strange Attractor pairing, with both Jack and the Monster lowering Desmond to the base of the waterfall and into the Source.

The configuration of Jack's relational map will cause some of you to wonder about the accuracy or completeness of Hurley's map. Didn't Libby's death at Michael's hands indicate Hurley was without a Constant? Wouldn't he then have to seek out a new Constant? Based on evidence presented in the final scenes in the church, it appears that Constancy survives death in the world of LOST. The premiere example is the Jack/Kate Constant Pair. Kate survived for years or decades after Jack's death, but she remained his Constant. Extrapolating to Hurley, he remained Libby's Constant, even following her death. For this reason the relational maps indicate no "Executioner" function for Constant relationships.

Without a Constant, no one can live, and no one gains the privilege of "moving on." I don't know with certainty that having developed a Strange Attractor relationship is necessary to "moving on," but it seems likely that without a Strange Attractor twin one cannot survive, at least in the LOST world. At the very least, without a Constant and without a Strange Attractor, one is Lost.

As Damon Lindelof said in 2007, "This show is about people who are metaphorically lost in their lives, who get on an airplane, and crash on an island, and become physically lost on the planet Earth. And once they are able to metaphorically find themselves in their lives again, they will be able to physically find themselves in the world again." (IGN interview, January 16, 2007)

Jack anchored himself with a Constant, fulfilled his destiny through Strange Attractors, and was no longer Lost. Once Jack found himself, he was free to acquire a new Strange Attractor, or die. He faced a happy death, not because of the agonising wound in his abdomen, but because of Faraday's Variable—the agent no one expected, the person who destroyed the Strange Attractor link between Jack and the Smoke Monster.

FARADAY'S VARIABLE

Jack's relational map is complex, but it is simplicity itself compared to the five-dimensional map required to understand Faraday's Variable. I refer to Faraday's discussion with Jack (Episode 5.14, "The Variable"):

FARADAY: I studied relativistic physics my entire life. One thing emerged over and over—can't change the past. Can't do it. Whatever happened, happened. All right? But then I finally realized... I had been spending so much time focused on the constants, I forgot about the variables. Do you know what the variables in these equations are, Jack?
JACK: [Chuckles] No.
FARADAY: Us. We're the variables. People. We think. We reason. We make choices. We have free will. We can change our destiny.

Faraday thought of human beings in general as capable of exercising volition to effect physical change. He believed they could disturb spacetime in a big way. By detonating a thermonuclear device they would create that disturbance—a boulder thrown into the stream of time—that would prevent the crash of Flight 815 in 2004. Faraday's Boulder would cut a new channel in time, and life would return to normal, free of the Island.

Faraday turned out to be incorrect in the particulars, but correct from a broader point of view, in ways he could not have expected.

The detonation of the thermonuclear device did not result in an explosion, but rather combined with the catastrophic release of electromagnetic energy to push the survivors thirty years into the future. The survivors' histories had not changed, but they were presented with the opportunity to fulfill their destiny.

The thing that Faraday understood is that people are the variables. He missed the obvious completion of this idea, though, and this lack of vision led to his erroneous interpretation regarding the variables' proper place, and the proper outcome of a true variable's actions. Perhaps if he had been privy to the names and numbers on the cave wall he would have intuited the complete equation.

What Faraday did not grasp is that the variables of human history are not catalysts of change. Rather, in the LOST world, we are the change we seek. We do not act as agents, wielding fulcrums and pulleys and levers to drop boulders into spacetime to effect diversion of the stream. We are the variables. We are the change. We are the boulders.

Most of us act as pebbles in the stream of time. Occasionally a large rock makes a little ripple. In every age, though, a handful of great leaders shake the very foundations of human civilisation, diverting space and time by sheer force of will. In our story we have called this leader Shakti, or Joan of Arc. Most of the time, we use her given name: Katherine Anne Austen.

THE GREAT MAN THEORY, REVISED

Kate was the Great Man, the person who determines the course of history simply by virtue of her identity. In the standard nineteenth century interpretation of the Great Man theory, a hero has unique insight into the workings of the world. As revised by LOST, the Great Man has unique Constant and Strange Attractor connections that render her hyper-effective at tasks critical to historic events.

Kate's beginnings were in wanderlust. She never had a chance to cultivate stability; moving from place to place became the expression of her incomplete, Lost soul. Even as a twelve-year-old, her best friend, Tom, knew she always had to run. Her biological father ran from one tavern to another, from one woman to another. Her stepfather ran from one war to another, trotting across the globe, serving the country he loved first in Korea and then in a dozen conflicts around the world. She thought she could settle down as "Monica" with Kevin Callis, but when she missed a menstrual period and thought she was pregnant, the illusion of being able to endure stability collapsed around her. "I almost had a baby, Kevin. Me, a baby! I can't do this! Taco night?! I don't do taco night!"

The thing she most feared was being tied down as a mother. It was this fear, not fear of being caught by Agent Ed Mars, that caused her to run again, away from the man she had illegally married. Years later, on the Island, Claire forced her to confront her worst fear.

KATE: You're so good with him.
[CLAIRE giggles.]

KATE: What?

CLAIRE: Just...the last thing I thought I'd be good at was being a mum. You know, you should try it sometime.

Only days after this conversation at the barracks, Kate was holding Aaron in the helicopter, committed to his safety and nurturing.

Relational Map for 51 Kate Austen

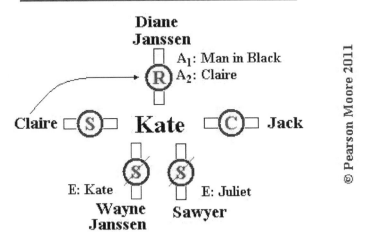

Kate's Constant was Jack, so (Kate) C (Jack). Her first Strange Attractor was her biological father, Wayne, so (Kate) S (Wayne), but she didn't want to believe that she was like him, that she could ever become involved in a sick relationship with a man, that she had to jump from place to place as Wayne did, so she killed him. That he abused her mother was the only excuse she needed, though not the real reason. On the Island she became involved with a con man, Sawyer. That Sawyer was Wayne's Strange Attractor replacement was proven in Episode 2.09, when Sawyer grabbed Kate by the neck and yelled, "You killed me! Why did you kill me?" Later, Kate tried to rouse Sawyer from sleep. She said, "Sawyer," but he did not move. Only when she said, "Wayne," did Sawyer finally stir.

Kate's choice of Strange Attractor relationships was unhealthy. A Strange Attractor had to incorporate opposing characteristics, not similar or identical traits. In Claire, Kate finally found her true Strange Attractor. Claire had been stable, predictable, the perfect mother to Aaron. In late 2004, at the barracks, Claire would have been the perfect Strange Attractor for always-running Kate. Three years later, when Kate was finally able to see the benefits of settling down with a baby boy, she realised she was not Aaron's mother. Just as Jack's son, David, was imaginary to flesh-and-bone Jack, Kate was imaginary to flesh-and-bone Aaron. Because she loved Aaron, she had to risk her life to bring his mother back. Even though Kate was by now "domesticated," she remained the perfect Strange Attractor for the new "feral" Claire Of The Jungle.

Kate's redemption was not through Jack or Claire, but through the Man in Black. She had destroyed her relationship with her mother, to the point that when Kate visited Diane in the hospital, the only emotion Diane felt was primal fear. The scene near the end of Episode 3.15 ("Left Behind") when the feeble, bed-ridden Diane Janssen summoned the energy to yell, "help!" was one of the most gut-wrenching scenes in the six years of LOST.

Kate found an unlikely kindred soul in her need to reconcile with her mother.

KATE: You... didn't have to bring me down here.
MAN IN BLACK: Sure, but then I wouldn't have gotten to talk to you. You referred to me as a dead man. I am not a dead man. I know what you're feeling, Kate. I know what you're going through.
KATE: And how do you know that?
MAN IN BLACK: Because... my mother was crazy. Long time ago, before I... looked like this... I had a mother, just like everyone. She was a very disturbed woman. And, as a result of that, I had some growing pains. Problems that I'm still trying to work my way through. Problems that could have been avoided had things been different.
KATE: Why are you telling me this?
MAN IN BLACK: Because now Aaron has a crazy mother too.

What a feeling Kate must have had after this intimate bit of sharing. It must have been similar to the feeling one has watching someone pick her nose, and then suffering the social obligation of having to shake hands with her. Or perhaps it was more akin to knowing the person sitting next to you on the plane enjoyed torturing dogs or abusing children, and then having to hear that you and she shared similar childhoods. Is it any wonder that when Kate got hold of a gun she pumped lead into his non-corporeal body?

The Man in Black was neither Constant nor Strange Attractor for Kate. He catalysed reconciliation with Kate's mother, but for Kate the Man in Black was, above all else, the origin of everything evil.

THE BOSS STONE

The Man in Black should have won. He had been calculating and conniving not for months or years, but for millennia. Jack was the one. After so many hundreds of years of figuring out every angle, it was almost disappointing to the Monster. "Jacob being who is, I expected to be a little more surprised. You're sort of the obvious choice."

Jack did end up surprising him when he slugged him in the mouth and drew blood. Still, it was not enough to thwart the Smoke Monster's plans. The Man in Black was stronger, more motivated. His desire had been building for over two thousand years, and it was the single force guiding thought, action, and will. Jack was a newcomer to this test of wills; how could he possibly prevail against unstoppable force?

The Man in Black thought he had everything figured out, with tolerances so generous that he could proceed even though Desmond's work had rendered him temporarily mortal. But he had in fact underestimated Jacob. Even in death, his arch-nemesis had a plan—a secret weapon so formidable he had never spoken of it.

The cave under the cliffs was the game house Jacob shared with his twin. Jacob wrote Candidate numbers and names on the ceiling and the Man in Black crossed them out whenever they died or failed. The Man in Black took great pleasure in crossing out one particular name in the cave: Kate Austen. Little did he know, Jacob maintained a second set of numbers and names in his lighthouse. The names on the lighthouse wheel were likewise crossed out whenever a Candidate died or failed. Kate's name should have been crossed out. She left the Island, played full-time nanny to Claire's baby, and was apparently so involved in these pseudo-motherly duties that she was oblivious to anything else. But her name was not crossed out. Jacob knew she would return. The Island made it so.

Damon Lindelof provided this observation during the Official LOST Audio Podcast of March 11, 2010:

"However, there's also this lighthouse, where... the names seem to correspond with angles or degrees on this rotating mirror. So, is it possible that we know that in the lighthouse Jacob seemed to be watching these people as candidates but he was also writing their names down in a cave? *Why would he do it in both places?* Is it possible, Carlton, that maybe he wanted his nemesis to find the cave and that there's a little bit of misdirection going on here? That maybe he crossed off Kate's name in the cave to throw the Monster off his scent? Is... it possible, Carlton?"

The great multi-dimensional cathedral that is LOST was held together with a Boss Stone, the same stone used to force the even distribution of weight in a gothic cathedral. Without that single stone, the entire edifice falls apart. But with the stone properly in place, a cathedral will resist any earthquake, any tornado, standing undisturbed for thousands of years. The Boss Stone—Faraday's Boulder—looks like the Cork Stone, but as I wrote earlier in the chapter, we do not use fulcrums and pulleys and gears to throw the boulder into the stream of time. We do not manipulate boulders. We are the boulders.

The Man in Black's downfall was his inability to think in as many dimensions as Jacob. Jacob didn't even understand as many dimensions as the two leaders, the lovers, the Constant-pair who became the Boss Stone in the great cathedral that required six years and four hundred skilled craftspeople and thirty million viewer-participants to build.

Jack attacked, Kate delivered the lethal blow, and Jack pushed him off the cliff. But their work was not yet done. For the truth was, the stone Desmond pulled out of the Source was not a cork holding evil incarnate at bay. This was the feeble and entirely incorrect explanation that Jacob gave Richard in Episode 6.09 ("Ab Aeterno"). The stone was not a cork holding in evil wine. The stone was the Boss Stone, holding together the grand cathedral that housed the Light, that which all women and men seek. When Jack returned to the Source, which now glowed with angry red energy, he replaced the Boss Stone, and the Light returned. The Cathedral glowed with the warm energy of peace and justice and every virtue of the human heart.

That silence may reign, and we may sleep. That harmony return, that a hero may die a noble death. That silence may reign, and we may sleep. That a child may grow in a mother's love, an aunt's care, a deceased but revered uncle's faith.

THE TRIUMPH OF APOLLO 13

Apollo 13 Mission Patch
NASA 1970 PD

The success of Apollo 13 in a period of four days was not due to the sudden discovery of new scientific principles or new insights into engineering. Gene Kranz attributed his team's success in the face of crushing odds to what he called the "human factor." In any of the missions he led, the variability of human response was the biggest factor determining success or failure. As he wrote, "They were people who were energized by a mission. And these teams were capable of moving right on and doing anything America asked them to do in space." Regardless of the challenge put in front of his team, they were able to overcome the obstacle. Test pilots called it "the right stuff." In LOST, we call it faith.

The Valenzetti Equation—the inevitable doom of humanity—was defeated not by the manipulation of the six terms, but by the addition of a seventh coefficient. Kate Austen, the seventh variable, was added to the equation at the last possible moment. She became the seventh nail in science's coffin. She was the unpredictable variable—the human potential for change—that Faraday referred to as the boulder in the stream of time.

The Seven Samurai. The Magnificent Seven. The Seven Candidates. In all three cases, seven were required to change the course of history. In all three examples, four heroes paid with their lives, and three lived to recount their deeds.

The importance of the Valenzetti Equation does not end with these revelations.

Kate killed the Smoke Monster, but she also killed the Valenzetti Equation, and with those deaths, she became agent and subject of the Island's thesis of hope: Human civilisation will never perish from this earth.

The Island relied on its own understanding of humanity as superior to any doomsday equation. The Valenzetti Equation was derailed by the inclusion of a seventh coefficient, by a woman who believed not in pre-ordained global self-destruction, but in one child's need for a mother. In seeking to re-unite Claire and Aaron, Kate freed the Island from the Smoke Monster's tyranny and gave everyone a new basis for optimism.

The bullet from Kate Austen's rifle killed the Smoke Monster, and it also killed the notion of the ascendency of science and rational thought. The Valenzetti Equation, predicting the inevitability of humankind's self-destruction, was entirely rational. Optimistic belief in the positive tendencies of human nature is irrational. The Island proved, through Kate, that irrational optimism is more firmly anchored in reality than the most scrupulously rational statement of scientific pessimism.

CHAPTER 18 ADVANCED TOPIC V:
THE MESSENGER

"White Rabbit"
Sir John Tenniel ca. 1889 PD

He spoke with an authority not his own.

"Follow me," he said. Neither invitation nor command, his words indicated something beyond himself and his followers, a voyage not only toward a location, but also onto an unknown and long-sought path. "You have a bit of a journey ahead of you." We knew he was preparing us for no Sunday drive in the park, but for an expedition, the grand journey of our desiring.

What if everything that happened here happened for a reason? What if everything we dreaded, everything we dreamed of, everything we longed for, bright and beautiful, dark and evil, mysterious and familiar, had origin and destination on a path unknown and long-sought?

The journey's the thing. We desire an origin, a destination, but we know only the dirt path through tropical forest, the soft sand along ocean shore, the trek to places beyond our understanding but close to our heart.

We hear him, see him, touch him. We should not tremble, for he cannot judge. We should not obey, for he does not govern. He is terrible and wonderful, fearsome and gentle, shock to our eyes, joy of our desiring. We obey, we follow his gentle command, and we tremble. For though he is neither magistrate nor king, he is sent by the one whom all obey.

Christian Shephard is the messenger.

FATHER AND SON

We know more about him than almost any other character in television fiction. We've met his father, wife, daughter, son, and grandson. We've seen him at work, at home, with his Australian lover. He's been sober and wise and drunk and foolish. He was a "minor" character for most of the six years we watched him, but his biography at Lostpedia consumes 4700 words.

With cruel and careless words Christian started Jack on his journey. "You just don't have what it takes," he told his son. Licenced to practice medicine, he should have been declared incompetent to the rigours of parenthood, for he understood not even the most fundamental responsibilities of the position.

We should be careful not to judge. Though his words were harsh, we know his heart was big. Sawyer uncovered the truth:

"About a week before we all got on the plane, I got to talking to this man in a bar in Sydney. He was American, too. A doctor. I've been on some benders in my time, but this guy—he was going for an all-time record. So, it turns out this guy has a son. His son's a doctor, too. They had some kind of big time falling out. The guy knew it was his fault, even though his son was back in the States thinking the same damn thing. See, kids are like dogs, you knock them around enough they'll think they did something to deserve it. Anyway, there's a pay phone in this bar. And this guy, Christian, tells me he wishes he had the stones to pick up the phone, call his kid, tell him he's sorry, that he's a better doctor than he'll ever be—he's proud, and he loves him. I had to take off, but—something tells me he never got around to making that call."

If he were only Jack Shephard's father, Christian Shephard would merit a central place in the analysis of LOST. Jack was the mythical hero, and arguably his greatest struggle, the conflict that launched his dangerous, angst-ridden journey, was the tormented connection with his father. The failures of paternity and the anguish this brought to daughters and sons was a major theme in LOST. Some analysts claim, with solid evidence from hundreds of scenes backing their words, that disconnection between fathers and children was the primary cause of the Lost, fragmented lives that were the subject of the series. If so, the relationship between Jack and Christian would become the starting point for every deliberate and thoughtful discussion of the work.

But Christian was not only Jack's father. His was the first face we saw and the last voice we followed. In a story rich with allusion and allegory, he was alpha and omega, beginning and end.

270

LOST began with Mobisode M.13, "So It Begins." If you have not yet experienced this episode, you will want to do so before reading further in this chapter. All thirteen mobisodes can be found with the Season Four DVD or Blu-Ray bonus features. As of March, 2011, they were also available at Youtube.com.

The scene adds only one minute thirteen seconds to the LOST canon, but they are arguably the richest seventy-three seconds of the series. We learn critical information about Christian, Jack, Vincent, and their relationship to each other that cannot be gleaned from the broadcast episodes.

The dog was the focal point of the scene. In fact, most of the scene was delivered from his point of view. This is a rare event in any fiction other than children's stories, and merits consideration all its own. It was not the last time we saw events unfold through Vincent's eyes. Early in the pilot episode (Act 2, Episode 1.01, "Pilot, Part One") we saw Jack, Charlie, and Kate cross an open field on their way toward the front section of the plane (Oceanic 815) from Vincent's point of view in the tall grass at the edge of the meadow. The scene was eerie in its intimation of intelligence beyond the normal constraints of canine awareness. As much as this scene appeared to beg credulity, it asked far less of us than the first scene of the series, which bordered the fantastic.

After the opening seconds of "So It Begins," Christian called Vincent, crouched down to the dog's level, grabbed him by the jowls, and gave him these instructions:

"I need you to go find my son. He's over there in that bamboo forest, unconscious. I need you to go wake him up. Okay? Go on. [Vincent whined and ran off. Christian rose to his feet.] He has work to do."

Why, in a serious piece of fiction, would the audience be asked to believe that a yellow Labrador Retriever understood a complex set of instructions and then focused on executing those instructions? Why would a dog understand what a "bamboo forest" was, or that a man was unconscious in that forest and that he was being dispatched to revive the man?

As weird as the series of events was, I find no way around the conclusion, corroborated by Vincent's appearance at Jack's side and the later scene in the open field, that the dog understood Christian. It seems certain, too, that we as audience participants were being asked to believe this fact was useful and significant to the story.

Christian knew the dog would understand and obey the complex instructions. From a purely mechanical point of view we can say that Vincent, in "So It Begins," was acting as Christian's agent. Christian had an agenda and he employed Vincent as his agent to fulfill the particulars of that agenda. The later scene from the edge of the meadow gave no indication of the larger plan, but we did get a glimpse around Day 66, when Charlie was constructing Mr.

Eko's church. Vincent carried a Virgin Mary statue in his mouth and dropped it at Charlie's feet (Episode 2.22, "Three Minutes").

That Vincent was one of the agents of Charlie's redemption, and therefore the redemption of each of the survivors, became clear when the dog brought Charlie to Sawyer's tent, where Charlie found all of the remaining Virgin Mary statues. He stuffed them into his pack, walked away from camp, and threw the statues into the ocean. It marked the end of Charlie's life as a drug addict and the beginning of his march toward martyrdom.

THE GOOD SHEPHERD

Mosaic of the Good Shepherd
Mausoleum of Galla Placidia
Ravenna, Italy ca. 430 AD

If Vincent was acting as Christian's agent, and it became Vincent's business to catalyse the redemption of the survivors, we are nearly obliged to conclude that Christian's agenda consisted in a grand plan to ensure the redemption of those he apparently considered in his care. Christian, Redeemer.

The image is striking. Though the words fit well together, they surely must bring anxiety as well as some sense of symmetry to our thoughts. We know well that Christian acted as shepherd to everyone in the church during the final scene of LOST. But we know too that LOST was not founded in syllogism. I have spent the better part of this book arguing—I hope convincingly—that science and logic constituted feeble and insufficient bases for the comprehension of LOST, and that LOST taught the inferiority of science to a non-scientific, multi-dimensional understanding of the world. To say then that Vincent was an agent of redemption, Vincent was Christian's agent, and therefore Christian was the architect of redemption employs the very tools of understanding that were long ago discredited in the pages of this book.

We need to consider all of the evidence, critical pieces of which will be found to indicate a role for Christian entirely incompatible with any position as author of redemption. However, much evidence supports a conclusion that Christian was, in fact, the Good Shepherd, and we will consider here some of the more compelling instances of support.

The strongest evidence occurred in Episodes 1.05 ("White Rabbit") and fifteen minutes from the end of Episode 6.18 ("The End"). In both of these episodes we saw Jack open his father's casket only to find it empty. His bewilderment was evident in both scenes. Despite the intensity of the event, Jack never told anyone what he had seen, perhaps out of fear. This sequence of events paralleled perfectly the description given in the Gospel of Mark, Chapter 16, Verse 8. In this verse, three of Jesus' disciples found the empty tomb, and they became "seized with trembling and bewilderment. They said nothing to anyone, for they were afraid."

The empty tomb is one of the strongest images of Christianity. That the image was used twice to reference the same person must be taken as nearly irrefutable confirmation that Christian's absence in the casket symbolised the resurrection of Jesus of Nazareth. We can cite several bits of corroborating support for this position. In Episode 5.09 ("Namaste"), Christian appeared at the abandoned Dharma Processing Center, saying to Sun and Frank, "Follow me." These words were frequently employed by Jesus in all four Gospels and can be considered a signature phrase. Certainly Christian's full name—Christian Shephard—and his position of spiritual authority during the final two scenes of the series could be taken as strong support for this idea.

It seems unlikely that the writers would have proposed that a drunk, ornery old man with a lover and an illegitimate child on the side who had neither the emotional bearing nor the raw ability to parent his son could serve as perfect exemplar of the Christian Deity. Yet Christian, in his Island apparitions, spoke with authority. We could consider that resurrection had somehow cleansed him of his temporal failings and that in this new perfection he represented the Redeemer. This would certainly make sense from a religious point of view, but the preponderance of evidence indicates a spiritual rather than a religious spin on the events of the series. I don't feel we can conclude that LOST wishes us to consider Christian Shephard as representing Jesus of Nazareth. He was a shepherd, symbol of the Good Shepherd, and in this capacity a symbol of the redemptive, salvific action of some higher power.

The question of Christian Shephard's on-Island identity centres on the notion of authority. Christian did not speak for himself. When Locke asked, "Are you Jacob?" Christian responded, "No, but I can speak on his behalf." (Episode 4.11, "Cabin Fever") When Christian appeared to Michael on the freighter, seconds before it exploded, he said, "You can go now, Michael," Michael asked, "Who are you?" (Episode 4.14, "There's No Place Like Home," Part Three) The question was appropriate, and it is the main question of this chapter. Because of the centrality of Christian, it is actually the main question of the entire series.

It is my intention to provide Christian's four-word response to Michael's question before the end of this chapter. In Christian's final words on the freighter, spoken as the C4 explosive went through irreversible chain reaction, we will tie together every piece of the massive puzzle that is LOST.

We saw Christian's dead body in a morgue in Sydney. Even though his empty casket indicated resurrection, bodily resurrection or reincarnation should not be considered the only possible explanation. The assumption that any of Christian's appearances on the Island were apparitions seems consistent with the nature of the appearances and their context.

The selective nature of the appearances and their limited duration indicates the possibility that the apparitions constituted a manipulation of Christian's image by another entity. We know that Christian's form was appropriated at least once, as confirmed by Carlton Cuse on May 23, 2010 during the nationally broadcast "Lost: The Final Journey":

"Once [the Man in Black becomes] the Smoke Monster, he only can assume the form of dead people on the Island. The Man in Black appeared as Christian Shephard."

The Smoke Monster had a distinctive aural signature in the ticky-ticky-ticky New York taxi-cab sound that was frequently heard when he moved about in his non-corporeal smoke form. We heard the sound several times while Jack was chasing Christian's form through the jungle in Episode 1.05. We also heard a faint ticky-ticky-ticky while Frank and Sun were at the Pala dock just outside the Dharma barracks in Episode 5.09 ("Namaste"). In both cases we saw Christian's apparition seconds or short minutes after having heard the Smoke Monster's signature. We are probably safe in assuming that these appearances were due to the Monster.

I don't believe we are justified in asserting the opinion that the Smoke Monster requisitioned Christian's form merely to advance his magisterium of fear and death. The Smoke Monster's appearance in Christian's form opens a line of inquiry we need to pursue if we are to understand the significance of Christian Shephard.

THE SOUND AND THE FURY

Just before the Kahana exploded, Christian stood opposite Michael behind a table loaded with C4 explosive. Michael peered at the spectre with an expression of pure bewilderment and posed the key question of the series.

CHRISTIAN: You can go now, Michael.
MICHAEL: Who are you?

We know the Smoke Monster had strong aversion to explosions. When the Smoke Monster pulled Locke into a "Cerberus Vent" at the end of Season One, it was Kate (of course) who threw a stick of dynamite into the hole. The explosion caused the Smoke Monster to release Locke. One might wonder why a cloud of non-corporeal smoke could be affected by anything as mundane as dynamite. We didn't learn the mechanism of action until Season Three, at the sonic fence. Sound energy was sufficient to keep the Smoke Monster from crossing land. Going up and over the fence was not an option; he simply could not deal with high-energy sound waves.

The highest of high-energy sound waves emanate from explosions, such as occur upon detonation of dynamite—or upon detonation of C4 explosive.

The entity occupying Christian Shephard's form stood behind a veritable mountain of C4 explosive. The table held enough C4, in fact, to sink fifty ships the size of the Kahana. The sound energy generated by the explosion was greater by orders of magnitude than anything produced by the sonic fence. It goes without saying that the Smoke Monster would not have voluntarily come anywhere near the freighter as long as it was rigged with that much explosive. The entity standing behind the C4 could not possibly have been the Smoke Monster.

The problem of the figure's identity is exacerbated by the fact that the freighter was in deep ocean water, several kilometres from the nearest shore.

MAN IN BLACK: We're taking a boat ride over to the other island.
SAWYER: What do you need a boat for? Can't you just turn into smoke and fly your ass over the water?
MAN IN BLACK: Do you think if I could do that I would still be on this island?

While we have no reason to trust anything the Smoke Monster said, we have no evidence that he was able to "fly his ass over the water" either. He didn't like being pushed into the water by Jack, and took the fastest route immediately out of the water. Whenever he crossed to Hydra Island, he did so in a canoe.

If Christian's form was occupied by the Smoke Monster, his form was not so occupied on the Kahana. Yet we have the word of Carlton Cuse testifying to the fact that the Smoke Monster, at least once, did take Christian's form.

Did different entities have control over Christian's apparitions, perhaps dependent upon venue, function, or objective? Although I consider this a possibility, I believe we ought to consider additional evidence before making our assessment.

BY THEIR FRUITS

Our earliest understanding of the Smoke Monster, in Season One, was as purveyor of random fear and death. Near the end of Season One, Danielle Rousseau referred to him as a "security system," and in Season Two, on the blast door map, we learned that members of the Dharma Initiative called him "Cerberus," after the three-headed guard dog of the gates of Hades from Greek mythology.

Smoke Monster Appearances

Form	Appeared To	Episode	Type	Issue
Yemi	Eko	3.05	Judgment	Eko's sin
Spiders	Nikki	3.14	Judgment	Nikki's sin
Smoke	Ben	5.12	Judgment	Ben's sin
Smoke	Kate	3.15	Judgment(?)	
Smoke	Juliet	3.15	Judgment(?)	
Alex	Ben	5.12	Coercion	Obey Locke
Locke	Ben	5.17	Coercion	Kill Jacob
Isabella	Richard	6.09	Coercion	Kill Jacob
Christian	Jack	1.05	Guide	Find water
Christian	Michael	4.14	Messenger	You can go
Christian	Locke	4.11	Guide	Move Island
Christian	Locke	5.05	Guide	Move Island
Christian	Sun	5.09	Guide	Find Jin

In Season Three we began to understand the Smoke Monster in quite a different way. In Episodes 3.05 and 3.14, the Monster acted as judge of Mr. Eko and Nikki and Paulo, using Yemi's form to admonish Eko, and the form of medusa spiders to judge and kill Nikki and Paulo for their sins against the old man in their care. In Season Five, when Ben believed he had sinned against the Island, he submitted himself to the Smoke Monster's judgment under the outer wall of the Temple.

It was not until Season Five that we experienced instances of naked coercion by the Monster. He took the form of Alex to coerce Ben into obeying "Locke" (the Man in Black in Locke's form). His initial use of Locke's body was a long-con to coerce Ben into killing Jacob. In Season Six, we saw him use Isabella's form to make Richard believe that Jacob was the Devil and had to be killed.

The appearances of the Man in Black in the form of Christian Shephard were unlike these other appearances in two important ways.

First, there was no element of judgment in Christian's apparitions, and neither were there any forceful commands. Christian acted consistently as a guide or messenger. I understand well the argument that Christian's pleasant appearance and air of helpfulness could have been nothing more than a ruse, another instance of a long con. I understand, too, that the judgments of Eko, Nikki, and Paulo could likewise be understood as cons. But I believe it is possibile that helpful information may be gleaned from at least a tentative acceptance of first impressions. At least for now, let us note that the apparitions of Christian Shephard were qualitatively different than apparitions of other dead people, and that Christian's purpose seemed to find expression as a guide.

Second, except for Christian's appearances to Jack in Episodes 1.04 and 1.05, he appeared to people who did not know him. Locke, Michael, Sun, and Frank had never met Christian, and didn't know his relationship to Jack. Locke figured out that Christian was Jack's father, but not because Christian told him directly. This is strange, since in every other case in which the Man in Black took human form, he was immediately recognised by the people to whom he appeared. Richard knew Isabella, Ben knew Alex, Eko knew Yemi, and so on. The appropriation of forms of loved ones would have been key to a ploy aimed at coercing people to take actions favourable to the Smoke Monster.

If the mode of action of the Man in Black was coercion, why did he dilute the force of his intention by providing open-ended assistance when he operated as guide and messenger under the form of Christian Shephard? Why did he further jeopardise long-term objectives by appearing in the form of a person to whom those receiving the guidance had no attachment whatever?

We might tentatively conclude that any theory postulating that the Man in Black's singular *modus operandi* was coercion toward his final objective is unsupported by the Christian Shephard apparitions. It seems equally unlikely, however, that the apparitions were without rhyme or reason. In fact, it seems possible, based on the evidence of Christian Shephard's apparitions, that the Smoke Monster, not his victims, was being forced to do something against his will. We need to dig deeper to understand.

THE LITTLE DUTCH BOY

Consciousness was not always limited to a single human form anchored in a single time and place. Desmond's consciousness was not attached to spacetime in the same way that most other persons' were. He was not alone in this respect. Proximity to the Island affected people in sometimes negative ways, and one of these ways was a disorienting disengagement of the consciousness from the body. George Minkowski suffered consciousness time travel and it ultimately caused his death.

But the skipping about of one person's consciousness from one spacetime to another was not the only type of spiritual leakage we observed in LOST. Recall in Episode 2.09 that Wayne Janssen either occupied Sawyer's form, or was channeled through him. As detailed in the last chapter, the unconscious Sawyer grabbed Kate's throat and yelled, "You killed me! Why did you kill me?"

Those on the Island would have required an army of little Dutch boys to plug the long list of leaks and cross-contaminations of spirits, souls, and consciousnesses that occurred on a frequent but unpredictable basis.

UNIQUE SIGNATURE

In Episode 6.04, the Man in Black was escorting Sawyer to the cave under the cliffs to show him Jacob's list of Candidates. En route to the cliffs, a boy with bloodied hands and arms appeared in the jungle. We later learned the boy was young Jacob, and the Man in Black chased him. At one point he tripped, falling to the ground, and the boy stood over him, as if in judgment.

BOY: You know the rules. You can't kill him.
MAN IN BLACK: Don't tell me what I can't do...
[The boy shakes his head and walks away]
MAN IN BLACK: Don't tell me what I can't do!

We've heard that seven-word phrase several times before. Sometimes we've heard variants of it (as with Eko's "Do not tell me what I can do."), but the exact seven words were uttered by only one person: John Locke. This seven-word command is as unique an identifier for Locke as the ticky-ticky-ticky sound is for the Smoke Monster, or "live together, die alone" is for Jack Shephard.

Perhaps we should not be surprised that the Man in Black used Locke's signature expression. After all, he was occupying Locke's form. But we need to be clear about what we are indicating here. The Man in Black did not occupy Locke's body. The body was elsewhere on the Island, and was eventually buried. What we are saying, in acknowledging the Man in Black's use of Locke's signature phrase, is that the Man in Black appropriated more than Locke's simple form. He incorporated into himself Locke's mannerisms, memories, and ways of thinking about things.

If anyone else were occupying another person's form we would feel justifiable confusion or shock. When Sawyer channeled the dead Wayne Janssen's words and emotions, we were shocked. When the Smoke Monster channeled the dead John Locke's words and emotions, we were not shocked.

The Man in Black had no corporeal signature, other than the worn phrase, "They come, they fight, they destroy, they corrupt," acquired from his adoptive mother. Nothing about him was his own—he didn't have a name, and Jacob took away his humanity. As discussed in Chapter 16, the Man in Black didn't even have an identity.

In acquiring the form of John Locke, the Man in Black was obliged to acquire also, as part of a "package deal," the identity of John Locke. The only thin aspect of identity that overruled Locke's predilections and sensibilities was the Man in Black's unbridled desire to leave the Island. In effect, the MIB/Locke became a kind of Anti-Horus, with the inclusive aspects of Locke's character subsumed to the selfish governing principle (Get off the Island!) of the Man in Black's character.

Simple syllogism allows us to extrapolate from the particular case of MIB/Locke to MIB/Christian: When he occupied Christian's form, the Man in Black incorporated into his character and projected the mannerisms, memories, and thought processes of Christian Shephard. We might imagine the Man in Black shouting not "Don't tell me what I can't do," when he was in Christian's form, but perhaps something more like, "Get me a drink!" This is quite simple logic, which of course means—it is entirely incorrect. Christian was not just another form to use willy-nilly according to the whims of the Man in Black. There were rules here, and the Man in Black was obliged to obey them as much as anyone else.

Something grand was in play whenever Christian Shephard was loose on the Island. In these strange apparitions we will find the key to understanding the deepest significance of LOST. We're almost there.

CANTON-RAINIER

Dogen's people held the wounded Sayid Jarrah under water until he lost consciousness and died. We did not know until several episodes later that he had died, but we received confirmation in Episode 6.06 ("Sundown") from the one person who would know: Corpse Whisperer Miles Straum.

SAYID: Apparently I'm evil. These people say I'm better off dead. Which is surprising, considering they were the ones who saved my life.
MILES: Well, actually, they're not. They...they tried to save you, but...you were dead man. For two hours. Trust me when...when you sat up they were just as surprised as the rest of us. So whatever brought you back, it wasn't them.

We know Jacob could not resurrect anyone, as he told us in his own words (Episode 6.09). And even if he were able to exercise such a power, he was already dead by the time Sayid was carried to the Temple. The Man in Black, on the other hand...

I suppose we are willing to ascribe to the Man in Black the power of resurrection because of the observed fruits of Sayid's resurrection activities. Dogen warned that Sayid had been "infected," and he tried to enlist Jack in the dark but necessary business of killing him before Sayid could become the Smoke Monster's zombie-agent. Dogen's fears seemed more than justified when Sayid slashed Lennon's throat, pulled Dogen into the pool and killed him, and prepared the Temple for the Smoke Monster's triumphal and destructive entrance.

But we need to reconcile these activities with Sayid's martyrdom aboard the submarine. He was no zombie in his final act on the Earth. If he had been infected, blindly serving the Smoke Monster's interests, he would have allowed the bomb to detonate in Jack's presence. The Smoke Monster's troubles would have ended on that submarine ride, just as he had been planning for so many centuries. But Sayid was not his agent, and never had been. He was never infected. He certainly was resurrected, though.

There really should be no puzzle regarding the cause of Sayid's resurrection. He had been held in the Island's healing waters—waters that had their origin at the Heart of the Island, the Source of life, death, and rebirth. That Dogen's hand failed to heal when he sliced it open and placed it in the pool did not reflect on the efficacy of the water, but only on the impotence of logical syllogism. The Island resurrected Sayid Jarrah. The Island gave him new life, but not new attitudes. He believed he was evil, because everyone had told him so. Carrying out the Smoke Monster's will in the Temple was not due to any influence of the Smoke Monster, but was the natural consequence of being told by Lennon and Dogen and Ben and Kelvin and anyone else who deigned to speak with a torturer that he was a horrible, bad, evil person. On the submarine Sayid finally rejected the decades of slurs against his character and asserted his true self. Sayid Jarrah was the best man one could ever hope to become.

AUTHORITY

The entity appearing behind the table of C4 assumed authority over Michael and over the fate of the Kahana. "You can go now, Michael" meant that the entity was in control of Michael's actions and his fate, and also the freighter's fate. The entity knew the C4 was just about to explode, and it knew Michael would die in the explosion. With those five words, the entity communicated to Michael that his work was done, that he had achieved the goal he had set out to achieve. Of course, this goal had nothing to do with the destruction of the Kahana, though this was the "accidental" (inconsequential) outcome of Michael's action. What had really transpired, as we now know, is that Michael had put into motion the series of events that would ensure his son's return to the Island, and Walter's intervention to secure Michael's release from Island limbo. All of that occurred simultaneously with Michael's death (as there is no time "here," as Christian said in 6.18).

The key provision upon which we base our understanding of the figure's identity is the fact of its authority. We know the entity is not the Man in Black, for the two solid, incontrovertible reasons cited earlier. We know Jacob never evinced the ability to change forms. Even in death, he appeared either as his younger self or as his older self and in no other form. He never took a loved one's form, for instance, and when he wished to visit anyone off-Island, he had to do so in the only form he ever possessed—his own.

Neither Jacob nor the Man in Black occupied Christian's form on the freighter. If we are to assign an identity to the occupying force, we must locate an entity having authority equal to or greater than that exercised by the two brothers.

OPPOSED VALUES, CONCERTED METHODS

Hurley detested falsehood, Ben embraced it. They worked together to lower Jack into the Source.

Jack was the Island's salvation, the MIB was the Island's destruction. They worked together to lower Desmond into the Source.

The MIB had no identity. The Source was pure identity. Together they discovered the one person who was key to Jack's redemption and ascension to faith.

The event had to occur on the sixth day, of course. The Oceanic Six, Jacob's Six, six Candidates, six degrees of perfection leading to the final seventh perfection, the epiphany of redemption that occurred on the lava cliffs. It was on the sixth day after the crash that the Island's redemptive power was channeled into the act that would catalyse a sequence of hundreds of events over three years, culminating in the Island's restoration. It was on the sixth day that the Island exercised its powers of rebirth in the resurrection of Jack's father, Christian Shephard.

"El Arbol De La Vida" Ignacio de Ries 1653 PD

If the Kahana had not exploded, these are the words we would have heard issue from between Christian's lips:

I am the Island.

The Smoke Monster was not an entity with independent identity or existence. The Island, too, became intimately tied to the Smoke Monster upon his creation at the Source. The Man in Black, after his transformation, drew identity and existence from the Island itself. Pure identity and pure non-identity were wrapped around each other in a twisted perversion of the Island's original majesty. When the Man in Black occupied Christian's form, the only identity he could channel was the Island, except now even his childish yearning to leave paradise was subsumed to the Island's desire to act as spiritual guide. We must not think that the Smoke Monster "wanted" to help the Island, any more than he "wanted" to help Jack when they collaborated in lowering Desmond into the Source. The Smoke Monster was physically and spiritually connected to the Island. When the Island felt a critical juncture had been reached requiring intervention, it mandated the commandeering of human form, and the Smoke Monster was obliged to comply.

When Desmond withdrew the Cork Stone—the Boss Stone—from the Source he effected the separation of the Smoke Monster from the Island. The Island was not yet in balance. The Source, however, was unaffected. It was never contingent in the energy it produced, and it projected the same intense force before and after the creation of the Smoke Monster. The Island was not in balance because it was not intended as a venue solely for the expression of the Source's power. It was the point of contact—the umbilical—between the world humans could understand and the much greater reality that will forever evade our comprehension. In order to restore the full function of the Island, the Boss Stone, inscribed with humankind's four commitments—the covenant statements—had to be replaced over the source. When Jack achieved this just before his death, he re-established the harmony of the world—something that had not been seen for over two thousand years.

I don't know that it matters much whether we think of Christian Shephard as representing the Island or its interests, or that we believe he embodied every aspect of the Island. At the very least, he was spokesperson for the Island, and that is all that matters.

Christian was shepherd to everyone on the Island, and especially to his son. He led his son to water, led him to question his reliance on logic and science, and led him, through John Locke, to grow into the man of faith who saved the Island and humanity's connection to the precepts of civilisation. Christian Shephard was the good shepherd. The Island led everyone from the wilderness of being Lost to finding themselves, and each other, and becoming the people they were destined to be.

CHAPTER 19 JUST FOR FUN:
THE SCIENCE OF LOST

"Magnetism" by Pearson Moore 2011

LOST is science fiction, but the "science" part of it is pure fantasy.

A sailing ship topples a 75-metre-high statue. The sky turns purple. Water fluoresces with an unearthly greenish glow. A compass needle is deflected more than twenty degrees by a mysterious force. And on and on, stretching our belief far beyond the breaking point. Pure fantasy. To believe a thirty-tonne wooden ship could knock over a 1500-tonne stone statue—why, we might as well believe the Cecil B. DeMille version of the parting of the Red Sea: Moses raises his arms and faster than you can say "Hollywood special effects", the sea is parted.

All of this might be considered the flight of fancy of a creative but not very well informed writing staff—except everything they wrote is true. LOST is firmly grounded in science fact and solid scientific theory. The wave the Black Rock rode in on would have knocked over the statue. The sky not only can turn purple, it is purple. Water fluoresces, exactly as depicted. Compass needles can and do go wild. And not even Cecil B. DeMille would believe it: twenty years ago, in a laboratory in France, a scientist pushed a button, and faster than you can say "Stranger than fiction," the waters parted.

Fasten your quantum electromagnetic seat belts. This is going to be one hell of a ride.

HOLLYWOOD SPECIAL EFFECTS
OR SCIENTIFIC TRUTH?

I enjoy watching "The Ten Commandments", the 1956 Cecil B. DeMille film starring Charlton Heston. I say this even after formal training in Biblical studies that demolished my childhood understanding of the parting of the Red Sea. It wouldn't have happened that way, our professors told us. The parting of the sea was much less dramatic than the Hollywood version. Perhaps the learned theologians were correct. Nevertheless, science says Cecil B. DeMille's version is entirely within the realm of reason.

Israel's Escape from Egypt
Providence Lithograph Co. 1907

I start with this scene from an ancient film to illustrate an important point about LOST. The science in LOST may seem far-fetched, but even the most fantastical elements—the time travel, the bizarre electromagnetic phenomena, the colour changes in water, earth, and sky—are firmly grounded in observed behaviour and well-accepted theory. The parting of the Red Sea has direct bearing on LOST because the modern-day recreation of that event relies on strange but reproducible magnetic properties that are at the core of our favourite television programme.

The Moses Effect was first reported by Eric Beaugnon and Robert Tournier to a highly sceptical scientific audience in the journal Nature in 1991 (1). Koichi Kitazawa reported the effect in pure water in 2001 (2); dozens of scientists around the world have corroborated the results. The effect is executed with simple application of a strong magnetic field (exceeding 10 Tesla) through a diamagnetic liquid, such as ordinary water.

The Moses Effect in Pure Water
(Kitazawa 2001)

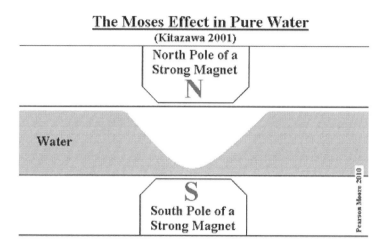

In the Moses Effect, a tube containing a diamagnetic liquid, such as water, is oriented between the poles of a powerful magnet (10-20 Tesla field strength). The poles are oriented normal (perpendicular) to the surface of the Earth. Upon activation of the field, water is pushed away from the north pole of the magnet, deforming the surface and the bulk of the liquid so that water forms an unsupported but stable column on each side of the field. Recent studies have demonstrated an effect at considerably reduced magnetic field strength by manipulating conditions such as pressure or by adding a second diamagnetic liquid.

Magnetic fields have unusual effects on ordinary household items. Water passed through a strong magnetic field mixed with cement and sand gives stronger concrete than identical mixtures prepared using untreated water (3). Oscillating magnetic fields are known to inhibit or even kill bacteria and mold in breads (4-5).

Phenomena of Biblical dimension are not confined to sixty-year-old movie relics. LOST presents us with even stranger effects, most of them centred around the peculiar electromagnetism of the Island. Many of these effects are well understood but not known to the general public, and some of them require a bit of background knowledge to comprehend. We're going to ease into this discussion, and I think there is no better way to start our adventure than with a healthy morning of spear fishing.

THE SPEED OF LIGHT IS NOT CONSTANT.

The hungry man in the illustration above wishes to spear cute little Nemo for lunch. Unfortunately, he seems to be operating under the mistaken belief that the speed of light is constant, and he will never achieve his goal. Nemo is going to escape. The fisherman is educated, majored in aquatic biology at the University of Alaska, took two semesters of university physics. The professor drilled this single truth into each of her students: The speed of light is constant. It is the most reliable, constant standard in the universe.

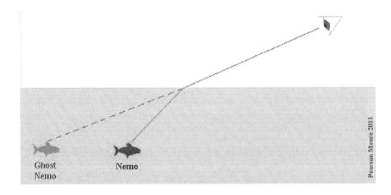

The professor's statement was incorrect, and she did her students a terrible disservice. Thanks to her sloppy pedagogy, the man above is going to go hungry, again. The speed of light changes. In fact, photons in water travel at only 75% of their speed in air. The slow-moving light reflected off the fish moves toward the surface of the water. Right there, at the water/air interface, a fascinating event occurs. The photon finds itself in a low-density medium and it zooms away, instantaneously increasing its speed. Concurrent with the increased velocity is an increased angle away from a line drawn normal to the point of incidence at the surface of the water. The fisherman, unfortunately, trusts his eyes, which tell him the fish is directly in line with the angle formed by his harpoon (that thing's going to make a bloody mess when it connects with a fish the size of Nemo). But the fisherman sees a phantom fish; Nemo is closer than he thinks, and it all comes down to the fact that light travels slower in water than in air.

The physics professor would have been correct if she had qualified her statement: The speed of light is constant *in a vacuum*. But the speed of light in real-world media changes all the time. Light travels through glass only 67% as fast as it does through air, for instance. Scientists have been able to slow light to less than 1% of its speed through empty space.

Light is not some amorphous material. It has definite properties amenable to manipulation, and it was heavily manipulated, in many ways, during the six years of LOST. The speed of light is only one of the properties that can be changed. The more interesting properties are key to our understanding of LOST, for they are centred on a quality at the core of every major dramatic event we witnessed: electromagnetism.

DANIEL'S DIFFRACTION DILEMMA

"The light... is strange out here isn't it? It's kinda like, it doesn't scatter quite right." Those were some of Daniel Faraday's first impressions of the Island in Episode 4.02. He noticed a peculiarity of light in a strong magnetic field--on the Island. If we are to understand Faraday's observations, we must first come to terms with the electromagnetic nature of light. One of the important electromagnetic properties of light is scattering, sometimes called diffraction.

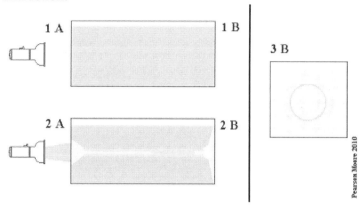

In Image 1 an aquarium is filled with water and a couple spoonfuls of milk are added and stirred until fully dispersed. A flashlight is placed at Side 1A. In Image 2, we turn on the flashlight. We see the beam pass through the tank. More important to our purposes, the water has acquired a bluish colour. However, if we walk around to the far side of the tank (Image 3B), we see yellow-orange colour and no blue at all.

We added milk to the aquarium to intensify diffraction. Note that when we see the liquid colour from the long side we are observing from a direction essentially perpendicular to the light source. When we move around to the far side of the tank, though, we are looking directly into the light source. This yellow colour is unusual. In fact, if we observe the tank from any perspective other than straight into the source, we will see blue colour.

The liquid acquires a blue cast due to light diffraction, or scattering. Understanding why the water turns blue and not red or white requires that we dig a little deeper into electromagnetic theory. When we understand how Faraday believed light ought to behave, we'll begin to appreciate why he believed light was behaving in a strange manner on Mittelos.

Light visible to our eyes occurs in a narrow band from red to violet, obeying the Roy G. Biv mnemonic we learned in grade school. Notice that wavelengths get shorter as we go from red to blue. Red has a wavelength of about 700 nanometres (abbreviated nm), which is 0.000000700 times the length of a metre, but violet light has a wavelength of 400 nm. Also note as the wavelength decreases, energy goes up. Microwaves are long wavelength (up to about 10 centimetres, abbreviated cm; 10 cm is 0.010 metre), and very low energy. Red photons have a bit higher energy, violet photons even more, and ultraviolet light, with very short wavelength (as low as 10 nm, roughly 50 times shorter than visible light) is extremely energetic. If you have sensitive skin and spend time out in the sun, you don't have to worry much about the red or green light beating down on you. But even a few minutes' exposure to the sun's ultraviolet light may be enough to give you third degree burns. In general, short wavelength radiation is most energetic.

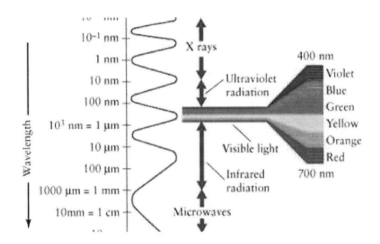

Light is electric. Light is magnetic. Light is a wave.

Light is affected by the electric and magnetic environments. This is because light has both electrical and magnetic properties. The light wave in the figure above is propagating toward the southwest. The wave comprises an electrical component (horizontal yellow wave) and a magnetic component (vertical green wave).

Electromagnetic Wave

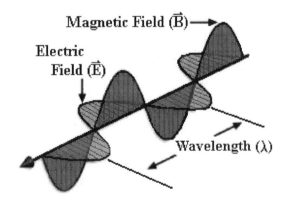

Now we're going to apply our spear fishing technology again. Recall the phenomenon that occurred when light reflected off the fish reached the water/air interface: the speed of light changed, and the photon suddenly veered away from a line drawn normal to the surface of the water. The phenomenon is called refraction. This same phenomenon is illustrated in the diagram below.

The incident ray and the emergent ray both describe wide angles (angle i) with a line drawn normal to the surface of the glass. Inside the glass the angles (angle r) to normal are sharp. That is, low-speed (low-energy) light propagates closer to a perpendicular to the surface than high-speed (high-energy) light.

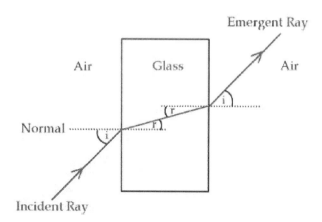

Now consider the case of a photon crashing into a molecule of nitrogen, the most prevalent gas in the air we breathe. A nitrogen molecule doesn't have much of a shape to speak of, so envisioning a line drawn "normal" to the surface is a bit of a challenge. For our purposes we can consider the incident photon to describe the line normal to the molecule.

The nitrogen molecule does not behave like a billiard ball. Recall from high school chemistry that the atomic constituents with any mass--the protons and neutrons--are located in a very small nucleus, and that most of the space is occupied by electrons zapping around. You could envision placing twelve or sixteen golf balls at the fifty metre line of a football field. Whizzing about the stadium you would have six or eight very small marbles, flying about so quickly that they seemed to be everywhere at once. In fact, we most accurately describe the sphere encompassing the stadium as the electron cloud.

When the wave of light hits the nitrogen molecule, for our purposes it interacts mostly with the electron cloud. Now, if you listen close enough during the course of this discussion, you will hear some science nerds shouting, "Hey! What about NMR? What about MRI?" Pay no attention to them. If they become too obnoxious, just ask them to explain the scientific basis for the Smoke Monster. That'll make 'em quiet down!

The electron cloud--being, ah... electronic—sees a kindred spirit in the electrically-inclined photon. They interact briefly, and the photon gets sent on its way, but on an energy-dependent trajectory. Low-energy waves (like red and yellow light) are not deflected much from their original course. High-energy waves (like blue and violet) are often diffracted at a large angle from the incident ray.

Rayleigh Scattering

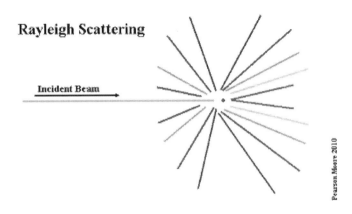

Incident Beam

Pearson Moore 2010

As with our aquarium experiment, if we observe the interaction of a mixed-wavelength beam of light with nitrogen in the atmosphere, we will see mostly blue colour, unless we are looking directly toward the incident beam.

Now we can begin to apply this to the Island. Consider the most frequent source of intense light on Mittelos: The sun. If we look toward the sun we see bright white or yellow light. If, however, we look into the sky away from the sun we see blue colour. The sky is blue because high-energy light diffracts at higher angle than low-energy light.

Now we're very close to understanding Faraday's statement that, "The light... is strange out here isn't it? It's kinda like, it doesn't scatter quite right." If we wish to understand LOST's über-physicist we're going to have to put on Dharma jumpsuits and take a walk over to the Swan Station. Desmond Hume will get us up to speed.

MY FILLINGS HURT JUST THINKING ABOUT IT

The Swan Station was intended to become the primary outpost for study of extreme electromagnetic phenomena. Instead it became the last and best hope to save the Island from electromagnetic destruction.

We spend our days in an environment having a magnetic field strength of around 50 microteslas (0.000050 Tesla; in scientific notation 50 x 10-6 Tesla). The normal field strength in the Swan Station is on the order of five Tesla—roughly ten thousand times higher than the most magnetically active regions of the Earth's crust. Recall that at ten Tesla we can induce the Moses Effect. At twenty Tesla we can force water to levitate vertically above a magnetic surface. The Swan Station is at the edge of some very strange magnetic behaviour.

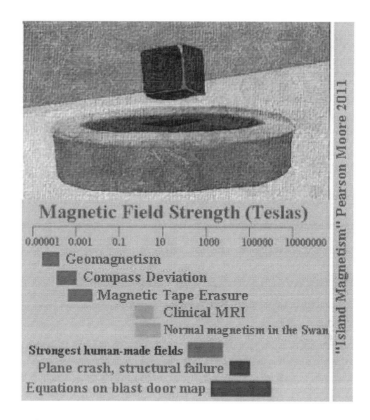

Magnetic Field Strength (Teslas)

LOST began when an Oceanic Airlines Boeing 777 was literally ripped apart during flight. The magnetic forces at play during this catastrophic event were on the order of tens of thousands of Tesla—hundreds of millions of times higher than the Earth's magnetic field. Aluminum and titanium—not normally thought of as magnetically susceptible—were pulled with forces nearly as great as the gravitational effects on a crashing airplane. Rivets popped out faster than bullets through water. Water molecules inside Desmond Hume's body were aligning with such rigid force the magnet was probably moments away from tearing him to pieces.

Silver-mercury amalgam—the metal composite of which fillings are made—is not magnetically susceptible under normal conditions. But at field strengths hundreds of thousands of times higher than normal Earth conditions—a typical condition in the Swan—even items not normally considered magnetic may undergo severe changes in behaviour.

With the in-flight destruction of Oceanic Flight 815 by forces without historic precedent, we venture into the realm of science fiction. Is there a scientific basis for extraordinarily high magnetic fields?

HARDHATS AND HO-HOS

"This... is 'the vault', constructed adjacent to a pocket of what we believe... to be negatively charged 'exotic matter'..." —Pierre Chang, Ph. D., as

291

"Dr. Edgar Halliwax," from the Dharma Initiative Station Six orientation video for "The Orchid"

Exotic matter is not antimatter. It is matter that violates the normal assumptions of quantum mechanics or is constructed of particles unknown to physics. This type of matter may be repelled by gravity, have negative mass, or exhibit other properties incompatible with normal matter. Exotic matter is most often invoked to explain the behaviour of Casimir Space.

The Casimir Effect, named after Hendrik Casimir, who discovered the phenomenon in 1948, constitutes the first instance of scientifically verified energy created from nothing.

Two perfectly smooth, uncharged metal plates are brought into close proximity (as close as one micrometre, or 0.000001 metre in width; sometimes abbreviated as 1 µm) in a perfect vacuum. Fields and waves of various types may exist or come into being in this vacuum.

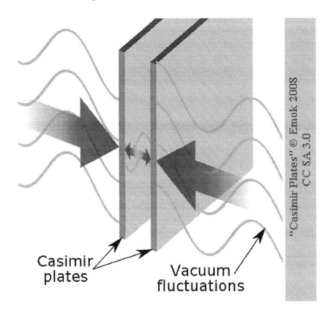

Casimir plates

Vacuum fluctuations

However, because of the narrow width between plates few waves will be able to exist in this squeezed region. The overall repulsive force between plates will be small, while the forces pushing the plates together will be comparatively strong.

The Casimir Effect has been verified several times (6), with numerical values typically achieving 85% to 95% of theoretical. This is not science fiction, but the real consequences of the phenomenon are among the strangest in physics. If placed in vacuum with frictionless surfaces, the two plates will quickly be forced together. However, if plate separation is maintained, extraordinary events might be expected.

Between the two plates there can be no substantial light-speed activity, since force and wave activities are substantially constrained. Some elegant solutions to the Casimir Effect require the assumption of exotic matter or faster-than-light travel. The fact that energy can be created from nothing is more than a little disconcerting to the physics community. Negative exotic matter or tachyonic movement, by cancelling out energy surpluses, obviates the disagreeable business of having unaccounted-for energy. According to the Special and General Theories of Relativity, faster-than-light travel would have to be considered travel by backwards chronological movement; Casimir Space may be the world's first time travel machine.

How could a Casimir Space have found its way onto Mittelos? We'll have to accompany Hugo Reyes on a shopping spree to find out. We're looking for Ho-Hos.

HURLEY'S HO-HO QUEST

In Episode 4.01 we find numerous occurrences of two letters of the alphabet: HO. When Hurley goes shopping, just before jumping into his Camaro for the police chase, he sees Charlie standing next to the Ho-Hos. Later, in the Santa Rosa Mental Health Institute recreation room, he stands in front of a conspicuously displayed set of building toys spelling out "Ho". Near the end of the episode, Hurley and Jack play horse on the basketball court, but they only get as far as "O"--again they have spelled "HO". "H" and "O" have significance to LOST in and of themselves. "H" is the 8th letter of the alphabet, and "O" is the 15th letter. These are two of Hurley's numbers, also Jacob's numbers, corresponding to Hurley (8) and Sawyer (15) respectively. They might also be taken to indicate Flight 815, the entry point for Jacob's final set of Candidates.

However, many analysts, including Doc Arzt (7), believe the two letters taken together may have a special significance. Lost Chicka made explicit the thought that many had a couple years ago after viewing the episode: "There are references to fertility and magnetism research relating to holmium. The island is a big holmium deposit." (8) Most important to the mythology of LOST is this fact:

Holmium has the greatest magnetic susceptibility of any element in the periodic table.

The most magnetic compounds known to humankind contain holmium or holmium alloys. If you wish to construct an Island rich in extreme magnetic phenomena, you could do no better than to build your civilisation on top of the world's richest deposit of this relatively common but extraordinarily powerful metal.

Holmium is a relatively abundant element. It is fifteen times more abundant than silver, and the richest ores are located more easily than those of even the most common metals. It is somewhat difficult to purify, but due to its great abundance, it is not terribly expensive. Holmium sells for around a thousand dollars (USD) per kilogram, roughly forty times cheaper than gold. If there were any significant market for the metal the price would almost certainly drop substantially.

The presence of high-purity holmium ores or the native metal may suffice to account for the high degree of electromagnetic activity on the Island and the presence of Casimir Space under the Orchid. It is also possible that volcanic phenomena would contribute to the intensity of the effect. Volcanic activity was probably known in historic times on the Island, certainly within the memory of Jacob. Magma chambers can be located as high as a kilometre below the surface. The richest sources of electromagnetic activity on the Island are known to occur underground at a depth of several dozen or even several hundred metres. Thus, magma chambers and occurrences of highly magnetised rock could occur in close proximity.

Convective currents in the magma chamber, displacing cool slurry to the bottom of the chamber while moving hot melt to the top, are a normal feature of all such volcanic chambers. The regular flow of magma could be expected to cause magnetic alignment in highly susceptible materials. As holmium is the most magnetically susceptible material known to science, the effects of highly directional and repeating magma flow on the rock would be extraordinary. Astronomically high magnetic activity could be expected in such an environment.

The extreme electromagnetic environment created by magnetically aligned holmium might be expected to provide a stable home for exotic Casimir matter.

THE VACUUM CATASTROPHE

Scientist-critics of LOST justifiably point out moving an entire island through time would cost enormous amounts of energy. Dr. Michio Kaku, physics professor at the City University of New York, calculated "the amount of exotic matter necessary to build a time machine would be about the mass of Jupiter" (10). However, Dr. Kaku and others do not take into account all of the possible (or likely) peculiarities of Casimir Space, and they neglect to mention the most important impediment to honest appraisals of Casimir limitations: the vacuum catastrophe.

The vacuum catastrophe refers to an extreme discrepancy--some 107 orders of magnitude--between calculated and observed strengths of vacuum energy density. This discrepancy has been called "the worst theoretical prediction in the history of physics" (9).

Vacuum energy density, of course, is precisely the unique characteristic of Casimir Space that may allow the existence of exotic matter, time travel, or other strange effects. That physicists cannot determine vacuum energy brings into question the validity of any conclusion regarding the cost of energy movement through the system.

Time travel as specified by the writers of LOST remains within the realm of plausible conjecture, with firm basis on the sturdy underpinnings of several phenomena confirmed to be integral to the Casimir Effect.

Several phenomena examined during LOST do not require the invocation of exotic matter, exotic metal, or exotic conditions of any kind. One of the first such phenomena was the deflection from expected bearing that Sayid found in the compass he received from Locke (Lost 1.13).

SAYID: Let me ask you something—which way do you think North is?
JACK: Sorry?
SAYID: North? Which way is it?
JACK: Uh, okay. [He looks around and points.] The sun's going to set over there, so that makes that West. [He points in another direction.] That'd be North. Yeah.
SAYID: Correct. That's where North should be. [He pulls Locke's compass out and shows Jack that North doesn't show up correctly on the compass.] Yet that is North.
JACK: I'm not...
SAYID: A minor magnetic anomaly might explain a variance of 2 or 3 degrees, but not this.
JACK: What are you saying?
SAYID: I'm saying this compass is obviously defective.

It's hard to determine the extent to which Sayid feels the compass may be deviating from expected north. From Sayid's and Jack's hand gestures, it looks like they may be considering an angle of twenty or thirty degrees. Such a large deviation may seem unreasonable, but such deflections are routinely found in lava-rich environments. As they make their way forward lavas cool and reach their Curie temperature. This is the temperature at which materials become paramagnetic—that is, the materials are easily magnetised. Lavas may stay at or around their Curie temperature for days, all the while pushing forward and continuing to force alignment with a single magnetic field. The result can be enormous local deviations from expected compass orientation; deflections of up to twenty degrees have been recorded in Hawaii (11).

GREEN GLOWS THE WATER

The green glowing water was a tough mystery to crack. I may be a chemist, but I am not conversant in all sub-branches of my discipline; water fluorescence is not a pressing concern of the Food and Drug Administration, so it doesn't become a topic at strategy meetings. But under the right conditions water does indeed fluoresce; in fact, the colour of fluorescence depicted in the final scenes of the light cave might even be correct, given the conditions of the cave.

When water is exposed to metastable argon, radical hydrogen (H) and a peculiar type of hydroxyl radical (OH ($A2\Sigma+$)) are produced (12), giving greenish-blue fluorescence (13).

$$Ar (3P2,0) + H2O \longrightarrow Ar + H + OH (A2\Sigma+)$$

One might reasonably ask how such fluorescence could occur; fluorescent water is not something one typically sees coming out of the tap or at the neighbourhood swimming pool. The air we breathe contains about one percent argon; in the presence of very high electromagnetic fields argon could be expected to reach the metastable excited state required to effect the splitting of water into hydrogen radical and high-energy hydroxyl radical in the A2Σ+ state. The fact that the glow coming from the light cave is decidedly yellowish-green rather than the expected greenish-blue may have to do with the presence of the subterranean red glow. Another possibility is that unusual conditions, especially the extreme electromagnetism, could push the fluorescence toward the longer-wavelength end of the spectrum.

THE TAWARET TSUNAMI

While we're marching through the easy ones, let's quickly dispatch the Tawaret Tsunami.

At a height of 75 metres, Tawaret is no ordinary statue. Even the Americans' Statue of Liberty in New York Harbour is only about 46 metres high. Tawaret is enormous. Certainly no tsunami could approach such a height, could it?

While it is true that tsunamis generally do not exceed ten or fifteen metres in wave amplitude, rare and memorable megatsunamis have been recorded. The 1958 Lityua Bay Tsunami had a maximum wave amplitude dwarfing even Tawaret. Although difficult to believe, the Lityua Bay Tsunami reached a recorded, confirmed height of just over half a kilometre--525 metres. The short and entirely plausible answer is that a 70-metre tsunami could easily visit the Island. Whether the Black Rock is riding the crest of the wave is immaterial. The forward momentum of ten metres of water is sufficient to tear out bridges, destroy houses, and raze entire villages. The catastrophic advance of seventy metres of water—hundreds of thousands of tonnes of pure destructive force—is going to wipe out the statue or Tawaret, even if the Black Rock decides to come in on a later wave. The Black Rock didn't destroy the statue of Tawaret. The water did.

PURPLE SKY

On a cloudless day the sky is neither blue nor even violet. It's ultraviolet. This is what birds would tell us, anyway, since they see well into the ultraviolet range.

The daytime sky contains much more violet and ultraviolet colour than blue. Recall our earlier discussion regarding light diffraction. High-energy colour is scattered at wider angles than low-energy colour. Ultraviolet and violet, being the shortest-wavelength major constituents of sunlight, are diffracted more broadly than blue. There is more violet to be seen—we just don't see it.

Human beings have colour vision, unlike dogs, who lack colour cone receptors, and see the world in black and white. We have three types of cones in our eyes: Yellow, Green, and Blue, at wavelength maxima of roughly 570 nm, 540 nm, and 440 nm respectively. The lowest wavelength receptor is firmly in the blue region of the spectrum, and drops off quickly on the violet side of the slope. Violet and deep red are among the colours human beings find most difficult to discriminate. We are most sensitive to greens, due to the close wavelength proximity of two of the three cones we use to distinguish colour.

The biophysics of the human eye explains why we see blue sky, not violet, but it does not explain why the survivors have experienced several occurrences of purple sky. We will need to return to Dr. Faraday for an answer to this question.

The electromagnetic field in the Swan Station is tens of thousands of times higher than normal ambient Earth conditions. The field strength averaged across the Island is probably on the order of half a Tesla; roughly a thousand times higher than typical ambient conditions anywhere else on the globe.

When Daniel Faraday looked into the sky, he probably saw a bit more violet there than he was used to seeing. Being a physicist, he would probably tend to be more aware of colour nuances than the rest of us.

The slight colour shift in diffracted light on and around the Island is due to the intense electromagnetic field. In particular, the violet shift can be attributed to the enormous contribution of the strong magnetic field.

Recall that light is ruled by both electric and magnetic fields.

The Lorenz equation, $F = q*(E + Bv/c)$ is the formal descriptor of total force on a particle, but after soberly invoking the equation, physicists will invariably neglect any mention of the magnetic component, Bv/c, since the magnetic field strength, B, is typically very small. In physicists' minds, then, the equation collapses to $F = q(E)$, which is much easier to work with, meaning one can take a longer lunch, maybe head over to the chemistry lab and laugh at the poor pharmaceutical chemists, who rarely even get a lunch...

But on Mittelos, with field strengths sometimes millions of times greater than those found anywhere else, the B term becomes terribly important. The total force on a particle may be several times higher on the Island than anywhere else in the world. With higher force comes greater energy, and with greater energy comes more scattering. Thus, as magnetic field strength increases, the sky becomes more and more purple, even to our violet-insensitive eyes.

In extreme cases, as with the Incident, the crash of Oceanic 815, or the Swan Station implosion, magnetic field strength can climb into the hundreds of thousands of Tesla, threatening the survival of everything on the Island. In these situations, the sky becomes decidedly purple, though people may not even notice, grimacing as they are, trying to keep their heads from exploding. Magnetic spikes on Mittelos are not relaxing events.

TIME DISCONTINUITY

The "payload" from the ship was a rocket. It should have arrived in less than two minutes. Instead, the supersonic missile, with no more than ten minutes' worth of fuel, required two hours 45 minutes (Island time) or three hours sixteen minutes (rocket time) to reach the Island.

Not only did the rocket require a hundred-fold more time than Faraday would have guessed, there was a thirty-one minute discrepancy between the two timers.

This was not the only example of a time discontinuity affecting events on and off Island. The helicopter ride from the Island to the freighter took about thirty minutes according to clocks on the helicopter. The freighter, though, and the people on the Island, experienced Lapidus' journey as a 32-hour marathon.

The most perplexing discontinuity had to be the one that involved neither helicopter nor missile, but slow working of the waves. Doctor Ray of the Kahana washed up on shore, face in the water, his throat slit, having been killed hours or days before. A telephone call to the Kahana immediately after finding the corpse revealed the good doctor was doing fine, tending to patients.

I don't think we can assess with complete certainty the cause of temporal discontinuities between the Island and the outside world. Certainly the extraordinary electrical and magnetic fields engulfing the Island must be the major causes of time shifts.

I envision the Island as being surrounded by a kind of double-walled bubble or sphere. Travel on the Island and within the inner sphere is performed in the normal manner, and the results are more or less as expected. The same is true, of course, for travelers outside the outer sphere. But within the two spheres we encounter very strange phenomena.

Consider the hypothetical case of a woman walking from the Island along a brown runway constructed across the ocean and through the time discontinuity.

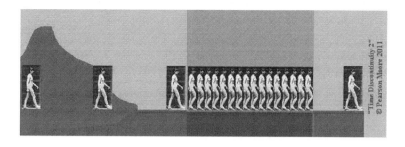

Starting at the far left, we use the convention that every instance of the woman's photograph constitutes ten minutes of walking. Everything is fine until she reaches the dark blue time discontinuity at middle right. She may experience the time inside the discontinuity as not more than ten or twenty minutes, but to an outside observer, the time she requires to traverse the discontinuity may run into dozens of hours—perhaps even a day or two. When she crosses through the outer sphere of the discontinuity her pace seems unaffected in her estimation, but an outside observer records a ten- or twenty- or fifty-fold increase in apparent walking speed.

The discontinuity ought to look something like the magnetic lines of force surrounding a magnet, perhaps something like this photograph of iron filings surrounding a magnet.

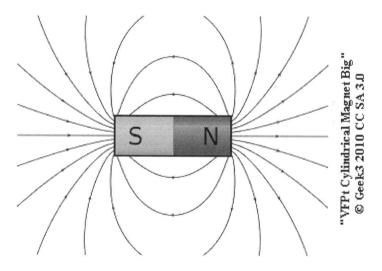

But the Island is not a uniform magnet like the one above. The Island contains regions of greater and lesser electromagnetism. Rather than having two regions of low temporal disturbance, the Island apparently has only one such corridor.

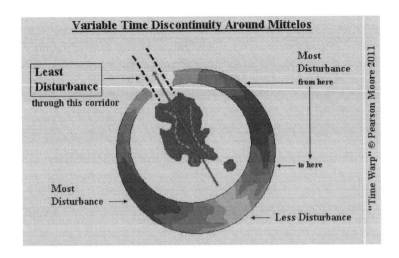

Variable Time Discontinuity Around Mittelos

Least Disturbance through this corridor

Most Disturbance from here

to here

Most Disturbance

Less Disturbance

"Time Warp" © Pearson Moore 2011

In the region of greatest disturbance an object may require hundreds or even thousands of hours, as measured by an outside observer, to complete a trip the traveler experiences as lasting not more than an hour. The same one-hour trip through the corridor of least disturbance may require not more than three hours. This is the reason that maintaining a precise bearing was critical. The bearing changed at least once during the course of the six years, from a heading of 325 to 305.

WHAT IT ALL MEANS

I hope this very long exercise was at least mildly entertaining and educational. I learned a lot in researching this book, and I found myself surprised by many tidbits. For instance, I knew nothing about the Voyager spacecraft having proven the so-called "vacuum catastrophe", and the enormous significance of this fact to predictions regarding events in Casimir Space.

The most enduring significance, though, I think, is the meaning that attaches to the plot developments and character growth that occurred as a result of interacting with Island phenomena. Even as a professional scientist, I find myself much more interested in character development than in the nuances of electromagnetism in the Swan Station. And more than the fascinating character arcs, I find deepest enjoyment in contemplation of the rich philosophical and spiritual positions of the writers, especially since they are considerably at odds with my own understanding of the world. Fiction holds a mirror up to us, shows us the rich complications of the human mind, the human psyche, the human condition. I have truly enjoyed examining the depths of our cultural heritage, as reflected back to us from the mirror put together by writers, directors, and actors.

After a very long couple of months at the keyboard I am more than ever aware of the painstaking effort that had to be involved in the construction of such a rich mythology as the one developed for LOST. Indeed, this book could easily have been three times longer than it is, not only because I am unnaturally verbose (though this is certainly a fair accusation), but more than anything because the mythology of the show is complex, profound, and highly consistent. The writers were certainly not experts in quantum mechanics, Egyptology, cosmology, physical chemistry, theology, botany, biophysics, and the dozens of other disciplines amply represented in this series. But they consulted experts. This was evident to me years ago, but became a real source of admiration as I worked my way through one question after another in preparing this book. Even a series like Star Trek does not have nearly the internal consistency of LOST.

To those who stayed with me over the course of 111,000 words, congratulations! For those who (certainly not without justification) threw in the towel, be of good cheer! In a few months we will begin the real work of LOST: Understanding the characters. Thank you. Namaste. And good luck!

Citations for Chapter 19

1. Braithwaite, D.; Beaugnon, E.; Tournier, R. Nature 1991, 354, 134.

2. Kitazawa, K. Physica B 2001, 294, 704-719.

3. Su, N.; Wu., C. Cement & Conc. Comp. 2003, 25, 681-688.

4. Barbosa-Cánovas, G.; Gongora-Nieto, M.; and Swanson, B. Food Sci. Int. 1998, 4, 363-370.

5. U.S. Food and Drug Administration (FDA), 2000, as reported in 2004 by EMR Labs, LLC. http://www.quantumbalancing.com/news/usda_magnetic_fields.htm

6. Bressi, G.; Carugno, G.; Onofrio, R.; Ruoso, G. Phys. Rev. Lett. 2002, 88, 041804.

7. Doc Arzt, 1 Feb 2008, at his website. http://www.docarzt.com/lost/lost-theories/lost-solved-its-all-about-ho-hos/ (accessed 6 Sep 2010).

8. Lost Chicka, as recorded by Ghost Rider in the comments section, March, 2008. http://www.lostblog.net/lost/tv/show/the-economist (accessed 6 Sep 2010).

9. Hobson, M.; Efstathiou, G.; Lasenby, G. General Relativity: An introduction for physicists (Reprint ed.). Cambridge University Press, 2006; p. 187. 2006.

10. Kaku, M; Time-Travel Expert: Lost Finale Opens New Trap Door in Space, Popular Mechanics, Published online May, 2008. http://www.popularmechanics.com/technology/digital/fact-vs-fiction/4266335

11. Baag, C.; et al. J. Geophys. Res. 1995, 100, 10013-10027.

12. Parr, T.; Martin, R. J. Phys. Chem. 1978, 82, 2226–2231.

13. Edery, F.; Kanaev, A. Euro. Phys. J. D. 2003, 23, 257-264.

The greatest collection of LOST expertise ever gathered in one book.

What if all your favorite LOST authors and bloggers were gathered in one place, accessible anytime you wished, day or night? What would you talk about with them? What fascinating ideas would they bring for your consideration?

What if you could talk with people who never left the Island, who never will leave the Island—whose job it is, in fact, to live, breathe, touch, and see LOST 24 hours a day, seven days a week?

There are such people, and there is such a magical place, in a book: LOST Thought. The best-known experts in the LOST community are here:

Bloggers and Authors:
Nikki Stafford (Finding Lost)
Jo Garfein (Jopinionated)
Pearson Moore (LOST Humanity)
Sarah Clarke Stuart (Literary Lost)
Sam McPherson (Lostpedia.com)
Erika Olson (Long Live Locke)
Ryan Ozawa (The Transmission)
Andy Page (Dark UFO)

Nationally Recognized Literary Scholars:
Amy Bauer, Ph.D. (Professor of Music)
Cynthia Burkhead, Ph.D. (Professor of English)
Jeffrey Frame (Professor of Theater and Film)
Julia Guernsey-Pitchford, Ph.D. (Professor of English)
Michelle Lang, Ph.D. (Professor of Art)
Antonio Savorelli, Ph.D. (Film and Literary Studies)
Paul Wright, Ph.D. (Professor of English)
Jamie R. Smith (Professor of English)

LOST Scholars:
Jennifer Galicinski (Theology)
C. David Milles (Literary and Film Studies)
Delano Freeberg, Ph.D. (Analytical Scientist)
Erin Carlyle (Women's Studies)
Gozde Kilic (Cultural Studies)
Kevin McGinnis (Religious Studies)

Available now at bookstores everywhere!

A novel unlike any other

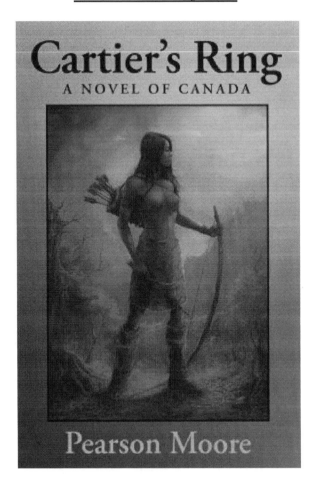

"Exquisite historical detail...Excellent novel."
—**J. A. Beard, Good Book Alert**

"I read Cartier's Ring cover to cover—right through the night, in fact—for the simple reason that I couldn't put it down. Pearson Moore has given us lasting love, bloody war and a clash of cultures...and leaves his readers dying to know what happens next...Cartier's Ring is a superbly researched, marvelously written book..."
—**Paula Cohen, bestselling author of *Gramercy Park***

"Myeerah is the real heroine, a young girl...who's forced to grow up very quickly...I'm not ashamed to say that a few times I had a lump in my throat as I read...I could almost feel...the camps and forests and ships. The battle of the characters became my battle, too. From the first page to the last, the story is gripping. A tale of love, of family, of honor and of power, it's fitting tribute to the birth of a nation."
—**Barbara Elsborg, bestselling author of *Strangers***

Made in the USA
Lexington, KY
05 December 2012